The Economics of *Emancipation*

KATHLEEN MARY BUTLER

The

Economics of

Emancipation

Jamaica & Barbados, 1823–1843

The University of North Carolina Press • Chapel Hill and London

The paper in this book meets the guidelines for permanence and durability of the Committee on Production Guidelines for Book Longevity of the Council on Library Resources.

Library of Congress Cataloging-in-Publication Data

Butler, Kathleen Mary.

The economics of emancipation : Jamaica and Barbados, 1823–
    1843 / by Kathleen Mary Butler.

p.   cm.

Includes bibliographical references and index.

ISBN 0-8078-2194-2 (alk. paper)

ISBN 0-8078-4501-9 (pbk. : alk. paper)

1. Slaves—Jamaica—Emancipation. 2. Slaves—Barbados—
    Emancipation. 3. Slavery—Economic aspects—Jamaica.
    4. Slavery—Economic aspects—Barbados. 5. Jamaica—
    Economic conditions. 6. Barbados—Economic
    conditions. I. Title.

HT1098.B88   1995

326'.097292—dc20   94-36129

                         CIP

Kathleen Mary Butler is assistant professor of history at
Rollins College.

99 98 97 96 95   5 4 3 2 1

For Lynn, Simon, Tom, and Michael

Contents

Tables

Figures and Maps

Acknowledgments

Many colleagues and friends have helped bring this study to a successful conclusion. My biggest debt of gratitude is to Franklin Knight and Colin Palmer for their continued faith, friendship, and support over the years. Their penetrating observations and editorial guidance have helped me to utilize my research to its fullest extent. More importantly, they believed in me.

Very special thanks are due to Mary Turner, whose sustained hospitality enlivened my research in London. Other friends also deserve special mention, in particular, Keith Hunte, Alison Worrell, Eugenia Ekejuba, and Carl Campbell, who gave emotional support at a time of personal crisis in Jamaica. Tony and Sylvia Phillips and Woodville and Dawn Marshall offered friendship and hospitality and smoothed my path in numerous ways in Barbados. Ronald Hughes, the Barbadian historian, willingly and unreservedly shared his extensive knowledge of the plantocracy and I thank him for his kindness. Verene Shepherd, Swithon Wilmot, Milton Thomas, Sheena Boa, David Beckles, Jennifer Adams, Cecilia Karch, George Lamming, Eric Armstrong, and many others too numerous to mention individually helped make my research in Jamaica, Barbados, and Trinidad a memorable experience.

A fellowship from the Organization of American States financed my initial West India research, and I acknowledge their generosity. A summer stipend and a travel-to-collections grant from the National Endowment for the Humanities, together with assistance from the Colgate University Research Council, enabled me to expand my research and devote time to writing.

Researchers cannot function without the efficient cooperation of the personnel of the many libraries and universities at which they work. I extend a special thanks for their unfailing patience and courtesy to the librarians and staff of the Institute of Jamaica at Kingston; the Jamaican National Archives and the Island Record Office at Spanish Town; the Department of Archives and Public Library of Barbados; the Barbados Museum and Historical Society; the University of the West Indies at Mona, Cave Hill; and St. Augustine; the British Library; the Public Record Office; Fulham Palace; the Guildhall Library; and the Universities of London, Bristol, and Oxford.

Nigel Bolland, Patrick Carroll, Ann Lane, Jay Mandle, Woodville Marshall, Colin Palmer, and Marli Weiner, all generously took time away from their own work to read and comment on an early draft, offer suggestions, and provide moral support. Michael Butler and Peter Jorgensen kindly helped with the computer programming. All have my respect and heartfelt thanks.

I am also indebted to my outside readers for their helpful comments and suggestions, and to the editors at the University of North Carolina Press, especially Ron Maner and Maura High, for their patience as I struggled to complete the inevitable revisions and at the same time move across the country to a new home and a new position.

Finally, this book is dedicated to my family, in recognition of their continued support and encouragement.

Introduction

Until the middle of the eighteenth century the sugar islands of the Caribbean ranked foremost among British colonies. Euphorically described as the brightest "jewels" in the British Crown, they provided the economic springboard for a new aristocracy of planters and merchants. For over a century, owners of West India plantations reaped handsome returns from their slave-grown sugar and coffee. Profits derived from sugar built English country estates, financed parliamentary seats, and helped to ensure the continued development of the cities and towns that catered to every aspect of colonial slavery. Assured of a protected British market, overconfident planters saddled their estates with a prolific array of legacies, annuities, and settlements.

Yet from the very beginning the sugar colonies carried the seeds of their own destruction. The entire economic structure operated on credit: credit to meet expenses at home and abroad, credit to buy land and plantation supplies, and credit to replenish the slave labor force. Until the early eighteenth century, planters who faced unexpected operating expenses simply borrowed from friends and family, but as credit patterns changed in the 1740s, planters became heavily dependent on British credit and services. When sugar prices began their long-term decline in the 1790s, they found it increasingly difficult to meet the liabilities secured against their once-profitable plantations. By 1820 few West India planters owned unencumbered estates. The majority struggled in a complicated web of debts and multiple mortgages as they attempted to continue production.

As British merchants became more deeply involved in the colonial credit structure, their economic power and prestige replaced the social power and prestige of the planters. With less possibility of recouping their original investments, British merchants began withdrawing from the West India trade and turning to more lucrative investments elsewhere. Few planters were prepared to admit that poor management and overproduction might have contributed to their downfall. The reopening of the slavery question in 1823 gave them the scapegoat they needed. Both planters and merchants quickly blamed the abolition movement for their economic problems and made it abundantly clear that they expected to be "adequately" compensated for the inevitable loss of their human property.

After prolonged negotiations the British government officially eliminated slavery in 1834 and agreed to compensate all owners of West Indian slaves. It awarded the slave owners £20 million and apprenticed the ex-slaves to their former masters for at least another four years. Such generous compensation was unprecedented. Critics charged that the government intended to compensate slave owners twice over. But most government officials, and indeed many abolitionists, believed that uncompensated emancipation would be unconstitutional and would set a dangerous precedent in Britain, a rapidly industrializing nation in constant need of land for essential railroads and canals. Despite angry complaints from disgruntled planters and merchants the government considered the grant and the complementary apprenticeship complete and adequate compensation.

The expectation of compensation offered British creditors a unique opportunity to recoup at least a small part of their capital outlay. The influential merchants, and many private individuals, who had invested heavily in sugar and coffee plantations demanded that their deeply indebted clients use their awards to reduce their long-standing debts. For their part, planters hoped that repaying at least part of their outstanding debts would encourage continued investment and make new working capital available. The extent to which these expectations were met had a direct bearing on the future development of the region.

All slave holders were eligible for compensation, regardless of the number of slaves they owned. The indemnity, therefore, had broader implications than the simple debt reduction. It affected many levels of British and colonial society, and its influence was felt as early as the 1820s.

This analysis of compensation uses a comparative framework to argue that the award had a significant short-term impact on two of Britain's premier sugar colonies: Barbados, a mature plantation economy with a predominantly resident planter class, and Jamaica, a plantation economy with the potential for further development, where the majority of the planters were absentees. It examines three interrelated aspects of the compensation award from a colonial perspective. First, it explores the impact of the indemnity on planter indebtedness and the availability of credit. Second, it analyzes the effect of compensation on the value and ownership of plantation land and the extent to which the ex-slaves gained access to land. Third, it examines the broader ramifications of the award for international trade and the transfer of capital.

Compensation formed the cornerstone of the government's abolition plan. From the moment Thomas Fowell Buxton reopened the question of slave emancipation in 1823 until the end of the apprenticeship in 1838 the issue generated heated debate in the British parliament, in the colonial legislatures, in select committees, and in the colonial and British press. The British radical press, in particular, roundly denounced the very idea of paying off the slave owners. Nevertheless, most historians have ignored the topic and concentrated instead on the apprenticeship with the result that the only full-length study of the grant is an unpublished Master's thesis written in 1932 by R. E. P. Wastell. More recently a few scholars such as Richard Pares, S. G. Checkland, and Michael Craton have referred to compensation as it affected specific families such as the Pinneys or the Gladstones, or particular estates such as Worthy Park. Richard Fogel, Stanley Engerman, and Barry Higman have consulted Wastell's work for their broader studies of slave values and prices and the general composition of the slave labor force. None of them, however, has related compensation to social and economic change within the colonies themselves.

Examining compensation from a colonial, albeit planter standpoint introduces a vital new perspective on the regional economies. It brings to light the hitherto unnoticed role of white women in the plantation economy and places them in the context of creditors and plantation owners. Uncovering the family, and sometimes purely business, links between these women and their clients adds another dimension to the economic canvass and expands our understanding of nineteenth-century colonial society.

The focus on the planter class reincorporates an element of society that has been largely deemphasized in recent studies of West Indian slavery. Both planters and slaves played important parts in the emancipation drama and in the changeover from slavery to free wage labor.

All of the plantations used in this study can be classified as large-scale operations; those used for Jamaica owned at least 100 slaves, while those for Barbados owned at least 50. The data for the analysis come from the official compensation records, deeds of land sales and mortgages, plantation accounts, attorneys' and merchants' letter books, and the virtually untouched records of the colonial courts of chancery. Despite the contemporary reputation for inefficiency and haphazard record-keeping of the colonial courts of chancery, their records remain one of the most important sources of information on the financial health of the plantations. Few masters in chancery were trained lawyers and many allowed the unauthorized removal and late enrollment of documents under their care. Nevertheless, the masters' records and the receivers' reports contain details of mortgage payments, estate expenditure, crop size, and prices. When estates were sold out of chancery extremely detailed accounts of the mortgages, liens, marriage settlements, and judgments against the property were recorded in the minutes or in the colonial deeds of conveyance. The chancery records often round out the picture of colonial indebtedness painted by plantation account books, attorneys letters, and private papers. The data thus enabled me to build a basic profile of over 900 Jamaican and more than 300 Barbadian plantations on the eve of emancipation and to develop an overall picture of the use and misuse of compensation.

Note: the term "of color" is used throughout to denote persons of mixed ancestry, although West Indian documents and slave registers sometimes used other terms.

All monetary values are in £sterling unless otherwise stated. £sterling was equal to £1.4 Jamaican or Barbadian currency throughout the period under consideration.

The Economics of *Emancipation*

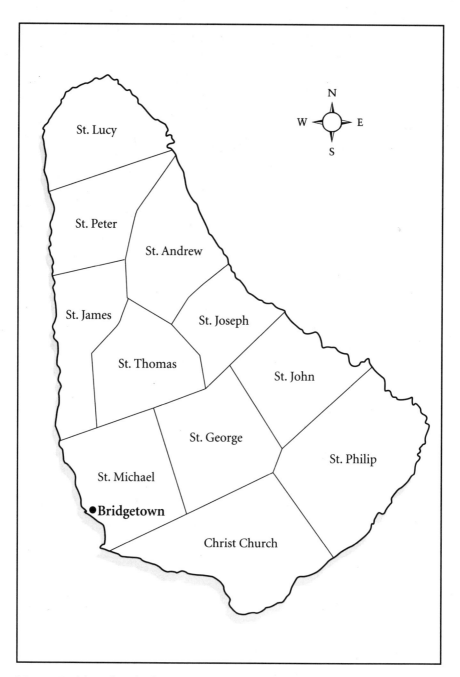

Map 1. *Parishes of Barbados*

Map 2. *Estates of Barbados*

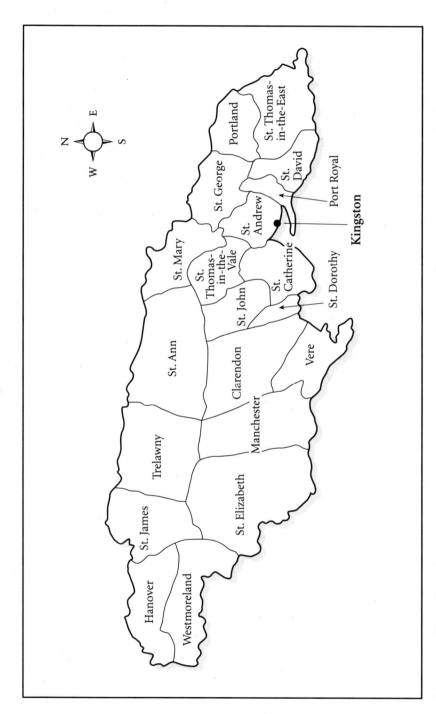

Map 3. *Parishes of Jamaica*

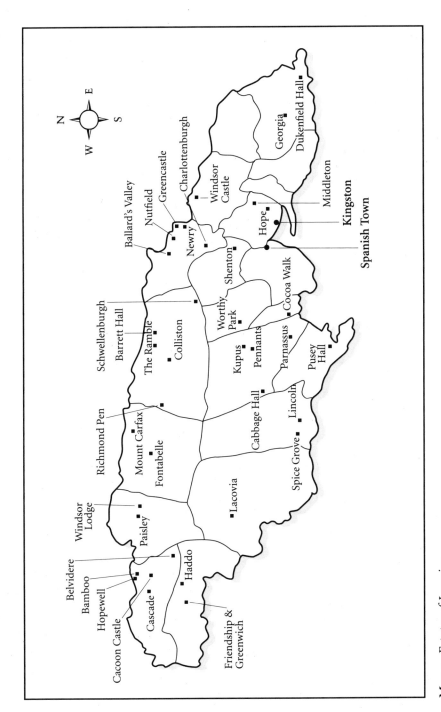

Map 4. *Estates of Jamaica*

1

The West India Lobby, 1823–1833

In 1823 Thomas Fowell Buxton led British abolitionists in a renewed attack on West Indian slavery and demanded the emancipation of all slaves held in British colonies. Anxious to maintain control of the issue, the British government agreed to emancipation in principle but argued that the slaves could only be freed when their well-being and the security of the colonies could be assured and *"with a fair and equitable consideration for the interests of private property."* [1]

The reopening of the slavery question gave West India merchants and the heavily indebted planters the scapegoat they needed. Both planters and merchants quickly blamed the antislavery movement for all their economic problems and immediately intensified the campaign for compensation that they had first undertaken some fifty years earlier, when abolitionists had called for the ending of the slave trade. Over the course of the next ten years, until the passage of the Slavery Abolition Act in 1833, representatives of the West India "Interest" lobbied vigorously for that "consideration." [2]

The Interest concentrated on two extremely effective arguments. First, it emphasized the depressed state of the colonial economies, the adverse effect of the abolition movement on West India property values, and the difficulty planters faced when trying to obtain credit secured against their estates. Second, it argued that the same laws protecting inanimate property also protected property in slaves. Therefore it would be both immoral and unconstitutional to emancipate the slaves without paying their owners adequate compensation. Such an action would set a dangerous precedent and endanger all British-owned property. Though the planters were not formally represented at Westminster, they could rely on the absentee proprietors who held seats in Parliament and on the lobbying efforts of their trade associations to protect and

further their interests. The most influential of these organizations were the
Society of West India Merchants, founded in 1750, and the Society of West
India Planters and Merchants formed in 1780 to combine the agricultural and
commercial aspects of sugar production and bring together the metropolitan
and colonial interests of the slave-based monoculture. The membership of this
interest group fell into three broad categories: the British sugar merchants, the
absentee planters, and the colonial agents appointed by the respective legislatures to represent the various colonies in England.[3]

The merchants who controlled the British sugar market lived mainly in
London, Bristol, Liverpool, Glasgow, and Dublin. They accepted shipments of
sugar on consignment and arranged for its sale to refiners and grocers. The
merchants deducted their commission, brokerage fees, insurance, and interest
from the proceeds of the sales and credited the remainder to the planters'
accounts. Against these accounts they charged the cost of the plantation supplies and luxury items that they shipped to the colonies. In the absence of
colonial banks, they honored bills of exchange and extended credit to cover
the slave purchases, annuity payments, and production costs that beset every
estate owner. In times of recession they provided mortgages, secured against
plantations and slaves, to enable the proprietors to continue production. By
the early nineteenth century, this cycle of credit and indebtedness had en-
gulfed the profits of countless estates. As colonial indebtedness increased and
British consignees expanded their influence, the composition of the Interest
became steadily more commercial, as merchants became mortgagees and even
proprietors of plantations.[4]

The political influence of the absentee planters reinforced the financial
prominence of the Interest. Many substantial proprietors lived in England and
coupled their colonial investments with the ownership of British country estates. As landed gentry they often served as members of Parliament and supported the conservative aims of their sugar-producing colleagues. At the time
of Buxton's motion for abolition, thirty-nine members of Parliament identified with the West India cause. Eleven West India merchants, including John
Gladstone and Joseph Marryat, represented London and the outports, while
the remaining twenty-eight members were the absentee owners of colonial
estates.[5]

The Interest's mercantile sector included Sir John Rae Reid, a financier and
merchant; John Gladstone, a Liverpool merchant, and Joseph Marryat, a London consignee. All three men linked their political and trading activities to
their positions as members of Parliament and absentee proprietors. Reid had
financial interests in Jamaica, Trinidad, St. Kitts, and the Virgin Islands. Joseph
Marryat was involved with estates in Jamaica, Trinidad, Grenada, St. Lucia,

and British Guiana, while John Gladstone had interests in seven properties in British Guiana and another six in Jamaica. Moreover, as an active member of the Liverpool West India Association, Gladstone exerted considerable influence over George Canning, the foreign minister and member of Parliament for Liverpool.[6]

The West Indian plantocracy also had several parliamentary representatives. Neill Malcolm, the member for Boston, owned nine estates and over 2,000 slaves in Jamaica. George Hay Dawkins-Pennant, the M.P. for New Romney, controlled four estates and nearly 800 slaves. Lord Seaford, the acknowledged leader of the West India Interest in the House of Commons, owned five Jamaican plantations. The Marquis of Chandos, the chairman of the Society of West India Planters and Merchants, owned two Jamaican plantations, served as the M.P. for Buckinghamshire, and further underscored the West Indians' involvement at Westminster.[7]

Moreover, the Interest could also count on the sympathetic support of many members of the House of Lords. Among the peers who owned colonial properties were the Earl of Harewood, with three estates in Barbados, two in Jamaica, and over 1,250 slaves; the Marquis of Sligo, later governor of Jamaica, with two Jamaican estates, and the Duke of Cleveland, who owned one estate and 230 slaves in Barbados.[8] At the same time other peers identified with the Interest's campaign for compensation by virtue of their common belief in the inalienable right to private property.

Additional political support came from the colonial agents who acted as parliamentary lobbyists for their West Indian constituents.[9] Among the most prominent agents were William Burge of Jamaica and John Pollard Mayers of Barbados. Mayers, in particular, worked tirelessly to obtain the highest possible indemnity for Barbados when it became clear that emancipation was inevitable.

Despite its impressive political and financial prestige, the Interest was not a completely cohesive group. Differences existed between planters and merchants, between London merchants and those of the outports, and among absentee planters and the agents of the crown and legislative colonies. Moreover, after 1827, a variety of financial and political events steadily reduced the number of M.P.s sympathetic to the West Indian cause. The continuing decline of the sugar economy and the Reform Act of 1832 removed the financial and structural base of at least twenty-seven of the Interest's traditional supporters. Some withdrew from Parliament when their backers declared bankruptcy, while others lost their seats as a result of the realignment of electoral boundaries.[10] Nevertheless, the issue of compensation appealed to a broad cross section of the population on the basis of the nature of private property.

When the Commons debated Buxton's proposal in 1823 the subject of compensation created a split among the members. William Smith, the M.P. for Norwich, spoke for many of his colleagues when he expressed his indignation that men could be defined as property. As long as people held this belief he argued that "the march of amelioration of the Negroes will be slow indeed." His words proved to be prophetic, for the condition of the slaves had scarcely improved when emancipation became a reality more than ten years later. Other members expressed their abhorrence of the slave system but continued to insist that slaves were the legal property of their masters. If the British government intended to abolish slavery, it should pay the slave owners adequate compensation for the loss of their property.[11] The broad-based agreement brought the debate to an end without a vote on Canning's resolution.

The consensus, however, was largely contrived. When the West India Interest learnt that Buxton intended to propose abolition, its members met with government representatives to discuss strategy. Eager to maintain control of the emancipation question rather than allow the abolitionists to take the initiative, the government drew up a program of amelioration with the aid of the Interest. To win the cooperation of the West Indians, the ministers agreed to amend Buxton's original proposal. The addition of the vital phrase "with a fair and equitable consideration for the interests of private property," ensured the Interest's approval and Canning's resolution passed unopposed.[12]

Nevertheless, the Interest urged its members to stay alert and to focus their attention on the two objectives it deemed "paramount to all other considerations": their right to property and their claim to compensation.[13] The Interest and its sympathizers continually reminded the public of the importance of protecting property rights. In petitions to Parliament and editorials in the conservative press they reminded all property owners of the dangerous precedent that uncompensated abolition could set.

In addition, the Interest argued that successive British governments had condoned and encouraged slave holding. Slavery had become a national sin, which could be absolved only by a national remedy: compensation for the injured proprietors. Newspapers, journals, petitions, and pamphlets frequently expressed this clever argument. On several occasions the *Quarterly Review* pointed out that various acts of Parliament had encouraged slave owners to spend vast sums of money to buy land and slaves. To deny them compensation, the *Review* believed, constituted a "flagrant breach of faith."[14] The proplanter *Glasgow Courier* put the point more forcefully when it declared that "the wrong was committed by the nation; by the wrong the nation has profited for a long series of years." If the entire country was guilty then it would be the grossly unfair to punish only the slave owners by withholding their just indemnity.[15]

These views were not confined solely to the Interest's metropolitan supporters. In a pamphlet published shortly after the abolition question was reopened, Augustus Hardin Beaumont, editor of the *Jamaican Courant*, explained the basis for the proprietors' claims. The crime of slave holding, he claimed, had originated with the British nation and had increased in direct opposition to "the interests, desires, and laws" of the West Indian colonies. The British people, he contended, should bear the expense of correcting this national wrong by providing slave owners with substantial compensation.[16]

Many of the free people of color who owned slaves also shared these views. In 1831, in St Ann's parish, Jamaica, the large community of color met to discuss the problems of abolition, property, and compensation. Benjamin Scott Moncrieffe, a wealthy estate owner and the recognized leader of the community, acted as chairman for the evening. Moncrieffe owned 400 slaves and three estates of his own and acted as the attorney for several other proprietors. Those attending the meeting objected strongly to comments that Stephen Lushington, the British abolitionist, had allegedly made to the effect that in Jamaica the free people of color had authorized him to emancipate their slaves. The members categorically denied giving any such authorization and stressed their determination to defend their property and to surrender it only for "the most full and ample compensation." They instructed Moncrieffe to send their resolutions to the Jamaican newspapers and to forward them to England for publication in *The Times* and in two of Britain's most rabidly proslavery newspapers, *John Bull* and the *Glasgow Courier*.[17]

The Interest complained about the commercial and financial distress so often and so effectively that in 1831 the British government appointed a select committee to investigate the economic condition of the colonies. When called on to present their case, members of the Interest catalogued the economic problems which beset the sugar colonies. They stressed the effects of the government's restrictive policies on West India trade and complained that increased production costs offset any advantage derived from their monopoly of the sugar market. They insisted that the continual discussion of the slavery question had led to a complete loss of confidence in the stability of colonial property with the result that since 1823 it had become virtually impossible to obtain credit secured against the estates.[18]

This argument was designed primarily to elicit higher compensation, for there is little evidence that the abolition movement adversely affected the amount of credit available to proprietors. Between 1823 and 1836, for example,

British merchants provided over £150,645 worth of mortgages to planters in Barbados alone. These mortgages were unrelated to the sale of property and were only part of the overall picture. As merchant credit declined after 1823, loans from private investors filled the vacuum. For the entire twenty-year period between 1823 and 1843, credit from British merchants accounted for only 20 percent of the total value of new Barbadian mortgages.[19] The credit argument clearly did not apply to private investment.

Planters also complained of the high costs of production and demanded a reduction in the duties on goods imported from Europe. Before the American Revolution, West Indian planters had bought many of their essential supplies from their mainland neighbors and paid for them with rum and molasses. After the war North American merchants were excluded from West Indian markets. In retaliation they raised their prices and demanded payment in specie or bills of exchange. Consequently the planters lost their cheapest suppliers of lumber, cattle, and clothing for their slaves and were forced to turn to the more expensive British and European markets. Fish and lumber, previously bought from the North American colonies, had to be imported from Canada and the Balkans. British merchants naturally passed the additional costs of freight and duty on to their clients in the form of higher prices. The planters, therefore, felt justified in complaining of the hidden costs of importing provisions from Europe and in seeking a reduction in the duties.[20]

Witnesses conceded that planters could buy most of their essential supplies in the alternative European markets. They could not, however, replace the convenient American markets for their rum and molasses. The improvement in Anglo-American relations in the 1830s did little to relieve the situation. The Americans refused to accept rum and molasses as barter for their goods and continued to demand payment in hard currency or bills of exchange. In 1817 the United States had imported an estimated 1,380,000 gallons of rum and over 1,120,000 gallons of molasses from the West Indies, but by 1831 American imports had virtually stopped. Moreover, between 1823 and 1831 the United States government encouraged sugar planters in Louisiana to increase production. In 1823 Louisiana had produced a little under 16,000 metric tons of sugar; by 1831 it had more than doubled its output. Since the United States was also the major importer of Cuban sugar and molasses and imported over 70 percent of the sugar produced in Puerto Rico, there was little likelihood of an American market reopening for West Indian produce.[21]

The Interest begged the select committee to recommend the removal of the restrictions on molasses and a reduction of the duties imposed on sugar. If brewers and distillers used molasses instead of grain in the manufacture of beer and spirits, it claimed, an extensive new market would soon replace the one lost in the United States. West Indian proprietors valued their rum at one-fourth the value of their sugar and used the profits from rum and molasses to pay production costs incurred in the islands.[22] Without a new market the profits from these by-products would be entirely lost. The creation of a British market for molasses, together with the reduction of the sugar duties, would assist the planters and save the colonies from imminent ruin. The Interest argued that a reduction of the duties would also lower the retail price of sugar, increase consumption, and allow the producer a reasonable profit.[23]

The figures that the Interest submitted for 1824 and 1830 did little to substantiate its argument. In 1824 British merchants bought approximately 3.8 million hundredweights of sugar at 58 shillings per hundredweight. By 1830 the price had fallen to 47 shillings per hundredweight but consumption had risen to only 4 million hundredweights. Though annual fluctuations in price affected consumption, the overall change was hardly dramatic.[24] Furthermore, the purchasing power of the public had a more direct bearing on the problem, and wage levels, rather than prices, influenced the level of consumption more acutely.

The planters' best hope of increasing consumption lay with the British working classes. Sugar was a relatively expensive item for industrial and agricultural workers. Lower prices might have allowed producers to tap this new market but the meager wages and often chronic unemployment of the period effectively prevented the laboring poor from buying more sugar even at greatly reduced prices.[25]

A more relevant argument claimed that high duties affected the planters' profits. Merchants made their profits on the wholesale-retail price differential but planters' profits depended on the difference between their production costs and the wholesale price of sugar. Difficulties arose when high sugar duties forced production costs up to the same level as wholesale prices and left the planter with no margin of profit.

Between 1815 and 1818 the difference between the lowest price of sugar and the lowest duty levied by the government was reasonably substantial, and planters could make between 17 shillings and 30 shillings per hundredweight before deducting their other operating costs. The price of sugar dropped between 1819 to 1831, but the duties remained constant. In 1823, for example, the lowest price paid for sugar was 27 shillings per hundredweight, the same as the duties imposed for that year. Planters who produced inferior sugar, or whose crop arrived late on a glutted market, had no profits from which to pay their expenses. Prices rose slightly over the next five years, allowing planters an average profit of 4 shillings per hundredweight, but when prices fell again in 1829, the profit margin disappeared once more. Although the duties were reduced in 1830, planters complained that they continued to lose 1 shilling on every hundredweight of sugar they produced.[26]

The Interest recommended that in addition to reducing the sugar duties the government pay a bounty on all refined sugar intended for reexport. A temporary bounty on reexported sugar, it argued, would stimulate both the metropolitan and colonial economies. The sugar duties yielded approximately £6.7 million per year. A bounty on refined sugar equivalent to one-twentieth of the total duties, would force up the price to the consumer and, at the same time, benefit the producer to the extent of 10 shillings per hundredweight. The bounty would also encourage refiners to produce more sugar for export and thereby benefit sugar-allied industry and shipping in the home country.[27]

The select committee raised the question of retaliatory action by foreign nations. The Interest replied that the most-favored-nation clauses incorporated into existing treaties made it illegal for foreign governments to raise their duties even if Britain increased the price of its exports. In any event, only a temporary bounty was needed because Britain's growing population would mean an increase in demand. At the same time the increase in slave manumission would inevitably lead to a decrease in production. Thus the problem would resolve itself within a few years. But unless the government took steps to improve colonial prosperity and protect the plantations, the restrictive commercial policies, together with the rising costs of production, would bankrupt the West Indian proprietors.[28]

Planters' production expenses extended far beyond the costs of buying slaves and equipment. The planter's metropolitan agent charged for his services at a near usurious rate. Usually the merchant received a 2.5 percent commission on the gross price of each shipment of sugar, 5 percent interest on any cash he advanced to his client, and 5 to 6 percent interest on any outstanding mortgages. In addition, the planter paid a 0.5 percent brokerage fee based on the long price of sugar, that is, the price of the sugar plus the duty, and a further 5 percent interest on the agent's commission. The merchant sold the sugar to refiners and retailers at the long price and was normally paid within two months. He, however, was not invoiced by his own suppliers for at least twelve months for any plantation supplies or luxury items he bought on behalf of the planter. Nevertheless, he invoiced the planter immediately and used both the duty and the interest for the intervening year. According to the calculations John Pollard Mayers presented to the select committee, if a merchant could turn over his capital five times each year, this practice netted him an annual profit of approximately 12 percent.[29]

The planter paid not only the merchant's charges and the government duty but lost part of his sugar into the bargain. He paid duty on the amount of sugar landed, but during storage in the warehouses, further drainage reduced the weight. Thomas Phillpotts calculated that producers paid approximately 7 pence duty on each hundredweight of sugar. After eighty days in the warehouse he estimated the loss from drainage at 6 pence per hundredweight. Moreover, any loss due to theft at the wharf, spoilage, or the bankruptcy of the buyer, was charged to the account of the planter.[30]

Several other witnesses testified to the high costs of production. All agreed that the abolition of the slave trade had added 15s. 10d. to the cost of producing one hundredweight of sugar. This figure represented both the direct costs of rearing young slaves instead of buying mature fieldworkers directly from Africa and the indirect expense of having fewer effective slaves in the labor force. Transportation and merchants' charges added another 8s. 4d. and raised the planter's costs to 24s. 2d., to be deducted from the price of sugar. With sugar selling for 23s. 8d. per hundredweight in 1831, the planter operated at a loss of 6 pence per hundredweight.[31] These figures, of course, are open to question, since the Interest frequently embellished its arguments for effect.

In many of the older colonies, an additional 4.5 percent tax on all exports further increased production costs. The British government had originally imposed the tax in the seventeenth century to offset the administration and defense costs that it assumed in place of the original proprietary owners. The tax created special difficulties for the smaller islands, such as Tortola and Antigua, where virtually all of the land was devoted to sugar. Over the previous century and a half Barbados alone had contributed almost £7,000 annually to the British exchequer. Repealing the tax, Mayers felt, would greatly assist the economic recovery of the islands.[32]

The Interest cited the increased competition from foreign producers as another factor contributing to the higher production costs experienced during the 1820s and 1830s. The abolition of the British slave trade in 1807 forced planters to rely on natural increase to supplement their slave labor force, while Brazil and Cuba, a relatively new producer, continued to take advantage of the slave trade. Planters in the British colonies asserted that Cuban and Brazilian proprietors paid £45 for each imported prime-age slave, whereas they had to maintain their slaves for fourteen years before they became useful field hands. This, they estimated, cost them £84 per slave. Since they also had to maintain the elderly, their serviceable labor force fell to forty-four per hundred, whereas the Cubans and Brazilians could count on the effective labor of sixty-four slaves in every hundred.[33]

The British proprietors conveniently forgot that they set their slave children to work at the age of six. They certainly did not maintain the children in idleness until they reached fourteen. They also downplayed the high death rate among newly imported Africans, which forced Brazilian and Cuban planters to buy twelve new Africans in order to gain eight slaves. At £45 each this raised the true cost of eight slaves to £540. British planters claimed it cost them £84 per slave, or £6 per year for fourteen years, before they could put these slaves to work. But since their slaves began work at the age of six, the planter had the benefit of the children's labor, albeit at a reduced rate, for eight years. Assuming that a six-year-old's labor was worth half that of a fourteen-year-old, it cost the planter £6 for the first six years and only £3 for the next eight. These creole slaves needed no "seasoning," so that, at a very basic level, it cost British planters £480 to raise eight slaves as opposed to the £672 they claimed. British planters, therefore, paid approximately 12 percent less than their Cuban and Brazilian counterparts, who continued to rely on the slave trade.[34]

Although the planters constantly complained of increased competition from Cuba, Brazil, Mauritius, and the East Indies, Britain imported less foreign sugar than they feared. Foreign sugar paid nearly three times the duty charged on West Indian sugars. The duty charged on Mauritius imports was not reduced to the same level as West Indian sugar until 1825, and only in 1835 did the government equalize the East Indian sugar duties. Thus the produce of both regions entered the British market at a distinct disadvantage. Nor did foreign sugar account for a great proportion of the total sugar imports: for the ten-year period from 1821 to 1831, foreign imports averaged 13 percent of the total sugar entering the home market; the proportion did not reach 23 percent until 1831.[35] Nevertheless it was to the Interest's advantage to depict as bleak a situation as possible in order to obtain the maximum compensation when emancipation eventually took place.

The West India Interest also returned repeatedly to its potent property argument in its campaign for compensation. Witness after witness testifying before the select committees on the colonial economies blamed the abolitionists for the deterioration in colonial property values. Since the reopening of the emancipation question in 1823, they claimed, the value of West Indian property had declined steadily and by the 1830s it was impossible to sell the plantations even at a depreciated rate. The constant pressure for the end of slavery discouraged British merchants from making further loans secured against either estates or slaves. The planters blamed the perceived lack of capital and credit for their inability to improve their property or meet long-standing financial obligations.[36]

Few nineteenth-century proprietors owned unencumbered estates. The majority struggled in a complex entanglement of annuities, legacies, settlements, and mortgages. Liabilities undertaken in the halcyon days of high prices and low operating costs became increasingly burdensome as prices began to fall in the 1790s. By the 1820s most estates carried multiple mortgages as their owners attempted to meet their financial responsibilities and continue production. In 1823 the Barbados Legislative Council complained that the recession had so affected their credit that many planters could not pay even the interest on their outstanding mortgages. The depression and the subsequent tightening of credit resulted in metropolitan merchants foreclosing on mortgages and forcing the sale of several estates through the Court of Chancery. The council cited six cases to illustrate the reduced value of estates which had passed through the court in the preceding year. One of the properties, The Adventure, had been sold privately in 1819 for over £22,142 but brought only £12,857 when sold in chancery a few years later. Similarly, when the Sion Hill estate had been sold privately in 1821 it brought £17,142, but when sold in chancery the following year its price had been reduced by half.[37]

Changes in the patterns of available credit complicated the lack of confidence in West Indian property. During the early eighteenth century most plantation owners simply borrowed from their fellow proprietors. By the 1740s they began depending heavily on metropolitan credit and services until, by the nineteenth century, British sugar merchants had become deeply involved in West Indian credit. Besides advancing credit against the consigned and expected crops, the merchants extended mortgages and accepted estates and slaves as collateral. By then, planters complained, profits barely covered operating costs and were rarely sufficient to pay the interest on long-standing legacies and annuities.[38]

The case of the Morgan Lewis estate in Barbados illustrates the tangled web of debts and liabilities surrounding many West Indian properties. In 1835 appraisers set the value of the estate and the unexpired terms of its apprentices at £16,171. When the Court of Chancery sold the estate six years later, nearly half of the £32,852 owed to the various creditors was in the form of legacies and annuities. The remaining debts consisted largely of open accounts to small creditors and mortgages to the British merchant house of Thomas and John Daniel. The sale price of £17,714 covered only the court costs and legacies and the sum of more than £8,571 due to the Daniels. The annuities and miscellaneous debts remained unpaid.[39]

Similar cases could be found throughout Jamaica, where the problem of planter indebtedness was equally widespread. In 1837 the Court of Chancery sold the Whydah estate which had been in receivership for fifteen years. The Master in Chancery reported that the property carried a mortgage of £20,090 dating from 1804, three legacies of £1,428 each, two legacies of £3,428 each, three gifts of £150, and other unspecified debts. In 1836 the owner's compensation amounted to only 7 percent of the total debt and hardly made an impact on the liabilities of the estate.[40]

The lack of a centralized banking system organized to provide and regulate credit forced planters to rely on mortgage arrangements with merchants and private individuals. The planters' involvement with British sugar merchants further complicated their problems. As mortgagees the merchants charged 6 percent interest on all mortgages; as consignees their charges were even greater. Taken together these charges accounted for rarely less than 10 percent and often as much as 20 percent of the planters' profits. If a planter wanted to consign his sugar to another merchant, he had first to pay off all outstanding debts to his previous creditor. Normally this was impossible, and merchant and planter remained locked together in a circle of mutual dependency: the planter unable to pay off even the interest on his debts; the merchant unwilling to foreclose and risk losing his entire investment. Merchants who decided to foreclose and force an estate through chancery were obliged to pay off the other creditors from the proceeds of the sale and often stood to lose more than they gained.[41] At the same time, proprietors argued that the uncertain future of colonial property made it even more difficult for them to get essential credit.

The belief that the abolition movement had depreciated West Indian estates had been voiced continually since 1823. When the owners of the Georgia estate had considered selling out in 1806, they expected to get at least £16,000 for the property, but by 1825 they doubted if the estate could be sold at any price. In 1830 a spokesman for Pitcairn, Amos, and Company, put the matter even more plainly. "I doubt," he wrote, "if we are justified in laying out a shilling on West Indian property, it appears as if the majority of the British nation was determined to destroy the colonies" by pressing the cause of abolition.[42]

While the select committee evaluated the evidence and prepared its report, abolitionist sentiment in Great Britain reached a new peak. Political reformers throughout the country pushed for the redistribution of parliamentary representation and in 1831 forced the government to act. The Reform Act of 1832 eliminated "rotten" and "pocket" boroughs and created new parliamentary seats to encompass the population of the growing industrial cities of Manchester, Birmingham, Leeds, and Sheffield. Deeply committed to abolition, these newly enfranchised areas pressured their prospective representatives to demand emancipation.[43] At the December elections few aspiring candidates were willing to risk defeat by adopting a proslavery stance.

The Reform Act extended the franchise and incorporated the cities but it also retained high property qualifications for election to Parliament. The newly elected Whig representatives of the industrial areas of the Midlands and the North proved to be as susceptible to the Interest's appeal to property as the conservative Tory gentry. The upheavals and riots of the preceding years had threatened the property of the gentry and factory owners alike, and even the abolitionists defended the principle of compensation. The social and political events of the early nineteenth century forced the government to recognize that most of the middle class would interpret uncompensated abolition as a direct attack on the rights of private property.[44]

Spurred on by public pressure, the cabinet met in early 1833 to discuss emancipation. It recommended that unless the colonial legislatures acted independently beforehand, the government should abolish the slave system by imperial order in 1837. When rumors of the possibility of uncompensated emancipation reached the West India Interest, it immediately took the offensive. It warned the government that if the rumors proved to be true "an immediate cessation of intercourse between the Mother Country and her colonies must ensue" and threatened to stop extending credit, honoring bills of exchange, or shipping out essential supplies. The resulting loss of confidence would have been disastrous for the new Whig administration because, in essence, the Interest threatened to destroy the colonial economies and to bring down the government.[45]

Unwilling to provoke a political or commercial crisis, Edward Stanley, the new colonial secretary, negotiated confidentially with the Interest before submitting any proposals for abolition to Parliament. Although the Interest refused to cooperate in drawing up a plan for emancipation, it made its expectations clear: nothing less than a continuation of the protective tariffs on colonial produce, a scheme to keep the ex-slaves attached to the estates, and extensive financial compensation would suffice.[46]

On 10 May, Stanley submitted a plan to the Interest for its comments: it provided for an apprenticeship of unspecified length for the ex-slaves and an interest-bearing loan of £15 million for the planters. Neither of the provisions satisfied the Interest. It pointed out that the slave owners would still have to feed and clothe the apprentices and to support the elderly and infirm. These obligations alone would absorb any possible profits. As for the loan, the Interest protested that West India property was valued at over £100 million and that the slaves alone were worth £40 million. It regarded a loan of £15 million as outright confiscation that merited no further comment.[47]

The outline of Stanley's plan appeared in *The Times* three days before he presented it to Parliament. Its appearance allowed him to test public reaction and to have sufficient leeway for future adjustments to the loan and the apprenticeship provisions. Four days later he presented his Abolition Bill to Parliament. The colonial secretary acknowledged that public opinion made it impossible to delay the settlement of the slavery question any longer. He hoped the bill would satisfy both the abolitionists and the slave owners. Its provisions freed all children under the age of six immediately, but all other slaves would serve a twelve-year apprenticeship to their former masters before gaining their unconditional freedom in 1846. The government proposed appointing stipendiary magistrates who would be sent from Britain to oversee the apprenticeship system and protect the interests of the ex-slaves. As compensation for the loss of their slaves, the owners would receive a £15 million interest-bearing loan.[48]

The members discussed each provision at length but paid the greatest attention to the apprenticeship system and the loan. The abolitionists among them objected strenuously to the terms of the apprenticeship. For twelve years the apprentices were to work three-fourths of their time for the master without pay but could hire themselves out for wages for the remaining hours. Out of their wages, the apprentices were expected to repay their masters one-twelfth of their value each year until at the end of twelve years they would be completely free. Stanley protested that he intended the apprenticeship to teach the ex-slaves industrious habits, to prepare them for their eventual freedom, and to introduce them to the system of wage labor. The abolitionists, on the other hand, protested that twelve years was too long to keep the apprentices in semi-slavery, and that it was the ultimate injustice to expect them to buy their freedom with their hard-earned wages. Whatever claims proprietors might have against the British people, they had no legitimate claim against the slaves. Forcing the slaves to pay for their liberty and, at the same time, extending a loan to the masters gave the owners double compensation. If the proprietors expected to receive compensation then, abolitionists argued, emancipation should be immediate.[49]

While the abolition party was most concerned with the apprenticeship, the Interest occupied itself primarily with the size and distribution of the proposed indemnity. It would have been out of character for the Interest to object to the apprenticeship, which it recognized as additional compensation. In fact, it would have been more advantageous to press for a longer term. The Interest, however, was composed mainly of merchants with West Indian investments at risk, and as John Pollard Mayers complained, "where the interest of the merchant is separable from that of the planter, it will generally be ascendant."[50] The representatives of the Interest, more concerned with recouping their financial losses, therefore concentrated their attention on the compensation clause.

Stanley based the suggested loan on the average annual net profits from the sugar, rum, and coffee produced in the colonies. The government calculated these at £1.5 million per annum and proposed advancing a loan equal to the value of ten years' profit. It based the calculation on figures that the Interest itself had previously submitted to the Board of Trade and considered the sum equivalent to one-fourth of the slaves' time. From the government's point of view, the loan, together with the apprenticeship, constituted full and adequate compensation.[51]

Both the size and form of the proposed indemnity aroused the Interest's indignant criticism. It adamantly refused to accept the offer claiming it was "a strange mode of remunerating a man for the loss of his property to favor him with a loan." The Interest expressed its dismay in a petition to the Commons. The loan, the petition stated, was totally inadequate and unrelated to the true value of West Indian property, which the Interest now placed at £47 million. Nor did it compensate proprietors who owned unencumbered estates or those who owned slaves but no land. Moreover, the interest repayments would swallow up all the planter's profits.[52]

The irrelevance of these arguments did not deter the Interest. For years it had insisted that it was absolutely impossible for planters to make a profit and that they in fact produced sugar at a loss. Now it expressed concern for those nonexistent profits. The plan tied neither the apprenticeship nor the loan to the ownership of land. If seen as a guarantee against the failure of abolition, the loan also helped the owners of unencumbered estates and therefore benefited all slave owners.[53] The West Indians had previously valued their property at £100 million. Now, perhaps afraid that by demanding too much it might get nothing, the Interest adjusted that value to a much lower figure. Only by returning to its property argument could the Interest publicly justify its continued discontent.

Representatives of the Interest met with the government again to discuss the provisions of the bill. They stressed their dissatisfaction with the amount offered and demanded a substantial increase. Apart from a grant of £20 million, they expected an additional £10 million loan. Planters could use the grant to pay off their outstanding debts, and the loan would provide encouragement and working capital. In making these demands the West Indians implied that failure to meet them would destroy all confidence in British trade and could affect the property of every British citizen.[54]

At the end of May Stanley informed the Commons that the government had changed the compensation from a loan of £15 million to an outright grant of £20 million. He expressed the hope that the members would support the proposed alteration and explained his reasons. Everyone connected with the colonies had agreed that the loan was insufficient. While West India merchants claimed they were loath to disturb colonial trade, they nevertheless made it clear that unless more money was forthcoming they would not hesitate to cancel credit and trade agreements in order to protect their own interests.[55]

The Interest made it clear that without adequate compensation the colonial legislatures would not cooperate in the difficult transition from slavery to freedom. As Ralph Bernal, a spokesman for the Interest, bluntly remarked in a later debate, the West Indians demanded the £20 million more to satisfy the disgruntled colonists and induce them to cooperate than to cover any financial losses they might sustain. The Interest's British representatives promised to use their influence in the colonies if the government met their demands. They set the price of their cooperation at £20 million. The government succumbed to the threat and gave in to the Interest's demand.[56]

Reactions to the proposed amendment came immediately from all sides. All shades of opinion, from ambivalence to outrage, were expressed at home and abroad. Critics and supporters of the grant aired their views in Parliament, the press, and in the colonial legislatures. In the Commons opinion was divided on the subject of the increased grant. For many members the problem lay with the size of the indemnity rather than with the principle of compensation: most believed it unconstitutional not to pay the slave owners for their loss, but some did not feel that the planters had proved that this loss amounted to £20 million.[57]

When the more radical members of Thomas Fowell Buxton's Anti-Slavery Society formed the Agency Committee in 1831, they took the question of abolition to the general public. Through lectures, pamphlets, rallies, and meetings, they reached many sections of the population untapped by the more cautious society. It was mainly because of the committee's efforts that voters forced prospective candidates for the Reformed Parliament to pledge their support for abolition.[58]

Although the Agency Committee pushed the idea of slavery as a national sin, it consistently opposed the payment of compensation. It saw any compensation paid to the slave owners as rewarding thieves for the loss of their stolen goods. If, on the other hand, the wages of sin were death, the committee believed that the wages of slavery should be the uncompensated death of the system.[59]

The Agency Committee and its allies expressed their outrage over the grant in a variety of ways. As early as 1831 advocates of factory reform had used the imagery of slavery to attack the abuses found in the factories and mills of the new industrial centers. They frequently drew comparisons between the treatment of the slaves and the treatment the laboring poor received in England.

Letters to the *Leeds Mercury* drew attention to the conditions that mill workers endured and accused mill owners of treating their workers like slaves.[60] Middle-class radicals were not alone in supporting the committee. Virtually all the working-class newspapers joined in the protest. The *Poor Man's Guardian* complained that the compensation money would be squeezed from the bones of those who worked as "white slaves" in England. Nor were these passing concerns, for as late as 1838 the *British Liberator* was still roundly criticizing the award.[61]

Despite the protests of the Agency Committee and its radical sympathizers, the compensation clause was incorporated into the bill. Buxton claimed that his strategy had been "to overthrow the apprenticeship at the price of the twenty millions." In exchange for this concession, the government shortened the apprenticeship from twelve to six years hoping that the increased grant would satisfy the planters and convince the Interest that it had not ignored their property rights.[62]

The colonies greeted the news of the increased compensation with ill grace. Individuals voiced their discontent in letters to newspaper editors, in private letters, and in the colonial assemblies. The *Barbados Globe and Colonial Advocate* complained that £20 million was insufficient and left the colonists uncompensated for over £27 million worth of property. Several metropolitan newspapers agreed with this view for the *St. Jago de la Vega Gazette* reprinted British editorials to the same effect. In a particularly virulent article the *Glasgow Courier* described the abolition bill as the work of "short-sighted and self-interested knaves" who, by forcing through abolition, would reduce thousands of intelligent whites to poverty and degradation.[63]

Private letters to England also reflected the slave owners' displeasure. Thomas W. B. Hendy of Barbados insisted that the colonies welcomed emancipation, but only adequate compensation could ensure the planters' cooperation and preserve the stability of the "beautiful" colonial superstructure. In words reminiscent of the abolitionists' attacks on slavery, he continued, the bill served only "to reduce men to the dismal necessity of dragging out their existence in misery and contempt, to make them curse the day of their birth, and sigh for that of their dissolution."[64] Hendy was not refering to the condition of the slaves but to the fate of the planters if denied full compensation.

In Jamaica, the proposals were denounced as "monstrous in the extreme," but in the legislature, John Mais attempted to pacify his more vocal colleagues. He decried the inadequacy of the indemnity and agreed that most of it would return to England. Nevertheless, he advised them to be cautious and pointed to the danger of giving the abolitionists any excuse to withhold the money. Unless the colonial legislatures passed the complementary abolition acts that the British government required, there was a good possibility that it would delay payment of the compensation indefinitely. He urged his colleagues to cooperate and to remember the old adage that "half a loaf is better than no bread."[65]

While the planters reacted with discontent, the colonial governors reacted with undisguised relief. With the planters even grudgingly satisfied, the governors' work of overseeing the transition from slavery to free wage labor became a great deal easier. The governor of Barbados, Sir Lionel Smith, assured Stanley that despite their protests the increase had given the planters a great deal of satisfaction. The home government's decision to leave the details of the colonial abolition acts to the individual legislatures proved even more gratifying. He reminded the colonial secretary never to forget that the planters loved their power over the slaves almost as much as they loved the slaves' labor.[66]

In the end the West Indians had the last word. For nearly a decade the Interest had lobbied for the "consideration" Canning had alluded to in 1823. The major debate over compensation had dealt less with the principle than with the size of the award. Buxton himself had little objection to compensation and denied that he had ever intended to bypass the subject.[67] Few politicians or abolitionists denied the validity of the Interest's property argument. The social and political unrest of the 1820s and 1830s caused all British property owners, great and small, to fear for the safety of their possessions. Farmers and factory owners alike felt personally threatened by the rash of riots, rick burnings, and machine breakings that erupted in 1830. Repressive laws were passed to protect property and prevent its destruction by the mill workers and agricultural laborers, who lacked access to the political process.

The relative minority that opposed compensation lacked sufficient power to do more than express its moral indignation. Those who held the power were themselves property owners and more likely to sympathize with the Interest's appeal. Small wonder that in July 1833 the *St. Jago de la Vega Gazette* triumphantly claimed the grant as "a complete admission of our right to property."[68]

2

Commissioners and Financiers

The Abolition Act brought the British government face to face with a major administrative challenge. Parliamentary approval of the grant created two immediate, interrelated problems: how to apportion the money equitably between the 44,000 individuals who owned slaves in nineteen different colonies and how to raise the money in the most efficient manner. Although the act established basic guidelines for dividing the money among the colonies and for classifying the newly emancipated slaves into various categories of apprentices, it did not set any precise rules for paying claims against the Compensation Fund or for the arbitration of disputed claims. Refining these guidelines became the responsibility of government-appointed commissioners of compensation.[1]

The complicated task of administering the fund began in late 1833 with the appointment of metropolitan and colonial commissioners. In London the Central Board of Commissioners supervised and coordinated the work of auxiliary boards set up in each of the colonies. Even before the government began its negotiations to raise the money, these boards set up the bureaucratic machinery necessary for distributing it smoothly and equitably.

The Abolition Act outlined the composition and duties of the central and auxiliary boards in general terms. It authorized the government to appoint the metropolitan commissioners but left the choice of the assistant commissioners to the governors of the individual colonies. All seven members of the Central Board had wide experience in legal and colonial affairs. Four were lawyers, while the others had close connections to the Colonial Office. Sir John Shaw-Lefevre's broad administrative experience, for example, complemented the knowledge of colonial affairs he had gained as an undersecretary to Edward

Stanley. Thomas Amyot was the registrar of slaves, and James Lewis had served as a former Speaker of the Jamaican House of Assembly.[2]

The two extra commissioners added in 1835 further strengthened the colonial connection. The new appointees, Robert William Hay and James Stephen, had both held permanent Colonial Office positions before joining the board. Hay had been the undersecretary for the Mediterranean and Eastern colonies before assuming responsibility for the West Indies in 1827. He remained at the Colonial Office until 1836.[3]

James Stephen was the best qualified of all the central commissioners and an acknowledged expert on West Indian law. His expertise combined the legal and colonial aspects of the board's work. Stephen had acted as unpaid legal counsel to the Colonial Office for over ten years before becoming the department's full-time legal advisor in 1825. His interest in the West Indies extended beyond his professional life and his long-standing association with the evangelical Clapham Sect reinforced his commitment to the abolition of West Indian slavery.[4]

In each of the colonies, the auxiliary boards of assistant commissioners worked in conjunction with the metropolitan board. The British government appointed the governor and attorney general of each colony as ex officio members of their auxiliary board and authorized the governor to appoint the remaining members.[5] Virtually all of the working members of the colonial boards were both commissioners and owners or managers of large estates.

In Barbados four members of the House of Assembly served on the board. Nathaniel Forte, the Speaker of the House, owned Bennett's and Warleigh Heights estates; Renn Hamden owned Rising Sun and Ball's estates and co-owned Small Ridge, and Joseph William Jordon owned the Burnt House and Walkers plantations. The fourth assemblyman, William Oxley, combined his duties as a commissioner with his long-standing position as the island's Master in Chancery. The final board member, Forster Clarke, owned Halton estate and acted as attorney for more than a dozen absentee proprietors. Between them the Barbadian commissioners owned over 2,056 acres and 1,392 slaves, while in his capacity as an attorney, Clarke supervised an additional 7,983 acres and 4,500 slaves belonging to his employers.[6]

The Jamaican assistant commissioners included the attorney general Dowell O'Reilly; John Mais, an attorney and owner of Mount James, Mount Pelier, and Hall's Delight plantations, and Hector Mitchell, the mayor of Kingston. Also serving on the board were Edward Wilson Panton, the advocate general and owner of Elmwood estate; William Miller, the attorney for Lord Seaford; Thomas J. Bernard, the attorney for James Dawkins; James Minot, the agent for the Caymans; and John Gale Vidal who served as the board's solicitor.[7]

This blend of duties was difficult to avoid in colonies, where suitable prominent residents invariably acted in several official capacities. Lord Sligo, the governor of Jamaica, was forced to apologize on several occasions for unavoidable delays in the commission's work. Many of the assistant commissioners also had duties at the assize court in Kingston and the grand court or the chancery court in Spanish Town. All their activities, he explained, often occurred within the space of a few weeks and the resulting backlog of work prevented the board from working more quickly.[8]

Several interrelated problems demanded immediate attention before any claims could be processed. First, the boards had to collect and evaluate the information necessary for determining the exact proportion of the grant due to the respective colonies; second, they had to assign the ex-slaves to their apprenticeship categories, and finally, they had to establish clear guidelines for submitting and paying claims. The responsibility for solving the first two problems fell by their very nature to the colonial boards.

The Abolition Act established that each colony's share of the indemnity depended upon the value and number of its slaves. The British government defined the value as the average price of slaves in each individual colony for the eight-year period from 1822 to 1830. To help them review the sales the assistant commissioners enlisted the help of the local officials directly connected with the sale or transfer of slaves. They also examined the records of the provost marshal, the registrar of slaves, and the registrar of mortgages and other evidence supplied by auctioneers, merchants, and attorneys. The government felt that forced sales reflected a disproportionately low value for the slaves involved, so the boards excluded these from their calculations and rejected sales between relatives and all sales for manumission for the same reason. The remaining sales fell into three general categories: registered slave sales, unregistered slave sales, and sales of slaves together with land or other property. Using the prices as the basis for estimating the value of the slaves did not always work to the benefit of the owners. In Mauritius, for example, the legislature collected a 2 percent duty on all slave prices, but buyers frequently avoided the duty by declaring a lower price. When the time for apportionment came, the slave owners of Mauritius found to their chagrin that the lower declared price had become the basis for evaluating their slaves.[9]

Once the boards had agreed on the average price, they multiplied it by the number of slaves recorded in the latest slave register for each colony. Next, they calculated this as a percentage of the total value of all slaves, which the government had estimated at £45,281,738 sterling. Each colony then received a percentage of the indemnity equal to the ratio that the value of its slaves bore to the total value of all slaves covered by the act.[10]

Table 2.1. *Value of the West Indian Slave Population, Selected Colonies*

Colony	Value of Slaves	Compensation
Jamaica	£13,951,139	£6,161,927
British Guiana	9,729,047	4,330,665[a]
Barbados	3,897,276	1,721,345
Trinidad	2,352,655	1,117,950[a]
Grenada	1,395,684	611,936[a]
St. Vincent	1,341,491	576,446[a]
St. Lucia	759,890	333,700[a]
Tobago	529,941	232,400[a]

Sources: PP, 1835 (420), 1837–38 (64). Wastell, "The History of Slave Compensation," pp. 70–71.
[a] Estimated compensation.

The prices and relative values varied greatly among the colonies. The Barbadian commissioners estimated the average price of their slaves at £47. When multiplied by the 82,807 slaves registered in 1834, this gave a relative value of £3,897,276, or 8.6 percent of the total value. Barbados thus received £1,721,345, or 8.6 percent of the fund. Jamaican slaves were valued at £13,951,139 which represented 30 percent of the total slave value. The colony therefore received £6,161,927, or 30 percent of the Compensation Fund. In more sparsely populated areas, such as Trinidad and British Guiana, where fewer slaves were available, the average prices ranged as high as £105 and £115, which gave a higher relative value for their slaves.[11] These colonies received 5 percent and 21 percent of the fund respectively (table 2.1).

When the government decided to distribute the money on an ad valorem basis, owners in the more densely populated islands immediately protested. Critics argued that the scheme was both costly and time consuming. The Interest and these colonies in particular pressed for a per capita distribution, which, they argued, simply entailed consulting the latest slave registers and would save the British government nearly £10,000.[12] The most sustained criticism came from John Pollard Mayers, the colonial agent for Barbados.

As early as 1833 Mayers began lobbying for the highest possible indemnity for his colonial constituents. Using a mixture of economic and humanitarian arguments he tried to persuade the government to increase the compensation allotted to Barbados. The island's large slave population, he claimed, showed they had been well treated and could reproduce their numbers naturally, but their very numbers in turn depressed their price. According to his estimate the government would penalize Barbadian planters for their kindness if it used slave prices as part of its calculations. Moreover, since the abolition of the interisland traffic in slaves, prices in Trinidad and British Guiana had been artificially inflated. Under the ad valorem system, British Guiana, where the slave population had decreased as sugar production increased, and Mauritius, which still carried on an illicit slave trade, would receive almost twice the amount due to Barbados. Mayers felt that these colonies should pay a bounty to Barbados instead of receiving extra compensation.[13] When these arguments failed to have the desired effect Mayers tried a slightly different approach.

Mayers pointed out that because all land in Barbados was held by individuals it would be totally unjust to change the existing system without paying an "ample indemnity." He put the same argument to Lord Goderich at the Colonial Office and again stressed the need for increased compensation for his island. Goderich reversed the argument, claiming that with all the land taken up there was none left for the ex-slaves to use and they would be forced to continue working on the estates. Consequently, since Barbadian planters had a secure workforce and could make the transition to free labor more easily, they would have less need for compensation.[14]

Not to be outdone, Mayers replied that 5,200 slave owners lived in Barbados and that 73 percent of these owned slaves but no land. He pointed out that at emancipation these people would lose their property immediately and suggested that all slave owners receive a flat £25 per slave. The remaining compensation could then be divided among the more highly valued colonies. Naturally, he neglected to say that 800,000 slaves at £25 each would use up the entire £20 million and leave no extra money for the rival colonies.[15]

Mayers obviously exaggerated his claim. The government's compensation returns, published in 1838, list 5,349 claims for 82,806 slaves in Barbados. This did not mean, however, that a different individual submitted each claim. For example, 241 large-scale proprietors submitted 7 percent of the claims. All of these were for 50 or more slaves, but the same people also submitted other claims for smaller numbers of bondsmen. The commissioners required a separate claim for each property, so one individual might submit as many as 8 or 9 different claims. William Prescod submitted 8 claims, one for each of his estates, while John Rycroft Best submitted at least 7. The practice was not confined to the larger owners. Jane Rose Hinds entered 14 separate claims for a total of 31 slaves, while Benjamin Robinson submitted 7 claims for a total of 34.[16]

Moreover, the mere fact that a person owned only a few slaves did not preclude the ownership of land. Indeed in several cases such proprietors owned at least ten acres. In a colony where respectability, the franchise, and land ownership went hand-in-hand, small-scale white proprietors attempted to acquire at least a few acres. William H. Cox, who submitted a claim for only 6 slaves, owned a ten-acre estate. Michael Corbin and James Sealy, who claimed for 7 and 4 slaves, owned seventeen and nine acres respectively.[17] Such examples indicate that Mayers probably inflated his figure for effect, perhaps by a factor of two.

Mayers also informed Goderich that the majority of the landless slave owners were people of color. In this he may have been closer to the truth, but he aimed at gaining greater and earlier compensation for Barbados rather than at underlining the position of the colored class. His rather specious argument was to no avail. Perhaps Goderich and the government agreed with Sir Lionel Smith, the governor of Barbados, who wrote confidentially that the Barbadians' disappointment over the proposed basis for apportionment resulted partly from their pride. "A Barbadian," he wrote, "can never be brought to understand that there is any other Colony of half the Value and Consequence to the Mother Country that this is . . . ," and Barbadian planters would never gracefully accept a scheme which awarded them less compensation than the other colonies.[18]

After collecting the necessary information for calculating the slave values, the auxiliary boards forwarded the data to the Central Board in London for the final analysis. The central commissioners then faced the problem of converting the various colonial currencies into sterling. As a basis for their calculations they used the Spanish silver dollar, exchanged at the rate of 4s. 4d., a rate that the British government had used for years when paying civil and military personnel serving abroad.[19]

With the problem of slave values solved, the assistant commissioners turned to their second task: classifying the newly emancipated slaves as apprentices. Since the length of apprenticeship and the ultimate value of each individual depended upon their classification, their assignment required on-the-spot supervision, to ensure as little abuse of the system as possible. The British government had established three major apprenticeship categories, which carried varying terms of service. The "praedial attached" category included all slaves commonly employed in agriculture on land belonging to their owners. Slaves engaged in agriculture on land owned by people other than their masters became "praedial unattached" apprentices. All other slaves became non-praedial apprentices. The two praedial classes carried a six-year apprenticeship, while the non-praedial group, which included domestics, dock workers, and artisans, was bound for a four-year term.[20] The central commissioners subdivided these three categories to reflect the true value of individual slaves as closely as

Table 2.2. *Apprenticeship Divisions and Classes, Jamaica*

Division	Rank	Subdivision	Compensation per Slave
Praedial	1	Head People	£31/00/06
attached	2	Tradesman	31/05/11
	3	Inferior tradesmen	20/13/07
	4	Field laborers	26/12/02
	5	Inferior field laborers	12/16/02
Praedial	1	Head People	31/00/10
unattached	2	Tradesman	31/11/02
	3	Inferior tradesman	20/17/11
	4	Field laborers	26/11/06
	5	Inferior field laborers	13/04/03
Non-praedial	1	Head tradesmen	30/19/02
	2	Inferior tradesmen	20/11/05
	3	Head People on wharves, shipping, etc.	30/05/05
	4	Inferior people as above	22/13/08
	5	Head domestic servants	29/03/01
	6	Inferior domestics	19/10/10
		Children under six years	5/07/10
		Aged, diseased, or noneffective	4/06/08
		Runaways [a]	

Source: *Royal Gazette and Jamaica Times*, 24–31 October 1835, Supplement 44.
[a] 7s.11d to the £ sterling of their value.

possible. Within each major group the Central Board created five subdivisions (table 2.2) and set their compensation value on a descending scale, but no standardization of the subgroups existed between the colonies. In Barbados, for example, "Head People" included rangers, drivers, cattle-keepers, and sugar boilers, while in the Bahamas no one owning fewer than ten slaves could claim a "Head Man." Faced with these inconsistencies, the Central Board decided that the problem of assigning the slaves to their particular division was beyond its scope and delegated the task to the individual colonial boards. In order to place the ex-slaves in their appropriate categories as accurately as possible, the colonial commissioners employed evaluators to supervise the classification. They divided the colonies into districts and assigned an independent evaluator to each. These evaluators were instructed to classify the slaves according to their employment during the twelve months immediately prior to emancipation and to check the alleged employment against their work as recorded in the latest slave registers. The evaluators assigned each slave or group of slaves a reference number for later use in identifying all claims and correspondence concerning the slaves in question. Until the evaluators' returns reached England, the central commissioners refused to accept any claims for compensation.[21]

The classification and evaluation system presented a number of problems. Theoretically, no evaluator worked in a district where he had either a personal or a commercial interest. In the smaller islands, where planters' interests spread across the entire colony, this was virtually impossible. Again, in theory, valuers were required to check the slaves' employment against the latest slave register. But theory and practice were difficult to reconcile. Given the close-knit white society and the desire to extract the longest possible apprenticeship, some deliberate misrepresentation was inevitable. It was mainly a matter of owners registering non-praedial slaves as praedial apprentices in order to gain two extra years of their labor. That the opportunity for misrepresentation existed is borne out by one important fact: several of the colonies, including Barbados and St. Vincent, did not compile their last slave register until 1834.[22] This was some time after the government had decided on the subdivisions and more than nine months after it had established the three major groups of apprentices. Moreover, the valuers' returns from Barbados did not arrive in England until 1835. That planters took advantage of the opportunity is also borne out by the many complaints that reached the stipendiary magistrates appointed to settle disputes between masters and apprentices.[23]

In the journal that he kept while serving as a stipendiary magistrate in Barbados and St. Vincent, Major John Colthurst recorded many instances of misclassification. The planters, he complained, had taken advantage of the difference in the length of the apprenticeship terms and made the problem "50 times worse, *by false registration upon oath*."[24] Many slaves who had never worked in the fields, either because they were too young or because they were really domestics, found themselves assigned to the praedial groups and condemned to serve the longer term. When the governor of St. Vincent asked him to check the registrations, Colthurst found blatant and, he suspected, deliberate misclassification of many apprentices. On one estate he visited, the owner claimed all his 150 slaves as field laborers, and Colthurst reported that almost all of the remaining estates had done the same. These deceptions, he felt, stemmed from a wish to demonstrate the planters' dissatisfaction with the amount of compensation. The planters hoped that the government would "bleed freely" to avoid trouble when the non-praedials' apprenticeship ended in 1838.[25]

In 1834 the Jamaican legislature passed laws allowing owners to change a slave's status from domestic to praedial, thereby forcing the apprentice to serve the longer term. Although James Stephen insisted that the Colonial Office disallow the Jamaican laws, similar problems existed in the other colonies. Between July 1837 and June 1838, the commissioners changed the status of approximately 1,166 Barbadian apprentices from praedial to non-praedial in cases of deception.[26]

Although most misclassification resulted from a desire to gain more labor, there was one area where an owner might gain financially. In Barbados, at least, owners appear to have understated the number of slaves categorized as "aged, diseased, or otherwise non-effective." Compensation for this group was the lowest of all, approximately £2 each. The Barbadian slave population numbered 83,149 in 1834 and of these 14,732 were children under the age of six years. Another 1,780 were considered "aged, diseased, or non-effective." After discounting the children, it becomes apparent that the Barbadian planters claimed compensation for 66,637 effective workers, leaving only 3 percent of the slaves registered as noneffective, as compared with 6 percent for St. Vincent and Jamaica. Such misrepresentation raised the question of collusion between slave owners and valuers. If, as some alleged, certain Jamaican valuers had allowed their clerk to add the names of slaves they had not seen to their completed list, how much easier it would have been to simply misclassify existing slaves.[27]

While the auxiliary commissioners wrestled with their appointed tasks, the Central Board addressed the final problem pressing for its attention. During 1834 and early 1835, the board compiled the general rules for submitting and paying claims against the Compensation Fund and clarified several questions concerning certain groups of slave owners. All slave holders were required to submit their claims in the colonies where their slaves were registered and to inform the assistant commissioners of the number of slaves involved, their normal place of residence, and the classification, value, and number the colonial evaluators had assigned to them. In addition, the registrar of slaves had to certify that the number of slaves claimed corresponded to the number registered, making due allowance for natural increase or decrease. In addition to sending details of the claims to London for a decision, the assistant commissioners circulated lists of claimants to local officials and newspapers to allow litigants to enter their appeals.[28]

In the case of contested claims, the rules were more flexible. Litigants could submit counterclaims either in London or in the colonies, provided that they clearly stated their interest or title in the disputed slaves. Claims based on liens, encumbrances, or mortgages detailed the original sum of money involved, the date and size of any payments, and the amount still outstanding at the time of the claim. After receiving notice of a counterclaim, the original claimant had three months in which to file a defense of his property. The commissioners set specific time limits for accepting both original and counterclaims. They refused to accept uncontested claims after 31 October 1840. No counterclaims lodged in the West Indies could be accepted after 1 May 1835, and no counterclaims originating in England would be considered after 1 July 1835.[29]

The first adjudication of all colonial counterclaims fell under the jurisdiction of the auxiliary boards, which based their decisions on the property laws of their respective colonies. The primacy of the various counterclaims received special attention. In most colonies this simply meant noting the dates of the liens, annuities, and mortgages and deciding which claims took precedence. In recently ceded colonies where French, Spanish, or Dutch property laws prevailed, the procedure was often more complicated. Settling counterclaims originating in England became the responsibility of the central commissioners, who made their decisions in consultation with their appropriate West Indian counterparts. Once the commissioners had made their decision, a claimant's only avenue for appeal was to the king-in-council. Of the thousands of decisions that the commissioners made, only six were appealed and only one overturned. After approving the rules, the government published them in the *London Gazette* and sent copies to the various governors for circulation among the residents and colonial officials. The board allowed a nine-month grace period for owners to register objections to the rules before they reviewed the first claims and counterclaims.[30]

The Central Board also clarified the position of several categories of slave owners who were not clearly covered by the Abolition Act. The owners of slaves who had been manumitted by virtue of having lived in England remained eligible for their share of the compensation. The owners of runaway slaves also received compensation, provided that they produced reasonable evidence of their ownership and of the slaves' continued existence. These owners, however, received compensation at a reduced rate. Maroon slave owners and owners of slaves in the Caymans were also eligible, even if they had never registered their slaves. The commissioners decided that for these owners at least, the failure to register did not constitute forfeiture of their right to claim compensation. The Abolition Act specifically excluded slave owners in Ceylon, St. Helena, and territories administered by the East India Company.[31]

Once it had established the rates of compensation and exactly who could submit a claim, the Central Board had only to decide on the place and method of payment. In the case of uncontested claims, claimants received interest-bearing certificates payable at the Bank of England and drawn against the West India Compensation Fund. The claimants, or their duly authorized agent, collected the award in the form of certificates or in government stock. In the case of litigated claims, the accountant general invested the award in 3 percent annuities until the claim could be settled, at which time the stock and accumulated interest passed to the successful litigant.[32]

Finally, the government paid all claims, regardless of size, in London. As early as 1833, delegates of the Interest had met with the government and made it clear that they wanted the compensation paid out in England rather than in the colonies. The method of payment had also worried the commissioners and colonial merchants, who urged the Colonial Office to pay the smaller colonial claims as quickly as possible. They suggested that these claimants receive a general power of attorney allowing them to dispense with the services of an agent in England. The government eventually issued colonial powers of attorney but the problem remained, especially for the smaller claimants.[33]

In the meantime the government set about raising the promised indemnity. In a country already burdened with a national debt of £800 million, this was an unenviable task. The Reformed Parliament had been elected to abolish slavery and reduce taxes. Trying to raise the money through direct taxation would be political suicide. Stanley himself realized that given the attitude of the general public it would be hopeless, and extremely unwise, to suggest giving slave owners any compensation that had been raised through new taxes.[34]

The £20 million represented 40 percent of the gross government revenue for the period.[35] Any effort to increase taxes to meet this new expenditure could have entailed a 4 percent increase across the board for ten years. It would have affected every aspect of life and all levels of society. Increased customs and excise taxes would have raised the prices of all imported goods while an increased stamp tax would have meant higher prices on all legal documents and newspapers. At the same time an increase in land taxes would have affected the aristocratic landowners, the humbler gentry, farmers, and the industrialists, as well as the agricultural and urban laborers who lived in rented property. To impose higher taxes may have required simple parliamentary legislation but any attempt to collect them could have led to revolution. The government, therefore, sought an alternative and turned to the great British financiers for help.

The government began its negotiations in July 1835. The Treasury wanted to raise a primary loan of £15 million without causing any unnecessary fluctuations in the national money market. The chancellor of the exchequer, Thomas Spring Rice, met with representatives of the leading financial houses to discuss a contract for a loan of £20 million. Present at the meeting were Sir John Rae Reid and members of the houses of Rothschild, Montefiore, Ricardo, Irving, and Baring. The government, Spring Rice explained, did not need to raise the entire amount during the current session of Parliament. The compensation payable to Barbados, Mauritius, and the Cape of Good Hope would not fall due immediately. The complementary abolition act required of Barbados had proved unsatisfactory and until the colonial authorities amended it, the government intended to withhold their compensation. In the case of Mauritius and the Cape of Good Hope, the government refused to pay any claims until the Central Board of Commissioners had received their evaluators' reports. These, he expected, would arrive in England sometime in early 1836, and at that time he would raise the additional funds.[36]

The chancellor proposed raising the loan in thirteen installments over a fourteen-month period. Payment of the initial installments was scheduled to begin in August 1835 and end in September 1836. For every £100 the bankers subscribed in money, the chancellor offered a combination of government stocks and annuities at 3 percent interest, and the usual discount of 2 percent per year. The bankers had the option of providing £14,701,875 in cash immediately, or the full £15 million spread over the proposed fourteen-month period. As a further incentive, Spring Rice invited sealed bids for additional deferred annuities that would expire in 1860. The interest on these annuities would be governed by the prevailing interest rate for similar public securities. As the meeting closed, Spring Rice asked the bankers to submit their bids at a second meeting to be held in early August.[37]

At the subsequent meeting, only the Rothschilds submitted a bid for the loan. Their first bid on the deferred annuities was higher than the chancellor was prepared to accept. After some consideration, the Rothschilds lowered their demand and brought it in line with the Treasury's sealed offer. The chancellor accepted the amended offer, signed the contract, and the Rothschilds began their own negotiations to raise the money from the international banking community.[38]

Some confusion arose over the exact amount the Rothschilds provided, and in 1838 the Commons demanded that the government clarify its position. John Finlaison, the Government Calculator, was ordered to explain the misunderstanding. In a lengthy and complicated series of calculations, Finlaison demonstrated the difficulty. The government had expected an initial loan of exactly £15 million, paid in fourteen installments. This meant that the Rothschilds would advance the government £15,304,170 in order to allow for the 2 percent

Table 2.3. *Compensation Awarded to Slave Owners, 1837*

Awards	Compensation
Awards to Uncontested Claims	£14,530,699/07/11
Awards to Litigated Claims	3,414,138/13/04
Paid into Chancery	497,139/13/11
Paid by Accountant General	227,423/15/05
Total	£18,669,401/10/07
Not Awarded	1,330,598/09/05
Total	£20,000,000/00/00

Source: PP, 1837–38 (215): 334.

discount. But the Rothschilds understood that they would deduct the discount from the £15 million, so that in reality, the government received less than it expected as a primary loan. According to Finlaison, the Rothschilds provided only £14,621,311, but made over £101,875 on the deferred annuities alone.[39]

By 1836 the Treasury had raised sufficient money to allow the commissioners to begin paying the uncontested claims. Over the course of the next twelve months the Central Board handled 39,790 uncontested and 4,651 litigated claims at a rate of almost 1,600 each week. When the board's commission finally expired in 1840, only 366 claims remained outstanding (table 2.3). These fell under the jurisdiction of James Lewis, who stayed on as the sole arbitrator of litigated claims, and in 1846 the £23,158 involved in these claims reverted to the public funds.[40]

The commissioners' decision to pay all claims in London provoked widespread criticism. Opponents of the policy quickly accused metropolitan merchants and creditors of pressuring the government in an effort to safeguard their own investments. Nevertheless, the commissioners argued that the method protected all legitimate claims, especially those of annuitants, trustees, and creditors living in England. Absentee estate owners and large-scale proprietors with family or business connections in England had no difficulty with the procedure. For them it simply meant issuing the necessary powers of attorney to enable their merchant-creditors to collect the money on their behalf. It was, essentially, just another aspect of the commercial relationship that already existed between the sugar planter and his merchant.[41] Indeed, in some instances, merchants insisted on receiving the power, perhaps not fully trusting their client to use the indemnity to pay long overdue bills or the interest on old mortgages. In 1837, for example, William Williamson gave his power of attorney to Stewart and Westmoreland, a merchant company based in London. Another merchant quickly challenged his action, claiming that Williamson had given him a power of attorney as early as 1833. He pointed out that he had already collected the compensation and intended to retain it until Williamson paid his outstanding debts.[42]

Not all of the eligible claimants benefited from the decision. From the point of view of the smaller claimants, the policy had definite problems. Thousands of West Indians owned few slaves: the commissioners had estimated that 30,000 people owned an average of only 3 each.[43] This meant that 30,000 people owned 90,000 slaves, or 11.25 percent of the total slave population of the British West Indies. The commissioners apparently equated the number of small claims with the number of small owners and assumed that a different individual submitted each claim. This was certainly not the case: since claims were made on the basis of where slaves lived, the owner of several estates submitted a different claim for each property. The same held true for urban slave owners whose slaves lived at different addresses within the various towns.

Seven percent of the 5,349 claims submitted for Barbados, for example, were for 50 or more slaves. A further 67 percent of the claims were for 11 to 49 slaves and the remaining 26 percent were for 10 slaves or less. Yet only 241 proprietors actually submitted the 368 largest claims, giving them an average of 1.5 claims each.[44] There is no reason to suspect that the Barbadian experience was unique. The problem of multiple claims led the commissioners to overstate the number of small proprietors. The commissioners' 30,000 owners were, in fact, 30,000 claims, many of which were submitted by the same people. If the Barbadian average of 1.5 claims per large-scale owner is applied to the figure for all of the West Indies, it reduces the number of small owners by one-third. Thus only 20,000 people might actually have owned the 90,000 slaves that the commissioners mentioned.

Few of these small slave owners had convenient contacts in England to whom they could turn. The cost of assigning an agent the requisite powers of attorney often meant a substantial reduction in their small awards. The stamp duty and commission charged on the document made little difference on awards amounting to thousands of pounds, but claims of £5 to £10 suffered considerably. In March 1836, *The Barbadian* published details of the costs involved in submitting a claim. Using the example of £89 due for 4 slaves, the newspaper showed that the costs of the receipt and stamp, postage, stamp for power of attorney, and commission at 1 percent amounted to £3 4s. 2d., or 3.5 percent of the award. It was hardly surprising these claimants became the obvious targets for speculators who were eager to make easy profits with little effort.[45]

From the very beginning, rumors circulated throughout the colonies that Britain would never pay the compensation. Several prominent spokesmen lent credence to this belief and to the fear that the commissioners' expenses would drastically deplete the fund. Richard Barrett, the Speaker of the Jamaican House of Assembly, attempted to convince his colleagues that the compensation would fall to £10 per slave. If such statements caused "a great deal of discontent" among the informed assemblymen, their effect upon less sophisticated slave owners often proved disastrous.[46]

Many small claimants were induced to part with their expected compensation in a variety of ways. Throughout 1835 and 1836, advertisements appeared in the local newspapers soliciting the sale of uncontested claims. Some, inserted by the more reputable merchants, offered top prices for any small unopposed claim. Other merchants offered to act as agents in England in exchange for a small commission and promised to pay their clients at the place of their choice. The editors of the *Royal Gazette and Jamaica Times* singled out the advertisements of Cavan and Company of Barbados, and Elin, Scott, and Company of Jamaica as examples of public spiritedness and concern for the less fortunate.[47]

Other advertisements, of a less generous nature, also appeared. Whitla and Cunningham inserted their notice in the *Barbados Globe and Colonial Advocate* in October 1835: in return for compensation claims the company offered their regular customers "advances in Dry Goods, at their established Cash prices," subject only to a small charge for expenses incurred.[48] Unfortunately it is impossible to check the prices of Whitla and Cunningham's goods for the years 1834 to 1836. Perhaps they would show an upward trend to offset the company's supposed generosity.

Not all speculators advertised their transactions in the public press, but their activities did not pass unnoticed. Complaints of extensive speculation soon appeared in official and unofficial reports. In late 1835 the Colonial Office informed the governors of charges that unscrupulous speculators had bought up claims at 50 to 60 percent discounts. The office urged the legislatures to do everything in their power to curb the abuse of the system. Speculation, it observed, affected the section of the community least able to bear the financial loss and whose willing cooperation was essential to the peaceful transition from slavery to freedom.[49] Lord Glenelg, the new colonial secretary, assured the assemblies that payment, though sometimes unavoidably delayed, was secured upon the "national faith" of Great Britain.[50]

While commenting on the extent of the problem, these official reports made no mention of specific cases, but John Colthurst vividly described the methods of the more aggressive speculators in his *Journal*. He recorded the case of an elderly woman who owed a Bridgetown merchant £20. The merchant threatened her violently, assured her "*that compensation would never be paid at all*," and terrorized her into parting with her compensation. In a similar incident, a woman owed a merchant £30, which she hoped to pay with the proceeds of her indemnity. The merchant, however, seized her slaves and sold them at auction. Her claim passed to the new owner, while the merchant made a profit of almost 400 percent on the sale. Colthurst mentioned these incidents not because they were the worst that came to his notice but because they illustrated the speed with which the "mercantile body" fell upon the poor.[51]

Not all reactions to the speculation were as indignant as those of the Colonial Office or John Colthurst. Although some felt that the legislatures should take care of the problem, others felt it was the commissioners' duty to rectify matters. The Colonial Office quickly pointed out that it was beyond the scope of the commissioners to take official notice of dubious claims and that it was virtually impossible to detect fraud.[52] Claims were often accompanied by a power of attorney which authorized the bearer to collect the money on behalf of the claimant. The commissioners could not possibly tell under what circumstance the power had been issued or if all the money reached the proper hands.

Other critics reacted much more cynically. In a letter to the *Royal Gazette and Jamaica Times* in 1835, "A Plebian" maintained that any attempt to curb the speculation interfered with individual rights. Citizens had the legal right to dispose of their property as they thought fit. Any interference with this right disturbed the normal vagaries of the marketplace and upset the balance between supply and demand. A second letter to the *Gazette* reinforced this view. The legislature could not take action, the writer argued, while the method of apportionment remained unsettled, while the place and time of payment were uncertain, and while negotiations for the loans to make up the £20 million were still incomplete. What is clear from the despatches, newspapers, and articles of the period is the general uncertainty many small proprietors felt about the payment of compensation. Although the more knowledgeable slave owners understood the problems the commissioners faced, the delays increased the doubts of the poorer ones. The commissioners could not make any payments until the returns from all the colonies arrived in London. They had set 1 April 1835 as the earliest date for the payment of claims, but the valuers' returns for Barbados did not arrive in England until September, while those from the Cape of Good Hope did not arrive until May 1836.[53] Given the uncertainty of the situation, many small claimants preferred cash in hand, or a reduction of their outstanding accounts with the local merchants, to the possibility of receiving nothing.

Although speculation undoubtedly occurred, it is difficult to document its extent accurately. The conveyances registered in Barbados show only transfers of compensation as part of legitimate sales. The Jamaican conveyances record similar legal transactions to pay normal debts. Nevertheless, some appear very dubious. The activities of Nathan Joseph, for example, give cause for suspicion. Joseph, a Jamaican merchant, registered eight conveyances of compensation in November and December of 1834. The conveyances, mainly from women, involved a total of £385 and are suspect for two reasons. First, no claim numbers appear, which is in itself unusual because legitimate purchasers took great care to record the identifying number in case of a later dispute. Second, all the claimants transferred not only the amount they knew they would receive but all rights to any future indemnity. This latter condition raises serious questions about the honesty of these transactions, especially in view of the fact that many colonists still entertained some hope of receiving additional compensation.[54]

The problem of speculation raised the question of possible alternative methods of payment, particularly regarding the smaller claims. On several occasions Sligo advised the Colonial Office that Jamaican slave holders wanted their compensation distributed in the island. He recommended that the auxiliary boards be allowed to draw checks against the Compensation Fund for those claimants with fewer than twenty slaves. These checks would have the same value as bills of exchange or bank notes and could be bought and sold in the same manner as other commercial paper. This system, he urged, would effectively eliminate the extensive speculation and discounting of claims which plagued the colonies.[55]

There was no sound reason for rejecting some method of local payment especially since the precedent and mechanism for such payments already existed. For many years the British government had paid the governors, military officers, and civilian officials abroad through the colonial military chests. The government had also used this method to pay the assistant commissioners and could presumably have extended it to accommodate the smaller claimants.[56] The danger involved in transporting the money was negligible. Payments to the military chests went by warship, as did the small amounts of coin that private merchants sent out to their agents. Once the Central Board had made a rough estimate of the number of small claims expected from each colony, it could have deposited the appropriate amounts in the various military chests. By authorizing the assistant commissioners to draw against these deposits, the government would have avoided most of the problem. Moreover, since most of the affected claimants would spend their awards with colonial merchants, the money would have entered the local economies.[57]

Despite the commissioners' error in equating claims with owners, the fact remains that an estimated 30,000 claims were submitted for an average of 3 slaves each. If each of the 90,000 slaves was worth £30, then £2.7 million would have found its way into the colonial economies. If each colony received the same proportion of this money as it had received of the Compensation Fund, Jamaica would have received £810,000, or 30 percent, and Barbados £232,200, or 8.6 percent. Even if the recipients were indebted to local merchants, the money would have circulated through the island economies before being returned to Britain to pay metropolitan suppliers.

Normally, colonial officials could not calculate the exact amount of coin or paper circulating within their jurisdiction at any given time.[58] Some other method of estimating the impact of the money on the local economies had, therefore, to be employed. Assuming that the supply of money available for trade was equivalent to the national exports, then a rough calculation becomes possible. For example, between 1833 and 1843, Barbadian exports averaged over £742,600 annually. The money paid to the smallest slave owners in 1836 and 1837 would have increased the island's money supply by approximately 31 percent. In the case of Jamaica, the average value of exports for the years 1832, 1837, and 1838 was over £2.5 million so its money supply would have increased 35 percent. If the compensation payments had been made in specie, the influx of hard currency would have greatly eased the shortage of specie, which the colonists continually complained about. In 1835 the receiver general of Jamaica stated that approximately £71,428 circulated in the island in the form of coins. This, he believed, was totally inadequate for trade purposes and at times the colony was "nearly drained" of all specie. Two years later he estimated the amount of coin circulating at only £70,214, so that the introduction of £810,000 in coin would have increased the available specie by a factor of eleven.[59]

Paying the larger claims was a completely different matter. British merchants and mortgagees clearly influenced the government's decision to make the payments in England. It was in their best interest to keep as much of the compensation as possible under their direct control. Once the central commissioners had made their awards, nothing short of litigation or an appeal to the king-in-council could alter their decision.[60] Thus, the need for many proprietors to employ an agent in England to collect their awards worked to the advantage of the creditors and proved a mere formality for the heavily indebted planters. Moreover, any proprietor who attempted to withhold the power of attorney risked the loss of all future credit and almost certainly faced an expensive lawsuit.

Given the determination of the merchant-creditors to control the payment

COMMISSIONERS AND FINANCIERS · 43

of the larger claims and thereby protect their investments, the extension of this control to the smaller claims made little sense. Smaller claimants were unlikely to owe large sums to British merchants. Nor were metropolitan merchants likely to extend them credit. A more liberal payment system would not have endangered the interests of the substantial British merchants and could have benefited the small claimants and the local economies.

Both the central commissioners and their colonial counterparts worked as quickly and efficiently as possible. The frequent delays were due to the government's restrictions rather than to the various boards. The problems connected with the colonial apportionments, evaluations, and speculation arose more from the original act than from ineptness on the part of the commissioners.

The influence of the West India Interest in framing the details of the act is nowhere more apparent than in the provision for paying all claims in England. The arrangement was not specified in the act, nor in the general rules that the Central Board established. Only concern for the metropolitan merchants and mortgagees can explain such a decision. Despite their competent administration, the commissioners were powerless to counteract an arrangement that served to confirm Mayers's complaint that the mercantile interest "most fearfully predominates over that of the planter."[61] Payment in London left metropolitan merchants and creditors ideally situated to protect their interests and ensure the prompt collection of outstanding debts. It also placed British merchants in a particularly good position to control the eventual investment of the funds.

3 Debt Reduction, 1833–1843

The government's decision to pay compensation had an immediate short-term effect on the island economies. For the first time in decades, West Indian proprietors such as Charles Nicholas Palmer of Jamaica and John Rycroft Best of Barbados could substantially reduce their long-standing debts to British merchants.[1] Palmer, for example, owned Rose Hill estate, which carried a mortgage for over £10,000 to Charles Payne and Son of Bristol. In 1824 Payne foreclosed on the property and forced the estate into chancery. The receiver used the proceeds from the annual sugar crop to maintain the interest payments and, by 1836, had reduced the outstanding principal slightly. The compensation awarded for the Rose Hill slaves in 1837 allowed Palmer to reduce the debt by a further 32 percent.[2]

In Barbados, John Rycroft Best managed his father's estates, Fairey Valley and Moonshine Hall. His consignees, Thomas and John Daniel of Bristol, held mortgages worth £14,500 against the two estates. When Best received £7,571 compensation for his father's ex-slaves in 1837, he used the award to reduce the interest accumulated against the estates. The Daniels allowed the debt against Fairey Valley to remain at interest and did not press for repayment of the principal. Nor did they force Best to sell the estates, since he had specifically used the compensation to meet the interest payments.[3]

The increased number of mortgages made available to planters following the award of compensation clearly illustrates the trend towards debt repayment and the extension of additional credit. For metropolitan merchants compensation meant more than a simple vindication of property rights. It represented a unique opportunity to recoup at least part of their colonial investments. After their ten-year lobbying efforts, creditors were determined to press their advantage and secure the repayment of outstanding debts. Getting possession of the compensation money was, as Hinton Spalding pointed out, the "great object" of all the creditors.[4]

Widespread indebtedness was the expected consequence of an economy based on credit. During the seventeenth and early eighteenth century, high sugar prices usually ensured that planters made sufficient profits from the annual crop to cover current operating costs and to guarantee payment of the debts charged against the plantations. But by the end of the eighteenth century, planters found it virtually impossible to meet their commitments. Whether their accumulated debts arose from an inability to pay inherited liabilities, from personal extravagance, or from an unexpected need for working capital, the result was the same.[5]

Metropolitan merchants demanded substantial collateral to protect their investments against default. Normally this took the form of a mortgage, at 6 percent annual interest, secured against the debtor's plantation and slaves. Generally, mortgages received priority according to the date of their registration. The West India trade did not recognize the English practice of "tacking," whereby a creditor could add later advances to his original mortgage, so merchants had little incentive to consolidate their clients' debts by buying up intervening mortgages. Consequently, estates often became encumbered with several independent mortgages. Some owners mortgaged their properties to three or more different creditors simultaneously, while others simply remortgaged them time after time to the same merchant house.[6]

If planters defaulted on their interest payments, a creditor had two options. He could either take legal possession of the estate or foreclose on the mortgage and file suit in the British or colonial courts of chancery. Neither alternative was completely satisfactory: they were generally used only as a last resort. As a mortgagee "in possession," the creditor installed his own agent to manage the estate and applied any profits toward reducing the debt. He assumed responsibility for reasonable repairs to the property and immediately became responsible to all other creditors. Although prohibited from selling the estate, the mortgagee could arrange with the owner to sell off surplus acreage. When Alexander Cowan took possession of the Hope coffee plantation in Jamaica in the early 1820s, he appointed James Daly as his agent. Daly kept detailed accounts of all plantation expenses and sales of produce and attested under oath to the accuracy of his bookkeeping. Between 1824 and 1830, Daly recorded the payment he made to William Peart for beef, to Stone and Roseberry for jobbing slaves, to Daly and Company for plantation supplies, and to sundry current and law accounts. The agent also recorded the sales of coffee and the application of the proceeds towards the liquidation of the two separate mortgages that Alexander Cowan held against the property.[7]

In December 1823 these two debts totaled over £13,700. Over the course of the next twelve months, the plantation produced 80 metric tons of coffee, which were sold in England for £4,172. The sale of some of the land for £2,100 raised the estate's income to £6,272 for the year and enabled Daly to pay Cowan just over £6,110 on the mortgage account and reduce the debt by 45 percent. Production fell precipitously, however, during the next two years: the estate produced only 25 metric tons in 1825 and a mere 21 metric tons in 1826. The income from these meager crops was not enough to pay both the operating expenses and the mortgages, so the interest for these two years was carried forward. The following year, production improved considerably and Daly sold 80 metric tons worth £2,211 on the British market and paid another £3,000 on the mortgage account. By then the account stood at £9,061, and although the payment reduced the debt by 33 percent, the total remained almost 80 percent of the amount owed in 1824. The sale of 45 metric tons of coffee in 1828 and 35 metric tons in 1829 brought the estate £3,186, but Daly could not make any further reduction to the mortgages before he registered his accounts in 1830.[8]

Problems involving legal title and the capital needed to put a run-down estate back in working order discouraged many creditors from taking possession of their debtors' property.[9] These creditors still had the option of filing a suit in the colonial courts of chancery. In 1832 mortgagees-in-possession held only 4 percent of the 948 Jamaican estates used in this study, while none of the 326 Barbadian estates were so registered. On the other hand, over 20 percent of the Jamaican estates and 3 percent of the Barbadian properties were in receivership.[10]

Unlike the mortgagee who took possession of an estate, the creditor who filed a chancery suit could demand that the estate be sold to satisfy his claim. In such cases the creditor entered a bill of complaint and foreclosure and the court appointed a receiver to administer the estate for twelve months. At the end of the year the receiver presented his accounts to the Master in Chancery. If the creditor persisted in his demand the master ordered the estate appraised and advertised for sale each week until the court received an acceptable bid. If the estate remained unsold after a year, it was reappraised and readvertised.[11] Once the property had been sold, the master ranked all of the debts according to their priority and paid them, the court costs, and receiver's expenses, out of the proceeds.

When Arthur Rollock defaulted on his mortgage in 1829, his principal creditors filed a bill of complaint and foreclosure in the Court of Chancery in Barbados. The court appraised Rollock's estate, Chance Hall, at £9,992 and ordered it to be sold for debt. Rollock died before the property could be sold, but his creditors persisted and, in 1833, petitioned for the revival of the bill against his heirs. William Bovell, the major creditor, then bought the estate at the new appraised price of £10,168. The proceeds covered £680 in court costs, £855 in administrator's fees, and 97 percent of the outstanding debts.[12]

Contemporary observers estimated that the price of a chancery estate was about half its true value. In 1822 the court sold six Barbadian estates, and in each case the price was approximately half the amount paid three years earlier, when each had been sold privately. The Interest used these examples to illustrate the depreciation in colonial property, but in reality they compared sales made under very different circumstances. Private sales took place at the convenience of the owner, whereas impatient creditors usually initiated chancery sales. The rules of the court also required the buyer to pay down at least 10 percent of the price at the time of the sale.[13] Under private conditions the buyer could, if necessary, secure the entire price with a mortgage. Moreover, there was little competition for chancery estates, and usually the purchaser made the sole bid for the property. In only two of the fifty-seven chancery sales transacted between 1823 and 1843 was more than one bid offered for any property.[14]

With little competition for chancery estates, the properties rarely sold above the appraised values. Between 1823 and 1843 the Barbadian court sold fifty-seven estates of which only fifteen (26 percent) sold for more than their appraised value. Another four (7 percent) sold for less, while the remaining thirty-eight (67 percent) sold as appraised. In only three cases was the price sufficient to cover all the liabilities charged against the property. Two of these estates, Black Rock and Dunscombe, were sold in 1825 and the third, Clifden, in 1832. The debts against Black Rock were estimated at over £5,880, but the estate was appraised at £5,482 and sold for £7,000. In the same year Dunscombe, with accumulated debts of over £28,000, was appraised at £27,857 and sold for £35,714 to Charles Thomas Alleyne, a member of one of the largest land-owning families in Barbados. In 1832 when the debts against Clifden were estimated at £12,500, the court appraised the property at £9,441 and sold it for £12,823 to Robert Haynes, another extensive land owner.[15]

The effectiveness and desirability of initiating a chancery suit varied from colony to colony. In Jamaica estates frequently remained in chancery for over twenty years. When the Duke of Buckingham bought the Middleton coffee plantation in 1830, it had been in chancery for almost fourteen years. Other estates fared even worse. A succession of receivers had administered Newfield for at least seventeen years before it was finally sold in 1841. In Barbados, on the other hand, the system was more efficient. Few estates remained in chancery for more than a year and most moved out of the court's jurisdiction within a few months. The Sunbury, Upton, and Hampton estates were placed in receivership in February 1832. They were advertised in June and sold later the same year.[16] The difference was due partly to the greater efficiency of the Barbadian court system and partly to the greater competition for available land in a smaller island where the majority of the proprietors lived on their estates. In the 1820s approximately 85 percent of all Jamaican planters were absentees, compared to 25 percent of Barbadian proprietors for the same period.[17]

Despite their widespread use, mortgages had several disadvantages. They could only be levied against real property, not against the produce of the estate, which the law classified as personal property. Thus creditors could not seize a planter's rum and sugar for debt. If consigned to another merchant, the produce was further protected by bills of lading and consignment agreements. Moreover, the loss of the estate through fire or the death of the slaves destroyed the value of the mortgage and left the creditor without recourse.[18] In many cases creditors extracted extra protection in the form of court judgments or additional collateral.

In Barbados, 183 private sales were transacted between 1823 and 1843. The types of collateral used fall into three distinct categories: in 29 percent of the sales, a court judgment secured the price. When Harbourne Gibbes Stragham bought Haynes Hall in 1832, for example, he paid £8,571 down and secured the remaining £3,428 with a judgment and a mortgage against the 115-acre estate. Henry Grannum made a similar arrangement in 1842 when he paid £15,000 for the Prior Park estate.[19] In a further 22 percent of the sales, the price was secured by a combined mortgage and judgment, and in 14 percent by a mortgage alone. In the remaining 35 percent of the cases, the method of payment was not specified or the purchaser paid in full.

A court judgment was considered a free admission of the debtor's obligation and was made for twice the amount of the new debt. For example, a judgment of £10,000 usually secured an advance of £5,000. Judgments had two advantages: first they could be executed at any time within a year of being issued, after which an appeal for a new judgment became necessary; second, they could be levied against both personal and real property, so that, when used in combination with a mortgage, the judgment gave a creditor short-term as well as long-term protection for his investment. In executing the judgment the colonial provost marshal confiscated goods or land to the value of the writ and sold them at public auction. Usually the planter could decide which lands would be affected and naturally chose to surrender the least-productive acreage. Out of sympathy for their neighbor, few planters attended such auctions, and overvalued goods sold at rock-bottom prices, leaving little surplus money to satisfy the creditor.[20]

The practice of demanding supplementary collateral was also widespread. In such cases the debt was secured against two or more estates, giving the creditor the opportunity to repay himself out of the proceeds of them all. When Robert Gladstone mortgaged his Great Valley estate in Jamaica in 1831, his creditor, James Shaw, wanted additional security for his £17,500 loan. He forced Gladstone to offer Canoe Valley, Rogers River Run, Golden Vale, and Gaultiers, as proof of his good faith and thereby secured his investment against five estates and over 1,000 slaves.[21]

By the time emancipation became a reality, few West Indian estates were free of all encumbrances. Complex liabilities, some dating from the early eighteenth century, fettered the majority of estates. In 1834 at least 37 percent of the 326 Barbadian properties surveyed carried at least one mortgage.[22] Earlier unpaid mortgages could well raise the percentage of estates still mortgaged at emancipation far higher. Thus, for many proprietors the prospect of compensation offered some small hope of reducing the entanglements.

The financial affairs of the Ellis family of Jamaica illustrate the complexity of colonial indebtedness. In the late eighteenth century the Ellis family's estates included Montpelier, Nutfield, Newry, and Greencastle plantations in the St. James and St. Mary parishes, together with several other properties scattered through the parishes of Trelawny, Westmoreland, St. Elizabeth, and Hanover. In 1774 John Ellis mortgaged Montpelier to secure loans totaling £4,200 from Cranfield Beecher and Henry Murray. Judgments and £200 annuities to each creditor afforded further protection for the loans. When Ellis died in 1781, he left the plantations to his two sons. Charles Rose Ellis, later Lord Seaford, inherited Montpelier and other property, while his younger brother, John Ellis, became the proprietor of the Nutfield, Newry, and Greencastle estates. Liability for their father's debts became their joint responsibility.[23]

By 1813 the younger John Ellis was heavily in debt and forced to mortgage Nutfield estate to his brother as surety for a £6,500 loan at 5 percent interest. John Ellis's financial situation continued to deteriorate, until by 1823 he owed £31,000 to Deffell and Son, his English consignees. The Deffells' refusal to advance a further £9,000 forced him to seek assistance elsewhere.[24] When, in desperation, Ellis appealed to the house of Timperon and Dobinson to take up the old debt and make the new loan, they agreed to do so only on condition that they received unusually large consignments of sugar. Ellis's brother, whose estates were unencumbered, agreed to assign his sugar to them to meet the requirement. Timperon and Dobinson accepted Nutfield and Newry as collateral for the £31,000 owed to the Deffells and advanced £9,000 on the security of Greencastle. In addition, they agreed to pay the interest on the earlier mortgage against Nutfield and to pay John Ellis £1,950 per annum for his maintenance. As long as they received Seaford's sugars all debts were serviced at 5 percent.[25]

By 1826 Ellis had fallen even deeper in debt. His account with Timperon and Dobinson had increased to over £44,800, and he was obliged to seek a new advance and to accept a greatly reduced allowance. In 1830 Timperon and Dobinson informed Ellis that his mortgage account had reached almost £50,000 and that since Lord Seaford had recently reassigned his sugars, due to the poor state of the market, the usual interest rate of 6 percent would apply to the entire debt. After receiving a letter from Ellis in France, the suspicious partners sought legal advice. Not only did they suspect him of disposing of produce in Jamaica, they also feared that Ellis was selling off property to avoid his obligations, and that his colonial agent was drawing excessively high bills of exchange on his behalf. They assured William Burge, their legal advisor, that they did not want possession of the estates, only further collateral.[26]

Meanwhile, Lord Seaford himself took legal action against his younger brother. In 1821 he sought a court judgment for over £32,600, which, he claimed, included John Ellis's share of the debts and annuities that remained outstanding at the time of their father's death. Under the terms of the will, Seaford was responsible for only four-sevenths of these liabilities, but he had paid the entire amount since 1784. The court granted the judgment and ordered that the debt should become the prior lien against Ellis's estates. These debts, together with those owed to Timperon and Dobinson, were still unpaid when Ellis died in 1832.[27]

In 1834 Seaford registered his counterclaim against his brother's property. Since the estates were also heavily mortgaged to Timperon and Dobinson, the central commissioners had to unravel the conflicting claims. Eventually, they awarded Timperon and Dobinson the £12,330 compensation due for the slaves on Nutfield, Newry, and Greencastle. A further £3,647, the compensation for Fort George, the plantations' livestock pen, went to Ellis's son, Charles Parker Ellis, who was obliged to share the money awarded for two other estates with his uncle, Lord Seaford.[28]

The financial conditions of other estates were similarly complicated, either through the actions of the owners or through the practice of transferring mortgages among creditors. In 1823 James Haughton James of Jamaica owed over £9,800 to Stirling, Gordon and Company of Glasgow. To secure the debt, James mortgaged two properties, Haughton Hall and Burnt Ground Pen, to the company. At the same time, he was a party in a chancery court case concerning Colliston, a coffee plantation in St. Ann. James held a mortgage of over £10,900 against Colliston and hoped to buy the estate through the chancery court. In 1824 Edward Trueman Gary, acting on behalf of James, bought Colliston for £7,142. To pay for the estate, James borrowed £7,857 from Hamilton Brown, a prominent local attorney. James intended either to mortgage Colliston to Stirling, Gordon, and Company as additional collateral or resell it and use the proceeds to repay the debt.[29] James apparently conveyed the new property to Brown to secure his debt and mortgaged its slaves to Stirling and Gordon.

In the same year Stirling and Gordon transferred their mortgages against Haughton Hall and Burnt Ground Pen to Hawthorn and Shedden of London who immediately instructed their solicitor to prosecute their claims for the compensation due for the slaves on all three properties. Although they received the compensation for the Colliston slaves, the £6,419 for the slaves at Haughton Hall and Burnt Ground Pen went to the James family. A final conveyance in 1836 remortgaged these two estates and transferred the compensation to Hawthorn and Shedden.[30]

Jamaican estates were not unique in the complexity of their credit arrangements. Those of Barbadian properties often proved equally tortuous. When Richard Parris Pile borrowed £5,571 from George Abel Deane in 1817 he secured it with a mortgage against the slaves on his Springfield estate. In 1827 Deane sold the mortgage to William Coppin. When Coppin died the next year, Pile's widow and executrix had to repay the outstanding principal of £2,857 to his estate. Charlotte Pile had kept up the interest payments since her husband's death in 1824 and had tried unsuccessfully for more than a year to sell Springfield. Although the net income of the estate had been estimated at £1,400 in 1825, Charlotte Pile could not raise the money to repay the mortgage. To satisfy her creditor she remortgaged the estate to Richard Haynes for the amount of the debt.[31] When the estate was sold in 1837, a loan of £1,428 remained among the outstanding debts, which then became the responsibility of the new owners. The compensation awarded for the Springfield slaves amounted to £3,907, and although Coppin's executors contested the claim, the indemnity went to the Pile family.[32]

Financial complications could also arise through difficulties with the buyers of colonial properties. In 1820, for example, James Holder Alleyne of Barbados sold Swans estate for £15,714 to Thomas Whitfoot Hendy. Hendy paid only £4,285 at the time of the sale and secured the remainder of the price with a mortgage. By 1829 Hendy had sold the estate to John Thomas Corbin, who quickly mortgaged it to Thomas and John Daniel. Three years later, Alleyne filed a bill of complaint and foreclosure against the estate, claiming that both Hendy and Corbin had defaulted on their payments and that over £7,142 remained due to him from the original sale. The action forced the estate into chancery, and Alleyne regained the property at a cost of £8,034, the appraised value. Although he regained the title to the estate, Alleyne received only £628, part of a lien of £2,679 that he held against the plantation. The rest of the money went to pay court and receiver's costs totaling nearly £1,428 and to pay off other debts and legacies incurred between the transactions.[33] The £4,651 mortgage that the Daniels held does not appear in the chancery records. Presumably they regarded Alleyne as a good risk and did not press their claim in court.

The merchants were, naturally, far more concerned with recouping their own losses than with the predicament of the beleaguered planters. The certainty of compensation virtually guaranteed that most of the money would return to the major creditors. Any proprietor foolhardy enough to offer serious resistance to his creditors' just claims risked lengthy and expensive court battles.

In 1838 the British government published detailed returns of all claims submitted to the commissioners of compensation. These lists, tabulated by colony, give the names of the recipients, the amount of money, and the number of slaves involved in each claim and distinguish straightforward claims from those settled through litigation.[34] The information provides the basis for calculating the percentage of compensation which Jamaican and Barbadian proprietors paid directly to their metropolitan merchants.

Estimates of the number of sugar estates operating in Jamaica in the early 1830s vary considerably.[35] The 948 properties surveyed here include at least 274 identifiable sugar estates, 157 coffee plantations, 86 livestock pens, and a further 21 growing a mixture of pimento, cotton, ginger, coffee, and sugar. They include most of the great sugar estates of the time and are spread across the entire island.[36]

By 1837, the owners of these 948 properties had submitted claims for 56 percent of the total compensation awarded to Jamaica.[37] Not all of this money went to the slave owners. Straightforward uncontested claims and many successful counterclaims put much of it directly into the hands of the influential merchants who controlled the metropolitan sugar industry and a substantial part went to the twenty-four merchant houses who dominated the Jamaican trade (table 3.1).[38]

Merchant houses such as W., R., and S. Mitchell and Company, W., G., and S. Hibbert and Company, Timperon and Dobinson, and other giants of the West India trade received at least 15 percent of the awards. The largest com-

Table 3.1. *Compensation Awarded Directly to Merchants, Jamaica*

Name	Awards from Planters	Compen- sation to Merchants	Location
W., R., & S. Mitchell	£83,449	£93,965	London
W., G., & S. Hibbert	55,587	59,545	Manchester
Judah & Hyman Cohen	26,542	38,247	London
Biddulph & Cockerell[a]	36,260	36,260	
Timperon & Dobinson	30,342	35,441	London
Currie, Pearse, & Tunno	36,256	35,406	London
Davidson & Barkly	28,059	35,122	London
P. J. Miles	24,547	28,188	Bristol
J. H. Deffell	25,537	26,804	London
T. & M. Hartley[a]	18,385	23,385	
Andrew Colville	19,324	20,830	London
John Gladstone	19,188	19,605	Liverpool
Sir John Rae Reid	19,400	19,400	London
Stewart & Westmoreland	16,254	17,361	London
Hawthorne & Shedden	12,177	15,520	London
Purrier & Purrier	15,211	15,211	London
Jegan & Rutherford	13,227	13,227	London
Dickinson & Harmon[a]	11,978	11,978	
Sir Alexander Grant	6,103	11,709	London
S. Boddington	8,765	10,413	London
Baker & Phillpotts	7,990	7,990	London
Barrow & Lousada[a]	6,730	6,730	
Charles Horsfall	5,196	5,196	Liverpool
Pitcairn & Amos	2,774	6,806	Yarmouth
Total	£529,281	£594,339	

Sources: PP, 1837–38 (215); Attorney's Letterbook: John Gale Vidal.
[a]Could not be linked to a specific location.

mercial collector of Jamaican compensation, the London-based Mitchell and Company, had business interests that covered the whole island and collected compensation for over 5,4176 slaves on estates in half of the twenty parishes. Altogether, Mitchell and Company collected over £93,900 from 27 major Jamaican properties and a variety of small pens and coffee plantations that employed fewer than 100 slaves.[39]

The Manchester house of W., G., and S. Hibbert and Company was the Mitchells' closest competitor. Their West India business dated from the early eighteenth century, when it supplied cotton goods for the African slave trade before expanding into the sugar industry. Its members included Robert Hibbert, owner of an extensive Jamaican plantation, and George Hibbert, the island agent. Although its investments were scattered across the island, at least 29 percent of the company's compensation came from the four Trelawny estates owned by Sir Simon Haughton Clarke. For the slaves on these properties the Hibberts collected over £15,230. Clarke's widow, Dame Catherine, received a further £27,515 for the 1,475 slaves living on their six other properties. When all the Hibberts' awards are taken into account, however, they received more than £59,500 from their Jamaican clients alone.[40]

Unlike the Mitchells and the Hibberts, other merchants concentrated their interests in specific areas. Philip John Miles, the Bristol merchant and banker, confined his attention to properties in the parishes of Hanover and Trelawny. Only one of the nine estates he was associated with, Golden Valley, was in another parish. As was so often the case, Miles appears in the slave registers as the owner of these properties although he held them only as the mortgagee-in-possession. In all, he collected over £34,800, 81 percent of which came from Jamaican estates. At the time of his death in 1848, Miles owned an estimated £1 million in real estate and personal property.[41]

John Gladstone's Jamaican connections accounted for only 18 percent of his total compensation. The remaining 82 percent was awarded for the slaves on his more profitable properties in British Guiana.[42] Although often registered as the owner, Gladstone was usually the mortgagee-in-possession of the estates for which he received compensation. Three of his awards came from the heavily encumbered property of Milligan, Robertson, and Company, which owned Holland and Shaw's estates in St. Elizabeth parish, and the Fair Prospect plantation in St. Thomas-in-the-East. Colin and Divie Robertson were Gladstone's brothers-in-law. When their company went bankrupt in 1826, he had advanced loans and bought up its unsecured bills of exchange in the hope of keeping it solvent. Gladstone's attempts to revive the company failed, and in 1836 he collected their compensation as the mortgagee of the plantations.[43]

The smaller partnership of Biddulph and Cockerell restricted its business activities by concentrating on one specific family. All of their Jamaican compensation was awarded for slaves owned by the Dawkins family, which was one of the largest owners of slaves in the island. The Dawkins papers illustrate the way one family used the indemnity to reduced long-standing debts.

Shortly before his death in 1812, Henry Dawkins bequeathed his Jamaican plantations to his eldest son, James. The inheritance included seven sugar estates, three livestock pens, and various smaller properties throughout the island. The plantations, which included Parnassus, Old Plantation, and Sutton's in Clarendon, and Dawkins Caymanas in St. Catherine parish, carried annuities totaling £40,000 for the benefit of his widow and younger children. The bequest stipulated that the estates should be mortgaged if their profits did not meet the expense. In 1817, the estate's trustees threatened to take possession unless James Dawkins raised the £40,000 or paid £8,000 annually towards liquidating the debt. Although his father had clearly intended the rents and profits to cover the bequests, James Dawkins was forced to mortgage the properties to Biddulph and Cockerell. By 1836 it was clear he could not pay off the principal, and the partnership collected over £33,400 in compensation and used it to reduce the debt.[44]

The detailed account books of Robert Gordon's Jamaican agent provide an even clearer picture of the system. These colonial accounts are unusual, for they deal not only with the daily expenses of Gordon's estates but also with his mortgage accounts with the Hibberts. Normally, the mortgage account of absentees like Gordon were kept separately, either by the merchant or perhaps the owner himself and would not have been the responsibility of the colonial administrator.

Robert Gordon owned two plantations, the 185-acre Paisley estate and Windsor Lodge, both in St. James, and consigned his sugar to Hibbert and Company. In 1827, Gordon's mortgage account stood at £11,098 with an interest rate of 5 percent per annum. Apparently he kept abreast of the interest payments and the principal remained the same until 1835. Soon after the commissioners began their work, the Hibberts submitted their uncontested claims against the estates. By April 1836 they had collected the indemnity for the 520 slaves and reduced Gordon's mortgage by £9,383. Nevertheless, Gordon was by no means out of debt. He still owed over £6,000 on his current and mortgage accounts and an additional £3,500 to the British government. This latter debt represented a loan from the imperial government to repair over £10,000 worth of damage to the estates sustained during the slave rebellion of 1831. Nevertheless the compensation award effectively halved his debt to the Hibberts.[45]

Similar trends in debt reduction can be seen in Barbados where slave owners submitted 5,349 claims for compensation. In contrast to the Jamaican case, the analysis of the Barbadian claims includes all claims for more than fifty slaves. Barbadian plantations were generally smaller than those in Jamaica and operated efficiently with fewer slaves. In Jamaica the average sugar estate was 900 acres and needed about 250 slaves.[46] The average Barbadian plantation, on the other hand, was approximately 250 acres and required 146 slaves. Drax Hall estate, the largest in the island, had only 187 slaves to work its 879 acres in 1834. Nevertheless, between 1825 and 1834, it produced an average of 163 metric tons of sugar and 4,845 gallons of rum per annum and brought the proprietor a net profit of £3,591 each year.[47]

Sugar dominated Barbados, and it is reasonable to assume that any group of 50 or more slaves worked either on the sugar estates or in sugar-related activities. It is unlikely that anyone owning so many slaves could have employed them in any other manner. In the 1830s approximately 69 percent of the total slave population worked in sugar production.[48] The remainder worked in fishing, shipping, in nonsugar agriculture, or in the towns. During the early 1830s sugar and its byproducts accounted for 98 percent of the value of the colony's exports, and although Barbados produced some cotton, aloes, ginger, and arrowroot as well, these items made comparatively minor contributions to the export economy.[49]

The 307 claims that Barbadian planters submitted were worth £971,995, approximately 56 percent of the compensation awarded to the island as a whole. The proportion of compensation awarded to large-scale claims relative to the total for the colony was the same for both Jamaica and Barbados. So, too, was the relative number of claims submitted by large estate owners. But far less of the Barbadian compensation went directly to merchants through simple or litigated claims.[50]

From the data it is possible to estimate the proportion of the Jamaican and Barbadian sugar trade and subsequent compensation that went to various British cities. In the case of Jamaica, the London merchant houses took 66 percent of the indemnity, the Hibberts of Manchester collected only 10.5 percent, and Philip John Miles of Bristol garnered another 4.5 percent. In Liverpool, John Gladstone and Charles Horsfall collected a combined 4.5 percent, while in Yarmouth Pitcairn and Amos accounted for 0.5 percent. The remaining 14 percent of the Jamaican trade went to merchant houses whose locations are unknown.

The compensation awards made to the seven major merchants with interests in Barbadian plantations are illustrated in table 3.2. The awards to Thomas and John Daniel have been divided equally between their London and Bristol houses. The data indicate that London picked up 38 percent of the Barbadian trade, followed by Liverpool, where John Gay Goding and Lee and Garner

Table 3.2. *Compensation Awarded Directly to Merchants, Barbados*

Name	Number of Slaves	Compensation	Location
T. & J. Daniel	1,413	£14,195	London
T. & J. Daniel		14,195	Bristol
Barton, Irlam, & Higginson	1,232	26,822	Liverpool
John Gay Goding	1,090	22,703	London
Blanshard & Morris[a]	527	10,660	
Brandon & Killick	185	4,004	Barbados
Gill & Louis	157	3,410	Barbados
Lee & Garner	112	2,239	Liverpool
Total	4,716	£98,228	

Source: PP, 1837–38 (215).
[a]Could not be linked to a specific location.

received 29 percent. The Bristol division of Thomas and John Daniel accounted for 15 percent and Blanshard and Morris, whose location is unknown, picked up the 11 percent remaining. A further 7 percent went to merchants who can be traced to Barbados but not to any British city.

Both Jamaican and Barbadian proprietors conducted most of their business with merchant houses in London. The Barbadians, on the other hand, preferred to send more of their sugar to Bristol and Liverpool, rather than to Manchester, the second choice of the Jamaican planters. Moreover, merchants trading with Jamaica differed completely from those trading with Barbados. Only Thomas and John Daniel had connections with both colonies, and their Jamaican interests were limited to one estate, Colbecks in St. Dorothy.

The merchants who traded with Barbados also received a smaller percentage of their clients' compensation. Only 26 (8.5 percent) of the 307 claims submitted on behalf of the large planters went directly to British merchants. These 26 claims totaled £98,228. The major Barbadian proprietors, therefore, paid only 10 percent of their indemnity directly to the merchants, as opposed to the 15 percent paid out by their Jamaican counterparts. The difference was due in part to the greater number of resident planters in Barbados.

Proprietors who lived on their plantations were in a good position to monitor expenditure and eliminate unnecessary costs. They avoided the need for colonial agents and attorneys and reduced the risk of fraud on the part of their employees.[51] Moreover, fewer opportunities existed in the colonies for the sumptuous life style for which West Indians living in England were so notorious. Greater fiscal responsibility, or lack of opportunity, often led to greater efficiency and a lower level of indebtedness. John Pollard Mayers estimated that 75 percent of Barbadian sugar planters lived in the island in 1824, and approximately 52 percent of the owners still lived there ten years later.[52]

Absenteeism is traditionally cited as a major cause of planter indebtedness. The estates of absentees were, of necessity, administered by "planting attorneys," who often lived at the proprietor's expense. The attorney charged a 5 to 6 percent commission on the sale price of every crop shipped to the British market. In addition, he received a 5 percent commission on the sale of any estate owned by the absentee proprietor. Innumerable opportunities existed for an unscrupulous attorney to enrich himself at the expense of his employer by inflating the price of stores or selling part of the crop on his own account. John Gladstone found that his Jamaican attorney drank heavily, was inefficient, and had cheated him for years. In 1832 Richard Barrett informed the Duke of Buckingham that for several years the overseer at Middleton had systematically stolen the plantation's corn and later complained that the previous manager had overspent on supplies for the great house. Nor was it unusual for attorneys to buy plantation supplies from their own companies.[53] With the great house and servants also at his disposal, a clever attorney who managed fifteen to twenty estates might make as much as £10,000 per year.[54]

In Barbados, Forster Clarke served as the attorney for at least twelve absentees, including Thomas and John Daniel, the Earl of Harewood, the Society for the Propagation of the Gospel in Foreign Parts, and S. W. S. Drax (table 3.3). Altogether he managed nineteen estates and was responsible for the wel-

Table 3.3. *Properties Administered by Attorneys, Barbados, 1823–1843*

Name	Number of Estates	Number of Slaves
Forster Clarke	19	4,300
Edward Thomas	19	2,764
Josiah Heath	6	945
George Hewitt	5	921
Total	49	8,930

Sources: Deeds and Conveyances, RB1/271–306; Slave Registers, T71/553–64.

Table 3.4. *Properties Administered by Attorneys, Jamaica,*
1823–1843

Name	Number of Estates	Number of Slaves
William Miller	42	8,817
Joseph Gordon	25	5,799
James McDonald	17	3,986
Simon Taylor	15	2,907
John Oldham	10	2,043
James Daly	8	1,439
Hamilton Brown	9	1,350
George Gordon	7	1,098
William Jackson	5	1,061
Henry Cox	8	828
Hector Mitchell	3	463
John Mais	3	436
Total	152	30,227

Sources: Deeds and Conveyances; Slave Registers.

fare of over 4,500 slaves.[55] In Jamaica, with its greater number of absentees, the drain on the income of the proprietors was substantially increased and the problem of indebtedness proportionately greater (table 3.4).

The letterbooks of John Gale Vidal illustrate the indirect and informal methods used to pay off creditors. As the Jamaican attorney for W., R., and S. Mitchell, Vidal was in an excellent position to record the various transactions of his employers and their clients. In 1833 Vidal informed the Mitchells that many of their debtors would be pleased to have the company take their compensation, their property, and the services of their apprentices in return for an appropriate reduction in their debts. Some had even suggested that the reduction should equal the value of the estates prior to the "interference of Parliament," though it is unclear whether they meant the value before 1823 or some later date. There is no record of the Mitchells' reaction to the suggestion but, in view of the tone of Vidal's later letters, it is unlikely that the company ever seriously considered reducing debts beyond the value of the compensation it received. At the same time, Vidal strongly urged his employers to obtain as much of the compensation as possible and "at any sacrifice," since he did not trust the owners to use the award to put their mortgaged estates on a sounder financial footing.[56]

To show his willingness to set his own affairs in order, Vidal asked Mitchell and Company to offset the mortgage against his estate. Vidal owned two plantations: Shenton in St. Thomas-in-the-Vale and Keith Hall in the adjoining parish of St. Catherine. The Mitchells held a mortgage of £17,380, plus interest, against the Shenton estate. Vidal suggested that they take the property, which he valued at £14,000, and the compensation, which he expected to be about £4,200, and promised to pay the difference between the mortgage and the value of the estate as soon as possible. The offer indicates that Vidal had not kept up his interest payments, otherwise he would have had at least £1,100 to his credit.[57] It is also clear that the Mitchells did not want to take over yet another property, even one belonging to their own attorney.

The following year, Vidal informed Mitchell and Company that he hoped to sell Shenton to his overseer, Charles Hosty. He asked the company to take Hosty as a debtor and to deduct the purchase price from his mortgage. Unfortunately, Hosty could not find security for the price of the estate and the proposed deal fell through. Eventually, in early 1836, Vidal announced that he had sold the estate, but not for cash. Instead, the purchasers offered to pay him £2,300 annually for the next five years. Shortly afterward, he informed his employers that the mortgage debt stood at £6,798.[58] Vidal could not possibly have reduced the debt so quickly unless he had used the £4,537 compensation for the estates, but where he obtained the other money is not recorded.

The Mitchells were determined that Vidal should reduce his outstanding debts to them and equally determined that others should do the same. In 1836 the company began proceedings against at least two of its clients. In both cases legal action resulted in the forced sale of the properties involved and the payment of the compensation to the Mitchells.

The Grange River Plantation, in Clarendon, had long been the subject of a dispute between the deceased owner's widow and Mitchell and Company. In February 1836 the widow's new husband, the Reverend Joshua Stoney, notified the company of his terms regarding the compensation due for their ex-slaves. He proposed that his creditors should receive the compensation, the estate, and unexpired term of the apprentices, together with part of another property, Cross Pen, towards the liquidation of a mortgage debt of approximately £10,000. In return, he expected the Mitchells to pay his outstanding debts to the value of £570 and to drop all further claims to his wife's estate.[59] Not surprisingly, the company rejected Stoney's offer and instructed Vidal to foreclose on the mortgage. The Master's Report for 1838 shows that the compensation for the Grange River slaves had been transferred to Mitchell and Company and had reduced the debt by 45 percent.[60]

The second case involved Bowden estate which had been part of a chancery suit since 1824. By 1836 the Mitchells had decided to take action. The 532-acre estate was appraised at £5,000 and advertised for sale by public auction.[61] The proceeds of the sale, together with the compensation, were used to reduce the deceased owner's debt of over £47,500 to Mitchell and Company.

The Mitchells' disputes over compensation were not isolated incidences. Although the commissioners had settled most of the litigated claims by 1838, over ninety-eight claims, involving almost £400,000, remained tied up in lawsuits. The property of many of the greatest Jamaican proprietors became the subject of disputes between their creditors and the heirs. John Tharp, one of the richest planters in the island, left eight estates in Trelawny and others in Hanover and St. James when he died in 1825. His entire property became the subject of protracted litigation among his many heirs. When the compensation payments began in 1836, over £48,000 due to Tharp's estate was placed in the hands of the accountant general for distribution when the suits were finally settled.[62]

The compensation due for the slaves owned by John Wedderburn, an extensive property owner in Westmoreland parish, suffered the same fate. So, too, did the awards due to John Rock Grossett, the assemblyman for St. George, who Sligo once described as "a man of poor understanding and immense property" who "never has a shilling and [is] much in distress."[63] Under the circumstances, it is unlikely that he received much of the £16,000 compensation for his newly emancipated slaves. The indemnity awarded to John Tharp, John Wedderburn, John Rock Grossett, William Shand, and A. G. Storer, five of the biggest landowners of the time, accounted for 34 percent of the money which remained tied up in litigation (table 3.5).

Although no attorney's letterbook similar to that of John Gale Vidal survives for Barbados, other records indicate that similar indirect methods prevailed there. The treasury papers and deeds of conveyance located in England and Barbados, together with the chancery records of the island, indicate that where counterclaims failed, or were withdrawn, creditors often relied on gentlemen's agreements to recoup their losses.

Barton, Irlam, and Higginson, for example, submitted a counterclaim against the Clermont estate owned by Charles Bradford Lane of St. Michael. The company based its claim on a debt of over £5,100, secured against the property. In 1835 the commissioners decided in favor of Lane, who almost immediately transferred his compensation to the merchants in partial repayment of his debt.[64]

Table 3.5. *Outstanding Litigated Claims, Jamaica, 1837–1838*

Name	Number of Slaves	Amount Claimed
John Tharp, deceased	2,505	£48,103
John Wedderburn, deceased	2,187	29,403
William Shand	1,148	19,266
John Rock Grossett	940	16,142
A. G. Storer, deceased	698	10,807
Total	7,478	123,721
Miscellaneous claims	11,177	238,236
Total	18,655	£361,957

Source: PP, 1837–38 (215).

George Hewitt, the executor for Apes Hill estate, and James Neil, the mortgagee, entered into a similar arrangement. The 460-acre Apes Hill estate had been unencumbered when George William Perch bought it from Thomas and John Daniel in 1816. Perch paid £26,000 for the estate and secured a mortgage for £12,857 from the Daniels. By 1829 Perch had paid off the mortgage but almost immediately remortgaged the property to James Neil to secure another loan of £7,142. Perch died before he could pay off the new mortgage, and in 1834, his executor claimed the compensation on behalf of the estate. Neil quickly challenged the action and entered his own counterclaim as the mortgagee. In 1836, when Hewitt agreed to honor the debt, Neil withdrew the counterclaim and relinquished all claims against the estate.[65]

In the hope of avoiding unnecessary delay, creditors occasionally allowed the slave owners or their agents to collect the compensation. Richard Barrett gave this as his reason when he attempted to collect the compensation due for the slaves on the Hope and Middleton estates. The two estates and the anticipated indemnity, owned by the Duke of Buckingham, were mortgaged to Ambrose Humphrys for over £11,500. Claiming that he acted on behalf of the duke, Barrett informed Humphrys of his action and pointed out that the respective claimants could resolve their differences in England. Humphrys challenged Barrett's action, responded with a counterclaim, and won the award for the Middleton slaves. The duke had to wait until 1844 before the dispute over the Hope compensation was settled and the money transferred to the estate's trustees.[66]

When counterclaims and gentlemen's agreements failed to have the desired effect, creditors had one final option. Recourse to a suit in the Court of Chancery frequently resulted in a judgment in favor of the plaintiff. Nevertheless, few creditors received full satisfaction and junior creditors or recent annuitants usually received nothing.

In 1832, Gibbes and Bright brought a chancery suit against Benjamin Storey of Barbados. The company hoped to recover over £5,365 in judgments and mortgages against Richmond Hill, the 132-acre estate that Storey had used as collateral. The estate was appraised at £5,709 and advertised for sale in December 1832. No one made an offer for the estate, and it remained on the market for the next fourteen months. Eventually, in 1835, the court reappraised the property and sold it to Joseph Bagley for £5,892.[67]

The Master in Chancery, William Oxley, ranked the Richmond Hill debts into nine individual liens totaling £10,033, with those of Gibbes and Bright in second, fourth, fifth, and eighth position. The money received from Bayley covered the court costs of £537 and the first three liens, leaving only £2,010 to pay off Gibbes and Bright. The case was not finally settled until 1837. By then the compensation for the fifty-five slaves at Richmond Hill had been paid to the accountant general in England. In his final decision, the master ordered the transfer of the compensation to Gibbes and Bright.[68] The records do not specify the exact amount but it could hardly have exceeded £1,500. Gibbes and Bright, Benjamin Storey's major creditors, thus received only £3,960, leaving them nearly £1400 out of pocket. Creditors who ranked after Gibbes and Bright were even less fortunate; they received nothing.

The parliamentary returns for the compensation awards reveal only the tip of the iceberg, and the dearth of merchants' letterbooks and planters' accounts precludes a more precise calculation of the amount of compensation paid to creditors through the more indirect conveyances and "gentlemen's agreements." Nevertheless, the data give a reasonably accurate indication of the different levels of indebtedness in the two colonies.

Credit and Creditors

If the drive for emancipation had significantly reduced the available credit, the mortgage records should show a steady decline in overall value after 1823. Yet this did not occur. It is more likely that, as Richard Pares has suggested, the abolition movement provided a convenient excuse for merchants to withhold credit from any particularly recalcitrant client.[1] The impact of the compensation payments on colonial credit can be judged from the mortgage deeds registered in Barbados during the twenty-year period between 1823 and 1843. These records include mortgages that formed part of estate sales and simple mortgages unrelated to the transfer of property.[2]

The deeds cover the 162 individual estates mortgaged between 1823 and 1843 and provide information on 256 separate mortgage transactions throughout the island for the same period.[3] Many of these properties were mortgaged more than once, and some were also sold through the Court of Chancery. Details concerning the source of the purchase money involved in chancery sales does not usually appear in the records, therefore judicial sales are excluded here.

The transactions can be separated into two distinct categories: sales-related and simple mortgages. Taken together their value amounted to slightly over £1,498,000 of credit for the twenty-year span. Nearly 58 percent, (149 transactions), fall into the sales-related group, where the buyer paid part of the price at the time of the sale and secured the remainder against the property and the slave labor force. These sales-related mortgages account for approximately 69 percent (£1,026,824) of the total value of credit for the period.

The simple mortgages, which were independent of a sale, make up the other 42 percent of the transactions. Planters frequently used these advances to buy supplies or slaves or to pay off other creditors, at least temporarily. At other times, West Indian proprietors mortgaged their properties in order to educate or further the careers of their children. John Prettyjohn mortgaged the Constant estate for this purpose on at least four different occasions. Although the plantation already carried mortgages and marriage settlements totaling more than £15,000, in 1839 Prettyjohn borrowed £1,865 to buy his son, Richard, a commission in the British army. The following year he remortgaged the estate for money to buy him the necessary uniform and accoutrements. A year later he again used the estate as collateral, this time to advance the career of a second son. In between times, Prettyjohn managed to raise an additional £2,857, so that in just three years he had mortgaged Constant at least four times to secure nearly £7,000 at 6 percent annual interest besides all his other liabilities.[4]

For the eleven-year period between 1823 and 1833, combined sales-related and simple mortgages carried an average value of £53,800 (table 4.1). The decline in mortgage values that occurred in 1824 followed a high level of investment during the previous year, a level of investment not reached again until 1837 and 1838, when the compensation payments affected colonial credit. Simi-

Table 4.1. *Value of Barbadian Mortgages, 1823–1833*
(£53,800 sterling = 100 percent)

Year	Average Value	Percent	Number of Mortgages
1823	£132,492	246	15
1824	12,421	23	4
1825	50,522	94	10
1826	43,942	81	10
1827	48,462	90	11
1828	92,173	171	16
1829	47,487	88	8
1830	101,779	189	15
1831	35,000	65	3
1832	19,595	36	3
1833	7,857	15	4
Total	£591,730		99

Source: Deeds and Conveyances, RB1/271–306.

lar drops occurred in 1832 and 1833, but they also followed an unusually high level in 1830, and factors other than the fear of emancipation affected investment at this point.

In 1831 events in British financial circles alarmed many West India merchants. The fear of bankruptcy haunted every merchant house connected with the West India trade. The uncertainty surrounding the repayment of colonial debts and fluctuating sugar prices could force even the most respected house to cease payment. In the thirty-six years between 1793 and 1829 over sixty West India firms went out of business, but in 1831 alone ten more companies declared bankruptcy.[5] With leading merchant houses such as Manning and Anderdon and Sir Edward Hyde East in difficulties, the Interest quickly blamed the slavery question for the problems affecting trade. In a letter to the West India Committee, John Pollard Mayers blamed the demise of Manning and Anderdon on "the depreciated value of West India property and the continued depression of the sugar market."[6] Yet Manning and Anderdon's problems appear to have been short-lived, for the Society for the Propagation of the Gospel in Foreign Parts continued consigning its sugar to them as late as 1836. Overproduction, competition from foreign producers, and the consequent fall in sugar prices were more to blame than the activity of the abolitionists. Certainly, James Stephen had little sympathy for the Interest's argument. If the abolition movement had caused the depreciation of West Indian property, Stephen believed it to be the "inevitable consequence of their own neglect of both their duty and their interests." If colonial proprietors had worked honestly for amelioration, he asserted, the debate over slavery would have ended years earlier.[7] The effect of the abolition movement on colonial investment was neither as drastic nor as long-term as the Interest claimed.

Between 1823 and 1843 metropolitan merchants provided Barbadian planters with fifty mortgages valued at £256,918. The leading British merchant houses extended 84 percent of these as simple mortgages. Thomas and John Daniel headed the list with £62,694 in credit spread across the period. The company had originated in Barbados in the eighteenth century but, like others before them, Thomas and John Daniel sought their fortunes in the metropolis. By the 1770s they had firmly established themselves as sugar merchants and brokers in Bristol and London. Together they rapidly gained control of a sizable sector of the West India trade and by the 1830s the company had become a major force in Barbados and the Windward Islands.[8]

Among their clients were the Codrington estates, owned by the Society for the Propagation of the Gospel in Foreign Parts. Thomas Daniel and Sons of Bristol had acted as one of the society's consignees since the 1780s.[9] In 1830,

Daniel and Company of London also solicited the society's business in the belief that the primary consignee, Marmaduke Trattle, had died. To its embarrassment the company learnt that the reports were unfounded and expressed the hope that Trattle would "long continue" to receive the society's business. Nevertheless, the following year the company wrote to the society again: "Mr. Trattle is now *really* dead and we therefore solicit the appointment of consignees of the sugars shipped to London from the Society's estate in Barbados." The company even offered to ship out supplies to the estates "freight free" in return for consignments of the society's sugar. Their appeal was not completely successful, for the society consigned its sugar to both the Daniels and to Manning and Anderdon.[10]

The Daniels received sugar from the influential Best and Alleyne families and were involved in the affairs of at least fifty other Barbadian estates. When the compensation awards began in 1837 they collected £117,383 for 3,953 slaves owned by their various clients (table 4.2) and continued trading in the Caribbean until going into voluntary liquidation in 1894.[11]

The Barton, Irlam, and Higginson partnership followed the Daniels closely in credit extension. Between 1823 and 1834 the company granted mortgages valued at £60,500 to a total of eleven different estates. The company operated out of Liverpool and traded in conjunction with an affiliated company in Barbados. When John Higginson, the sole surviving partner of the parent company, died in 1834, his son Jonathan replaced him. In Barbados the subsidiary company of Higginson, Deane and Stott protected the company's colonial affairs. This partnership included Richard Deane, Higginson's attorney and ex-

Table 4.2. *Compensation Awarded to Thomas and John Daniel*

Colony	Number of Slaves	Compensation
British Guiana	1,623	£71,326
Barbados	1,466	30,705
Tobago	310	5,883
Montserrat	270	4,800
Antigua	167	2,728
Nevis	117	1,941
Total	3,953	£117,383

Source: PP, 1837–38 (215).

ecutor, and Thomas Stott, a Bridgetown merchant.[12] The Liverpool company acted on behalf of thirty estates, including Forster Hall, Cottage, and Groves. These three estates were owned by Thomas Yard and together produced an annual average of nearly 170 metric tons of sugar and 5,833 gallons of rum over the period.[13]

The creditors themselves are as important as the level of investment during this period. All too frequently, the terms *creditor* and *merchant* are used interchangeably, yet advancing credit against West Indian estates had long been a way for private individuals to put their otherwise idle capital to work.

The willingness of such people to invest in West Indian property belies the Interest's assertion that credit was unobtainable. The eighteenth-century practice of planters borrowing from friends and relations continued into the nineteenth century. In the absence of a formal banking system to regulate credit, many private individuals invested in the colonial sugar economy, and throughout the period, more credit came from private sources than from British merchant houses.[14]

Between 1823 and 1843 well over 80 percent of the credit available to Barbadian planters came from private sources (figure 1). By contrast, less than 20 percent of the total invested came from merchants who conducted business with the island.[15] An even more striking picture emerges when the three years 1837 to 1839 are isolated from the overall picture. The central commissioners began paying claims in 1836, and the effects of compensation surfaced a year or two later. During the eleven years between 1823 to 1834, mortgages had averaged eight per year with each one worth an average of £6,154. Perhaps in anticipation of the compensation, the number rose in 1835 to eleven mortgages worth an average of £7,357 each. The next two years were record ones for investment, with thirty-five mortgages, with an average value of £6,628, recorded for 1837: a significant increase of 31 percent. In 1838 the number dropped slightly to thirty-two mortgages with an average value of £5,964. By the following year more of the compensation had filtered through the economy, and although the actual number of mortgages fell, their average value increased well above the previous level. The only time these figures had been surpassed was in 1823, when the average value was slightly over £8,800 for the fifteen mortgages of the year. Clearly, the payment of compensation stimulated investment, which in turn denoted continuing confidence in the future of the Barbadian sugar economy.

In Jamaica, one of the major private creditors was Abraham Hodgson, an influential assemblyman from St. Mary. In 1832 he accompanied Richard Barrett, the Speaker of the Jamaican House of Assembly, on a visit to England

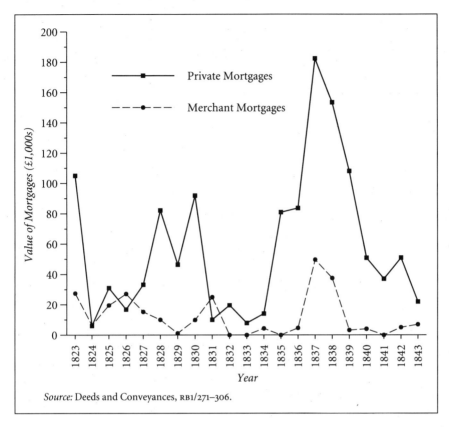

Figure 1. *Value of Mortgages, Barbados, 1823–1843*

where he met with members of the West India Interest and presented the demands of Jamaican proprietors to British government officials. In his private comments about various members of the assembly, Lord Sligo described Hodgson as an "independent, but bigoted, old planter" who was nevertheless the "cleverest and wealthiest man in the House."[16]

Hodgson owned four estates in St. Mary. His Halifax estate produced mainly sugar. The other three, Huddersfield, Swan, and Rio Nova Bay, operated as a single entity, producing pimento and livestock as well as some sugar. Ninety-three slaves worked on Hodgson's fifth property, Halifax Pen in St. Ann, which supplied the other four estates with meat and draft animals.[17]

Hodgson employed his son-in-law, Henry Cox, as the attorney for all four plantations. Cox registered the slaves and supervised the white employees but it is unlikely that Hodgson gave him any control over the financial concerns of the estates. Although Cox owned several estates and actually owned more slaves, he was in continual financial difficulties. His problems were apparently well-known, for in one of his less acerbic comments, Sligo described him simply as "very poor." Even though he owned over 850 slaves, Cox did not collect a single penny of the compensation due for them. Instead the money went directly to his father-in-law, no doubt to settle outstanding debts.[18]

Apart from the money he received for his own slaves and those of Henry Cox, Abraham Hodgson collected compensation for another 376 slaves. Whether these were his own property or those of his debtors is difficult to tell, but at least 140 of them clearly belonged to Grier Park, an estate owned by Hamilton Brown. The others appear in groups varying in size from 30 to 90 and raised Hodgson's total compensation to £31,374, 76 percent of which he received for slaves owned by his various debtors.[19]

Many British merchants did not reinvest their compensation in West Indian property. Some had already begun to withdraw their capital from the sugar colonies well before emancipation. Instead, they turned to investment possibilities in India and South America.[20] Those who preferred to keep their capital closer to home responded quickly to the opportunities that expanding canal and railroad construction offered in England.

By the late eighteenth century, the focus of British interest had begun to shift away from the Caribbean islands. In 1787 the East India Company moved into sugar production, and from then until the equalization of the sugar duties in 1846, the East India Interest challenged the West Indians' monopoly of the British sugar market. As early as 1814, John Gladstone had ventured into Indian trade, and although his West India investments remained paramount throughout the 1820s and early 1830s, he never lost his interest in India.[21]

In 1812 Gladstone had paid £11,000 for a half share in Success, a coffee estate in British Guiana. After acquiring the rest of the estate four years later, he immediately doubled the labor force and switched the plantation over to sugar production. The venture proved highly successful, and by the time he gained control of the Vreedenhoop estate in 1822 he was already a major force in the colony. He expected these two estates to provide a minimum net profit of £20,000 per year. So lucrative were his ventures that by the end of the decade he had invested approximately £300,000 in West Indian plantations and mortgages. Between 1829 and 1832 the Success plantation alone produced 0.8 metric tons of sugar per slave per year, while for the same period the slaves at Vreedenhoop each produced 1.03 metric tons annually. The average for the estates of British Guiana was 0.5 metric tons, and the far higher productivity of Gladstone's estates caused Lord Howick to cite them and John Moss's Anna Regina estate as examples of increased output leading to higher death rates among the slaves.[22]

With the equalization of the East and West India sugar duties in 1846, Gladstone shifted his attention to other areas. Although he received over £110,000 in compensation for his slaves in Jamaica and British Guiana, he did not reinvest the money in either colony. Instead, he used part of his award to buy ships for trade with India, but for his major investments he turned to England, investing in canals and railroads. His interest in canals and railroads dated back to the early 1820s. By 1828 he owned 20 shares in the Gloucester canal and 40 shares in the Liverpool to Manchester railroad. In 1837 he greatly extended his investments with the purchase of 300 shares in the new Grand Junction railway, which linked Birmingham with the cotton mills of south Lancashire and connected with the Liverpool-Manchester railway. He also bought £40,000 worth of shares in the Forth and Clyde canal, which made him the largest shareholder and gave him a controlling interest in the enterprise. His increased investments in transportation stock paralleled the decrease in his colonial holdings. The value of his transportation stocks rose from £3,500 in 1828 to £213,150 in 1843. His West Indian investments, on the other hand, fell from £336,000 in 1833 to £32,600 in 1848. By 1840 he had disposed of most of the estates in British Guiana, and by the end of the decade his only connection with the colony was an £18,000 mortgage on the Wales plantation, which he had held for over twenty years. His only remaining Jamaican investment was the controlling interest in the Lacovia and Holland estates, both of which were worked by tenant planters.[23]

In the early 1830s the Bristol merchant house of Pinney also began liquidating its West Indian assets. Like Gladstone, Charles Pinney did not reinvest his compensation in the sugar industry. Instead, he speculated in cotton and railroad stock, and by 1839 he had bought canal and dock shares worth £14,000 and invested a further £12,000 in the Great Western Cotton Works.[24]

If many of the foremost West India merchants concentrated on withdrawing their capital from the sugar colonies, the same was not true of private investors. During the early years of the Industrial Revolution, the British upper and middle classes accumulated wealth at an unprecedented rate. The amount of available capital outstripped the opportunities for investment in British trade and industry. Eric Hobsbawm has estimated that by the 1840s the nation had an annual surplus of £60 million available for investment. Those willing to risk large sums took advantage of the opportunities offered by the construction of the canals and railroads that linked the industrial north with London and the Midlands. In 1830 only a few miles of railroad had been built, all of them in Great Britain. Ten years later there were 4,500 miles of track, and by 1850 over 23,000 miles had been laid in Europe, the United States, Cuba, and Latin America, most of it built with British capital.[25]

If speculators and promoters did well on their investments in transportation, the small investor did not. Although John Gladstone earned 6.5 percent on his railroad stock, his bonds paid only 4.5 percent.[26] Smaller investors may have preferred the familiar risks of West Indian mortgages, at 6 percent interest, to the more speculative transport ventures. Moreover, canal and railroad stock required a large capital outlay, which eliminated investors with access to relatively small amounts of money.

The smaller British investors had few ways to increase their assets other than investing in the Caribbean sugar colonies. In some cases, such people had direct family connections with the plantations, but in others, no personal contact existed between the mortgagees and their debtors. Instead, a network of attorneys in Britain and the colonies made the legal arrangements between the principals.[27]

Whatever the reasons for the initial contact, there were enough private investors between 1823 and 1843 to make a significant impact on the shape of colonial credit. Each year during the twenty-year period, private investments outweighed those of British merchants, both in number and in value. Private individuals extended 82 percent of all mortgages secured against Barbadian plantations and over 83 percent of their total value.[28] For four of these years, 1832, 1833, 1835, and 1841, individuals continued to invest in Barbados while the traditional merchants withheld credit. If the increased drive for abolition in 1832 and 1833 alarmed the merchant community, it had little effect on the private sector. The transactions for these two years divide equally between sales-related and simple mortgages and do not reflect a rush by Barbadian proprietors to rid themselves of their estates.

Private individuals who accepted Barbadian mortgages invested an average of £6,000. Their only security was the colonial estate, and their only return the annual 6 percent interest that West Indian mortgages normally carried. As individuals, rather than merchants, they made no consignment arrangements and did not have the additional security of consignments of sugar to sell on the British market.

When simple and sales-related mortgages are separated into their distinct categories, a new factor emerges. Until 1835 most mortgages had been unconnected with the sale of estates, but in 1834 the situation began to change dramatically as the number of sales of Barbadian estates increased, a trend that continued until 1842. People who wished to sell off their Barbadian sugar plantations found willing purchasers. The properties in question had not necessarily been on the market for long, nor were they being sold for debt. Each purchaser found a seller willing and able to extend credit in the form of deferred payment of at least part of the price.

Although the West India Interest complained bitterly about a lack of credit, the data for Barbados clearly indicates that they overstated the problem. Land in Barbados was considered excellent collateral, and it was common practice to accept part of the price as a mortgage secured against the property. Such mortgages held good, regardless of the number of times an estate changed hands, and they simply became the liability of each successive owner.[29]

5
Expansion and Speculation

In 1806 the Georgia estate in Jamaica had a value of £20,000, but by 1825 the owner was advised that in view of the depreciated state of all colonial property he would be lucky to get half that amount. Six years later, when the owners of the Chiswick plantation thought of selling out, their agents also advised against the idea. "We never knew," they wrote "a worse time than the present to attempt a sale."[1] The Interest frequently argued that the antislavery movement made it impossible to sell colonial estates, even at drastically reduced prices, and by 1833 it blamed the uncertainty surrounding the compensation negotiations for the "very precarious" nature of West Indian property.[2]

The guarantee of compensation changed the situation radically. In 1836 Governor Sligo of Jamaica confidently asserted that people had regained their confidence in the value and security of their property, that rural property values had improved considerably, and that the value of property in Kingston had risen 50 percent. British merchant houses, he claimed, had commissioned several leading citizens, including John Oldham, a prominent solicitor, to buy land on their behalf. Moreover, the governor pointed out, Oldham had demonstrated his confidence in Jamaican property by investing over £10,000 of his own money in land since 1834.[3]

Sligo cited other recent purchases, particularly those of Richard Barrett, the Speaker of the House of Assembly. The governor made no secret of his intense dislike for Barrett. He firmly believed that there was not in Jamaica "a man more publicly known to be unprincipled in the highest degree, no man who has more passions than himself or makes less effort to prevent their mastering him."

Sligo gossiped frequently about the Speaker's morals and financial affairs.

He reported in his despatches that Barrett flaunted his white mistress but never allowed his wife to leave their home. He claimed that everyone knew of Barrett's financial distress, although he supposedly enjoyed an annual income of over £7,000. The compensation money, he assumed, had relieved Barrett's situation, satisfied his creditors, and enabled him to extend his property.[4]

Barrett may not have been as heavily indebted as Sligo believed. In 1833, when he applied to Mitchell and Company for temporary assistance, he saw no need to mortgage his plantations in the usual way and instead offered to secure the advance against the produce of his estates. Moreover, he stated that his marriage settlement was the sole encumbrance against his property. Indeed, when John Gale Vidal searched the records on behalf of the Mitchells, he could uncover only the settlement and one mortgage, which Barrett had already repaid.[5]

Despite his obvious disapproval, Sligo had to concede that few matched Barrett's astute business sense.[6] Certainly, he took advantage of the changing real estate market to expand his existing property by acquiring over 7,700 additional acres of plantation land. At emancipation he already owned Barrett Hall and Richmond Pen in the parish of St. Ann, and between 1836 and 1840 he spent more than £13,900 on his new purchases. In 1836 he bought the 300-acre Greenwood plantation from his partner, Philip Anglin Morris. The two men owned the estate as tenants-in-common and had mortgaged the property several years earlier. Barrett had already paid off most of the mortgage and took the estate, which bordered Richmond Pen, to satisfy the debt.[7] His major purchases, however, were made after April 1836 when he collected over £6,000 compensation for his 287 slaves. He used the money later in the year to put down a 50 percent deposit on the 2,386-acre Ramble estate and to buy the neighboring 1,693-acre New York Pen outright. Two years later, with the express idea of further enlarging the Ramble, he bought the combined 1,079-acre Dixon and Lime Tree Valley Pens, and the 357-acre Charlton Ring estate, thereby expanding his property by an additional 31 percent.[8]

The activities of Alexander Bravo and Hamilton Brown further underscored Sligo's assertion that "everyone is on the lookout for purchases." Bravo, a wealthy Jewish merchant, was a well-educated assemblyman, whom Sligo described as a "decided liberal" before his election to the House. Bravo derived part of his wealth from rental properties, which brought in nearly £6,500 in 1835 and 1836. His compensation award brought him a further £12,588 for the slaves on his three estates: Marley Mount, Knight, and Mount Moses.[9] In 1837 Bravo added a further 1,100 acres to his holdings when he bought parts of the Deeside and Cabbage Hall estates. Cabbage Hall seems to have been a marginal plantation and its owner in dire financial straits, for Bravo was able to buy nearly 600 acres for about 10 shillings an acre.[10]

Bravo continued to extend his property and in 1842 bought Sligo's own estates, Cocoa Walk and Kelly, for £7,892. Bravo claimed that the price exceeded the value of the estates and that they brought him little profit. The major problem, he explained to the governor, was the droughts that had destroyed the 1841 and 1844 crops. By 1845 he had spent more than £30,000 trying unsuccessfully to improve the plantations, and the expenses had left him over £6,500 in debt.[11]

Compensation improved the liquidity of Hamilton Brown, the attorney for Mitchell and Company and several other absentee plantation owners. Brown was an active member of the Colonial Church Union, the antisectarian and anti-British organization founded by the Reverend George W. Bridges in the wake of the 1831 slave rebellion.[12]

Brown owned four estates: Colliston, Minard Pen, Grier Park, and Antrim, but the compensation awarded for the slaves on these properties went directly to his creditors. Nevertheless, he collected over £7,600 for various slaves owned by others, and in 1838 his improved credit enabled him to buy Hounslow Heath, a 700-acre estate that bordered Grier Park to the southwest.[13]

The changing patterns of estate sales in Barbados between 1823 and 1843 underscore the impact of compensation on land ownership in a colony where the predominantly resident planters exercised direct control over their financial affairs. During this twenty-year period, 403 sugar estates of 50 acres or more operated in Barbados.[14] The deeds of conveyance and chancery court records indicate that 39 percent (158) of these estates changed hands either privately or as the result of judicial action. Moreover, at least 37 percent (59) of the properties were sold more than once. The data from the resulting 240 separate transactions provide the basis for an analysis of the land ownership trends in the island.[15] The Barbadian records show a substantial rise in the number of sugar estates sold in the three years immediately following the award of the compensation. The majority of the transactions concerned properties in St. Thomas and St. Michael (table 5.1). Most were private rather than forced sales, indicating that owners of estates in the more fertile parish of St. Thomas and the heavily populated parish of St. Michael had little trouble in disposing of their properties. The majority of the chancery sales, on the other hand, occurred in St. Philip, where the plantations were generally considered less productive and their owners less able to meet their financial obligations.

Chancery sales outnumbered private sales only twice, once in 1832 and again

Table 5.1. *Estate Sales, Barbados, 1823–1843 (by parish)*

Parish	Private	Chancery	Total
Christ Church	20	5	25
St. Andrew	11	2	13
St. George	20	1	21
St. James	16	3	19
St. John	11	2	13
St. Joseph	10	2	12
St. Lucy	4	6	10
St. Michael	28	9	37
St. Peter	14	3	17
St. Philip	20	15	35
St. Thomas	29	9	38
Total	183	57	240
Percentage	76.25	23.75	100

Sources: Deeds and Conveyances, RB1/271-306; Chancery Sales, 1825–64;
Minutes of the Court of Chancery, 1829–34, 1835–44.

in 1833 (figure 2). These two years marked the height of the abolition movement in England and the time of greatest uncertainty surrounding the size of
the award and the method of its distribution. Nevertheless, judicial sales never
accounted for more than 25 percent of the total sales for the entire period, a
dramatic contrast with the period from 1880 to 1920, when over two-thirds of
the Barbadian estates still in production passed through the chancery system.[16]

Chancery sales declined substantially after 1835. Whereas the court had sold
forty-five estates between 1823 and 1835, it sold only twelve during the course
of the next eight years. Seventy-nine percent of all judicial sales, therefore,
occurred before the compensation money had much time to affect the creditworthiness of the proprietors. Furthermore, these sales represent 81 percent of
the total amount paid for chancery estates (table 5.2).

Equally important was the value of the estates involved in these sales. After
the passage of the Abolition Act the increased value of plantation land in Barbados also aroused comment. When James A. Thome and Joseph H. Kimball,
the American abolitionists, visited the island in 1837, they heard many reports
about the improvement in real estate values. Plantation managers and local
officials alike claimed that land values had risen substantially since emancipa-

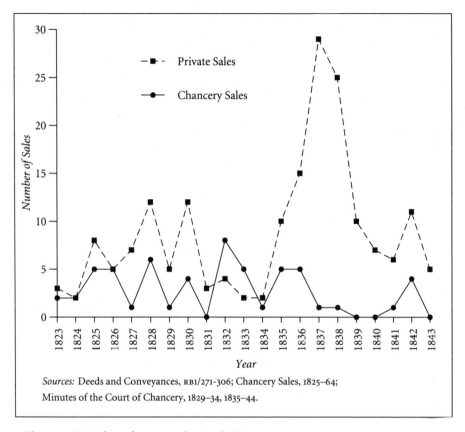

Figure 2. *Number of Estate Sales, Barbados, 1823–1843*

tion and that many plantation owners were improving their properties.[17] Although their information was often imprecise, the Americans were, nevertheless, impressed by the overall feeling of confidence in the future of the islands.

The deeds of conveyance and the records of the chancery court reinforce the impressions of travelers and government officials. The combined private and chancery sales highlight the effect of compensation on the value of the estates and their satellite pens (table 5.3). The indemnity's impact on land values is clearest between 1835, when the first payments began, and 1843, when the effect of the money had largely dissipated. Its influence is also apparent in the types of sales transacted. In 1838, just three years after the compensation payments began, the average price per acre for plantation land was already nearly 14 percent above the previous high of 1825. A year later the average price, £95 per acre, was 34 percent higher. The prices of eight of the ten estates sold privately in 1839 were uniformly high. Only two, the 185-acre Reid's Bay estate and the 226-acre Six Mens plantation, were sold for less than £70 per

Table 5.2. *Chancery Sales, Barbados, 1823–1843*

Year	Number of Sales	Total Price	Average per Acre
1823	2	£19,893	£40.43
1824	2	22,113	50.03
1825	5	78,722	76.36
1826	5	83,841	58.02
1827	1	11,258	37.53
1828	6	92,706	52.88
1829	1	11,143	37.77
1830	4	56,995	50.89
1831	0	0	0
1832	8	107,671	53.81
1833	5	38,169	30.83
1834	1	10,169	57.13
1835	5	27,268	37.15
1836	5	46,314	42.69
1837	1	16,882	48.93
1838	1	7,827	29.65
1839	0	0	0
1840	0	0	0
1841	1	6,518	52.14
1842	4	51,876	57.83
1843	0	0	0
Total	57	£689,365	£50.15

Sources: Deeds and Conveyances, RB1/271–306; Chancery Sales, 1825–64;
Minutes of the Court of Chancery, 1829–34, 1835–44.

acre. Four properties in St. George sold for an average of £98 per acre, although the 119-acre Golden Ridge estate sold for over £200 per acre. Two plantations in St. Thomas sold for an average of £112 per acre, while Pollards, the only estate sold in St. Philip that year, went for £149 per acre, the highest price for an estate in that parish for the entire period.[18] The high average prices of 1839 were due partly to the fact that all the properties involved were sold privately, and partly due to the location of these particular estates. Six of the ten estates were in St. George and St. Thomas, the most fertile of the island's

Table 5.3. *Total Estate Sales, Barbados, 1823–1843*

Year	Number of Sales	Total Price	Price per Acre
1823	5	£88,630	£70.57
1824	4	30,946	53.26
1825	13	175,952	71.79
1826	10	147,949	62.11
1827	8	80,676	61.63
1828	18	229,687	51.48
1829	6	67,203	55.04
1830	16	172,026	58.27
1831	3	22,983	42.48
1832	12	154,100	50.10
1833	7	48,255	34.25
1834	3	15,169	26.94
1835	15	181,982	56.05
1836	20	186,076	48.24
1837	30	394,294	63.29
1838	26	348,818	81.69
1839	10	157,964	95.85
1840	7	72,500	63.71
1841	7	45,504	42.65
1842	15	156,264	63.16
1843	5	64,622	79.29
Total	240	£2,841,600	£60.53

Sources: Deeds and Conveyances, RB1/271–306; Chancery Sales, 1825–64; Minutes of the Court of Chancery, 1829–34, 1835–44.

eleven parishes. The average price for estates in St. George between 1823 and 1843 reached £80 per acre, well above the average per-acre price for the colony as a whole.[19]

The overwhelming number of Barbadian chancery court records reveal the extent of the proprietors' indebtedness and the degree to which the sale price reduced the encumbrances against the properties. The debts secured against the forty-eight estates sold between 1823 and 1843 totaled approximately £924,000, while the proceeds from their sales amounted to £598,267, or

64 percent of their total debts. In the case of only three estates—Dunscombe, Black Rock, and Clifden—was the price sufficient to cover the court costs and the claims of all the creditors. None of the claimants involved in the chancery proceedings received prorated compensation, and many were left unpaid.[20] In 1830, for example, Mehitabelle Ann Simmons sold the Harrow and Four Square plantations for £38,557, but this covered only 68 percent of her deceased husband's liabilities. His major creditors, Gibbes and Bright of Bristol, who had initiated the suit, recovered 46 percent of their claim, but Thomas and John Daniel recovered only 14 percent of theirs.[21]

When the price of one estate was insufficient to satisfy the creditors, a planter could be forced to sell off other properties. In the twenty years between 1823 and 1843, at least ten plantations were sold in this way. In 1826 and 1827 Richard Smitten used Mangrove Pond and The Farm in St. Thomas, together with Black Rock in St. James, to secure one mortgage to Lee and Garner and another to Gibbes and Bright. When Lee and Garner sued in chancery in 1830, the court ordered the sale of all three properties. The proceeds from the sales covered 67 percent of the £44,664 secured against the properties in the form of fifty-three separate liens.[22]

Compared to the number of liens against Smitten's estates, those against John Barrow's plantations appeared quite modest. The same did not hold true for the total value of the liabilities secured against them. By 1832, Barrow owed a variety of creditors more than £82,885, over half of it due to Thomas and John Daniel.[23] In the ensuing chancery suit, the Daniels paid a total of £52,432 for Barrow's three estates: the 413-acre Sunbury plantation; the 348-acre Hampton estate, and Upton, a 242-acre property in St. Michael. The money paid off the seven liens prior to the Daniels', but left the partners with over £19,857 to carry as a bad debt.[24]

The chancery records and deeds of conveyance frequently provide detailed information concerning the liabilities of each estate that fell under the court's jurisdiction. In 89 percent (fifty-one) of the cases for which records have survived, it is also possible to identify the major creditors and calculate the frequency with which they bought chancery estates.

Metropolitan merchants acted as the major creditors for nearly half of the fifty-three estates that passed through the chancery courts between 1823 and 1843. Thomas and John Daniel headed the list with twelve estates, followed by Barton, Irlam, and Higginson, of Liverpool, with nine.[25] The merchant house of Gibbes and Bright held the major liens against four estates and Lee and Garner, also of Bristol, held a mortgage against one.[26] Yet these merchants did not invariably buy the estates when they fell into receivership.

Thomas and John Daniel bought only three of the twelve properties against which they held the major lien: John Barrow's Sunbury, Upton, and Hampton estates. Others such as Bagatelle in St. Thomas, The Pine in St. Michael, and Kirton's in St. Philip, passed to private individuals. Charles St. John bought the 165-acre Bagatelle plantation in 1832, although the Daniels had filed the motion for foreclosure. St. John paid £5,953 for the property, and although this did not cover all the estate's liabilities of more than £8,000, it paid off the Daniels' claim.[27]

When Bezsin King Reece bought The Pine in 1838, he paid over £7,800 for the 264-acre plantation. Thomas and John Daniel held two mortgages totaling £14,685, but because these ranked third and fifth among the seven liens against the estate, the partners recovered only 31 percent of their claim. On other occasions, of course, they recovered nothing. When Ralph Crichlow bought the 233-acre Kirton's estate in 1833, the property carried debts of £38,800, nearly half of it due to the Daniels. Although theirs was apparently the prior lien, the Master in Chancery excluded them and divided the money among the annuitants and smaller creditors instead.[28]

Barton, Irlam, and Higginson, on the other hand, bought eight of the ten chancery estates for which they were the major creditors. In 1823 the senior partner, Sir William Barton, paid £11,142 for the Sandy Lane plantation which had been appraised at £14,084 only three years earlier. When the estate appeared in chancery again in 1829, its liabilities to the partners alone had risen from £3,185 to over £23,500. On this occasion John Higginson, the sole surviving partner, bought it again, although this transaction may merely have been a transfer of the title, since the price of the property equaled the total debt due to the partnership.[29]

In 1832 Richard Deane, acting as Higginson's executor, bought the Grettons plantation out of chancery under unusual circumstances. Deane paid £16,860 for the estate, which had been mortgaged to Barton, Irlam, and Higginson on at least three occasions over the previous twelve years and which by 1832 owed the partners more than £10,600. The estate had originally been appraised at £25,682 and advertised for sale in 1827. When the court received no offers for the property, it reappraised the estate at £23,605 and put it back on the market. The records offer no explanation for the reduction in the appraised value over the five-year period. Presumably, the court lowered its evaluation because the estate had been in chancery an unusually long time for a Barbadian property. Shortly before his death, Higginson had agreed to buy the estate on condition that £5,000 remained in trust for the female relatives of the late owner. The master accepted his terms, but the women later entered a counterclaim for the compensation due for the estate's slaves. The commissioners considered their claim unjustified and ordered the money used to liquidate the estate's debts and encumbrances.[30]

An inventory made in 1835 of John Higginson's property put the value of his seven estates at £77,750, which included £17,485 for the services of 867 apprentices. The inventory valued the estates as follows: Joe's River in St. Joseph at £24,578, approximately 30 percent less than Higginson had paid for it in 1826; and Foul Bay at £14,592, about 14 percent less than the 1832 chancery price. The difference between the price Higginson paid for Joe's River and the later appraised value was partly due to the fact that the 239 workers had been valued at £38 each as slaves but at only £20 as apprentices. The appraisals for the 147-acre Rowans estate in St. George and 280-acre Congo Road in St. Philip were set at £7,678 and £13,850 respectively. Higginson had paid £11,365 for Rowans in 1829 and £16,071 for Congo Road three years later. The evaluators appraised Sandy Lane, a 296-acre property in St. James, at £8,057 and the 121-acre Cane Garden estate in St. Andrew at £7,792. The evaluation of the seventh estate, Castle Grant, covered only 50 apprentices, who may have been used as collateral for a mortgage by their previous employer.[31]

Both Sandy Lane and Joe's River, the two properties that Higginson bought through chancery, retained their value. The chancery court appraisal of 1826 and the inventory of properties made nine years later placed the value of Sandy Lane at between £21 and £25 per acre and Joe's River at between £36 and £37 per acre. These figures refute the West India Interest's claims that land values declined drastically after 1823 and that chancery prices were invariably far lower than the true value of the property.[32]

The affairs of Barton, Irlam, and Higginson remained closely tied to Barbados even after the deaths of the founding partners. A colonial subsidiary, Higginson, Deane, and Stott, continued to oversee its interest in the island. In February 1837 Thomas Stott bought Mount Clapham, a plantation that had been on the market for less than two weeks. He paid £16,882 for the property and paid off all debts due to Thomas and John Daniel and 90 percent of those owed John Higginson's estate. Within a year the partners resold the estate for £19,285 and made a profit of nearly 13 percent.[33]

Four years later, Jonathan Higginson bought another plantation that was heavily indebted to his father's estate. Palmers, in St. Philip, carried debts totaling £23,541, 36 percent of which was due to Barton, Irlam, and Higginson. The price the younger Higginson paid for the estate covered the court costs, Richard Deane's expenses as receiver, an outstanding mortgage to the imperial government taken out after the hurricane of 1831, the total debt due to the Liverpool partnership, and part of the debt due to Thomas and John Daniel.[34]

Compensation not only affected the ability of some Barbadian planters to dispose of their properties, it also modified the composition of the planto-cracy. By opening up the real estate market and easing the transfer of property, it allowed some proprietors to extend their current holdings and enabled oth-ers to become members of the plantocracy for the first time. Many prominent Barbadians who were not themselves planters nevertheless owned hundreds of slaves. They hired out these slaves at high cost to neighboring planters who were hard-pressed for labor during the planting and crop seasons. Like their indebted counterparts, these slave owners also benefited from compensation. But unlike those forced to repay persistent creditors, they had readily available resources that allowed them to take immediate advantage of rapidly changing conditions within the colony.

Individuals who bought sugar estates between 1834 and 1843 fall into three easily definable, though sometimes overlapping, categories. The largest cate-gory consisted of established proprietors intent on expanding their existing holdings. Such purchases accounted for 46 percent (63) of the 138 sales trans-acted during the ten-year period. Each buyer paid an average of £10,085, or approximately £57 per acre, for 155 additional acres. Individual purchasers bought fifty-two of the properties, four planters bought two estates each, and members of the powerful Alleyne family bought the remaining three estates.

In an important study of the Barbadian sugar economy in the late nine-teenth century, Cecilia Karch describes the Alleynes as the "archetypal plan-tocratic family," whose members were consistently prominent in the colonial legislature. The family continuously, and sometimes simultaneously, provided the island with councilors, assemblymen, justices, and officers of the militia. Its members intermarried with other influential Barbadian families.[35] The presence of the name Holder as a given name for their sons indicates the Alleynes connection with the Holder family, which, between 1660 and 1900, produced ten assembly or council members, one general, and five colonels of the island militia. At one point, the Holders owned property in several par-ishes, but they appear as estate owners only once in the final slave register of 1834. By then their property seems to have been reduced to John Alleyne Hold-er's 189-acre Lemon Arbour estate in St. John.[36] With the exception of Congo Road, which it owned until 1832, the family had disposed of its other property before 1823. No reference to a private or chancery sale of the Holders' estate appears in the later records.[37]

The patriarch of the Alleyne family, John Foster Alleyne, served on the leg-islative council at the beginning of the nineteenth century. His property con-sisted of four estates comprising 1,128 acres in the parish of St. James. At his death, sometime around 1820, the estates passed to his three sons. Charles

Thomas Alleyne inherited the 636-acre Porters and Mount Standfast estates, which were valued together at over £44,264; James Holder Alleyne received the Reid's Bay estate; while Samuel Holder Alleyne inherited an estate known as Cox's.[38] Over the course of the next fifteen years, the three sons made extensive additions to the family property.

Despite the West India Interest's gloomy pronouncements, the Alleyne family had enough confidence in the future to double its land holdings by 1834. Charles Thomas Alleyne had originally inherited Porters and Mount Standfast in partnership with Henry Alleyne, probably his cousin. In 1823 he bought Seniors, a 158-acre estate in St. Joseph, and two years later paid the chancery court £35,714 for the 365-acre Dunscombe estate in St. Thomas. By 1835 he had mortgaged the four estates to a variety of creditors, including Thomas and John Daniel and the imperial government.[39] Yet Charles and Henry Alleyne do not appear to have had any great financial difficulties. If the value of their land is based on the average price per acre for the twenty-year period, that is, £60, their 1,159 acres were worth approximately £69,540. Even with mortgages totaling £29,428, their land was mortgaged for only 42 percent of its market value. Nevertheless, the £12,767 they received as compensation in 1837, together with a deposit of over £2,000 from the sale of Seniors, enabled them to reduce their overall indebtedness by more than half. By 1838 Charles Thomas Alleyne had redeemed the mortgage that Thomas and John Daniel held against Dunscombe and over £10,000 in mortgages secured against Seniors. The compensation not only enabled Alleyne to reduce his liabilities, it improved his credit so that in 1837 he was able to buy up Henry Alleyne's half share of the Porters and Mount Standfast estates.[40]

The Alleyne brothers' expansion did not end with these purchases, nor did Henry Alleyne lose interest in sugar planting with the sale of his share of Porters and Mount Standfast. Between 1820 and 1834 James Holder Alleyne had bought Swan's and Gregg Farm estates in St. Andrew and The Spa plantation in St. Joseph, thus adding another 535 acres to the 185 acres that comprised Reid's Bay. By 1834 the family owned 2,028 acres and had doubled its original holdings. When Henry Alleyne bought the 484-acre Lancaster estate in 1840, he increased the family's property by 24 percent, thereby making the Alleyne family the largest owners of sugar estates in the island.[41]

With the exception of the Alleyne family, the greatest landowners of Barbados added little or nothing to their holdings after 1834. William H. Prescod, the largest individual proprietor, made no new additions to his 2,254 acres, probably because 90 percent of his compensation went to his attorneys and creditors.[42] The Haynes family, which owned slightly over 2,000 acres and ranked as the third largest landowner in the island, bought only one new estate, Mount Harmony, which added a mere 59 acres to their property. The family already owned seven major estates and three smaller properties of under 50 acres.[43] In 1837 Robert Haynes and his sons received over £35,000 compensation for their 1,293 slaves. The award was more than enough to cover the £17,000 secured against their Newcastle and Clifton Hall estates.[44] If the family had any liabilities other than normal operating costs, they do not appear in the records for the period. Fears of a diminished labor supply after the end of the proposed six-year apprenticeship perhaps played a greater part in the Haynes' decision not to expand than did a possible lack of funds and credit. John Rycroft Best, on the other hand, was more concerned with debt reduction than with expansion.

Best owned five plantations of his own and administered Moonshine Hall and Fairey Valley as his father's executor, which gave him control of more than 1,950 acres, mainly in Christ Church. His sole purchase after 1834 was the small 54-acre Harburton estate. Best used his own compensation to pay off outstanding mortgages to the imperial government, Thomas and John Daniel, and various other creditors. By 1841 he had used the £7,571 compensation awarded for his father's slaves to maintain the interest payments on the mortgages that the Daniels held against Moonshine Hall and Fairey Valley.[45] The £18,381 he received for his own slaves paid off private debts against Blackmans, which he had bought out of chancery in 1825, and redeemed other mortgages held by the government against his Greenlands, Rycroft, and Blackmans estates. When the Harburton plantation became available in 1837, Best was able to pay £5,000 for the property and to take responsibility for the £1,610 secured against it.[46] It was, however, the middle-sized proprietors who bought the greatest acreage, and paid the highest prices, after emancipation. The Alleyne family acquired 668 additional acres, but this was the exception rather than the rule among the major landowners; lesser landowners such as Joseph Lyder Briggs and Bezsin King Reece bought almost as much land, but at somewhat higher prices.

In 1834 Joseph Lyder Briggs already owned three plantations: the 324-acre Checker Hall estate in St. Lucy, the 233-acre Maynards in St. Peter, and The Fortress, an 86-acre property in St. Thomas. He had bought Checker Hall in 1830 through the Court of Chancery and by emancipation owned a total of 643 acres.[47] Three years later Briggs received over £6,000 compensation for his 219 slaves and shortly afterward began extending his property in earnest. First, he bought the Grenade Hall and Welch Town estates in St. Peter, thereby adding 430 acres to his existing holdings. Then, in 1839, he purchased the 226-acre Six Mens estate from Sir Fitzroy Maclean for £14,285. On both occasions he paid approximately half the money down as a deposit and secured the remainder with judgments and liens. Despite having sold The Fortress in 1835, Briggs thus owned 1,213 acres. The purchase of Six Mens gave him a total of 889 acres in St. Peter, in addition to his original holding in St. Lucy.[48] In a two-year period he had spent more than £44,280, increased his property by over 100 percent, and put himself among the top twelve landowners of the island.

Although Bezsin King Reece spent less than Briggs on expanding his property, he bought more land. With the exception of the Alleyne family, he acquired a greater acreage after 1834 than any other established proprietor. Reece was also a latecomer to the plantocracy, having acquired his first estate in 1830 when he bought Yorkshire, a 313-acre estate in Christ Church. Its 152 slaves were valued at £7,865, and Reece collected £3,054 compensation for them in 1837.[49] By then he had already begun to expand his property. In 1835 he bought Pickerings through the Court of Chancery. The 250-acre estate had come under the court's jurisdiction in 1831, when creditors claimed that its owner had reaped several crops but failed to pay the interest on his debts. Three years later the court ordered the estate appraised and sold. In order to buy the estate, Reece had to bid against other interested parties and eventually paid nearly 10 percent above the appraised value. By 1838 a neighboring estate was also in receivership. The 264 acres known as The Pine were saddled with debts of over £22,000, and Reece himself was among the major creditors, although Thomas and John Daniel probably initiated the writ of foreclosure.[50] When Reece bought The Pine for £10,958, the Daniels recovered 31 percent of their money and Reece more than doubled his holdings. The two transactions gave him one property in Christ Church and two contiguous estates in St. Michael.

An entirely new class of proprietors emerged after 1836. This second category of landowners included several plantation attorneys. None had owned estates before emancipation, but all took advantage of the social and economic changes in Barbados to establish themselves as members of the plantocracy for the first time. Between 1834 and 1843, twenty-nine new buyers paid £382,038 for 5,917 acres of plantation land in the island. Their purchases accounted for 28 percent (39) of all sales transacted during the ten-year period. On average a first-time purchaser paid £13,173 for a 204-acre estate, about 12.5 percent more than established planters paid for their new acquisitions.[51]

In their capacity as plantation attorneys, several prominent Barbadians, such as Eyare King, oversaw the estates of merchants and absentees. Prior to abolition, King had acted as the attorney for Howard Griffiths, owner of the Bright Hall and Husbands estates. Although he owned no land of his own at the time, King was sufficiently wealthy to be able to make loans to a variety of planters. When the Court of Chancery sold the Prior Park estate in 1832, he recovered 65 percent of a lien which he held against the property. Four years later he received the compensation award for the slaves at Husbands and for those at Pools, an estate owned by Edward Lake Hinds.[52] The following year, in 1837, King used his award to buy Hopeland, a 216-acre estate in St. Michael. The Brandon and Killick partnership, the owners of the property, wanted £14,142 for the plantation. King paid a deposit of £4,285 and secured the remainder in the usual manner. The purchase seemed wise, for during the early nineteenth century Hopeland had produced a net income of £1,771 per annum, and with careful management, King expected it to continue making a profit.[53]

This purchase did not limit King's investment in land, however, for the same year he also bought the Waterford estate. The plantation cost £21,428 and increased his holdings in St. Michael by another 319 acres. In 1840 he acquired a half share in Sturges in St. Thomas and in Mallards, a smaller property on the border of St. Joseph and St. Andrew.[54]

The 146-acre Sturges estate, together with The Hill and Neils plantations, had belonged to William Bryant Worrell. At the time of his death, colonial law barred Worrell's wife, a foreign national, from inheriting the properties. The estates were escheated to the Crown, which instructed the receiver general of Barbados to offer them for sale at public auction. King and an associate, Christopher Gill, bought Sturges for £10,500, paid £3,547 down and mortgaged the estate for the balance of the price. Under the terms of the sales the widow, Marie Ann Worrell, received the purchase money less the costs of the sale and escheatment. Within a year King had sold his share of Sturges and Mallards to his partner. Gill paid £1,428 for King's half interest and undertook to pay off all outstanding debts against the properties.[55] In the course of his transactions, Eyare King had paid £43,214 for 535 acres.

The general easing of credit after 1836 allowed other men to profit from the upswing in the real estate market. Neither Thomas William Bradshaw nor William Lucien Warren had owned estates before emancipation, nor did they receive compensation for any slaves. Nevertheless, both men seized the opportunity to buy land as the market opened.

Thomas William Bradshaw's purchases illustrate how one man took advantage of the situation to become a proprietor and make a profit at the same time. In 1838 Bradshaw paid £14,285 for the Highland estate in St. Thomas. Within a year he sold the 197-acre property to Nathaniel Forte, the Speaker of the House of Assembly, for £15,714. The following year, Bradshaw used the 11 percent profit he had made on the sale as part of the deposit on the smaller Endeavour estate in St. Thomas, which he bought for £8,000.[56]

William Lucien Warren made his first purchases in partnership with Richard Inniss. In 1836 the partners paid £4,297 for the Grenade Hall estate and an additional £14,000 for the neighboring Welch Town plantation. In all they paid approximately £18,297 for a total of 430 acres in St. Peter. Two years later, Warren sold his half share of the properties to his partner for £12,857 and made a 29 percent profit on the sale. After selling Grenade Hall and Welch Town, he retained his position within the plantocracy and in 1839 bought Cane Garden, a 169-acre estate in St. Thomas. Richard Inniss proved to be almost as astute. Once in complete control of the two plantations, he immediately sold them at a 27 percent profit to Joseph Briggs.[57]

The distinction between purchasers like Bradshaw, Warren, and Richard Inniss and simple speculators is sometimes blurred. At times the two groups overlap, but the major difference is one of timing and motive. All three men bought their first estates after 1834, apparently with the idea of joining the plantocracy and improving their social standing. Thus, they clearly belong with Eyare King as first-time buyers and overlap with speculators because they made a profit along the way.

The third category of purchasers, therefore, consists of those who bought estates with an eye to quick and profitable resale. Such speculators were either already established as plantation owners before 1834 or operated as merchants in Barbados. Their purchases account for approximately 9 percent of the 138 sales transacted between 1834 and 1843.[58]

Speculators usually kept their estates for less than three years. Resident planters had the advantage over absentees and were better able to adjust to changes in the real estate market. Their familiarity with local conditions and the financial situation of their neighbors allowed them to buy and sell to the best advantage. Although no vast fortunes resulted from these transactions, it was often possible for the speculator to make a profit of £2,000 or £3,000. It was, moreover, the owners of relatively small properties, who collected less than £3,000 in compensation, who speculated in land at this point.

In 1837, for example, James William Biddy sold a substantial property and bought a smaller estate. He sold Lammings, a 111-acre plantation in St. Joseph, to James Thomas Rogers for £10,000. Rogers paid a deposit of £8,571 and undertook to pay off the outstanding debts against the estate, rather than give a mortgage in the usual way. With the proceeds from this sale, Biddy purchased the Endeavour estate in St. Thomas. The estate cost him £5,357, which he paid immediately. A year later he sold the 53-acre estate for over £5,700.[59] Although much of the price was secured by a mortgage, Biddy nevertheless made a healthy profit on the combined transactions. If Lammings was an average estate and worth the same as other plantations sold in St. Joseph that year, that is, £71 per acre, then Biddy's profit margin was approximately 21 percent on the first sale and an additional 6 percent on the second.

Other proprietors also speculated in land during this period. James Holligan, who owned two estates in St. Michael, used the compensation paid for his Bank Hall slaves to pay off part of the property's £4,285 mortgage. In 1838 Holligan and his partners, Benjamin C. Howell and Benjamin Howell Jones, bought the 229-acre Mangrove Pond estate for £17,857. Later the same year, Holligan and Jones paid Howell £4,642 for his share of the property.[60] Holligan bought a second property, Cox's, in 1838. When he bought the plantation from James Holder Alleyne, he paid £27,000 for the property and Alleyne agreed to pay off the only outstanding debt, a mortgage of £5,000 held by the imperial government. By 1839, James Holder Alleyne had begun to regret the sale and proposed buying back the estate. Holligan agreed and resold Cox's to Alleyne for £21,428, making an 11 percent profit in the process.[61]

Only two of the merchant companies that traded in Barbados during the period logically fall within the confines of the speculator group. Each resold property within two years of the original purchase and each made a profit on its transactions. Higginson, Deane, and Stott capitalized on their purchase and resale of Mount Clapham. When the company disposed of the property in 1838, it made a 13 percent profit.[62] Lee and Garner enjoyed similar success.

In 1836 Thomas Lee paid the chancery court £16,428 for the Mangrove Pond estate. Within two years he resold the property to James Holligan and his partners for £17,857, thereby making a profit of roughly 8 percent. During the same period, Lee profited from another judicious transaction. In 1835 he had paid Joseph Tudor £14,285 for the Lightfoots estate. Apart from the property, the sale also included the compensation due to Tudor for his 139 slaves. Thus, besides the 206-acre estate, Lee gained Tudor's £2,700 compensation award. When Lee advertised the estate for sale two years later, Nathaniel Cave offered him £14,285 for the property. Although this was the amount he had originally paid for the estate, Lee accepted the offer and a deposit of £1,428, thereby still realizing a reasonable profit by acquiring the compensation money and a substantial cash deposit.[63]

With plantations in Barbados finding ready buyers, the Interest's claims that colonial property values were severely depreciated and that the estates had been rendered virtually unsaleable were clearly unfounded. Barbadian estates sold quickly, often within a few days of being put on the market. Private individuals intent on extending their existing property, or on joining the plantocracy for the first time, bought 74 percent of all estates offered for sale after 1834. Sales to known merchants or speculators accounted for just under 10 percent of the total sales, and even then the land reverted to private ownership within two to three years.

More than half the sales transacted in Barbados occurred after Stanley's bill had passed through Parliament. By then West Indian proprietors could easily calculate the amount of compensation they would receive. The compensation award had a critical impact on the ownership of land in the sugar islands. By injecting £20 million into the planter economy, the indemnity increased the proprietors' liquidity and improved their overall financial standing. It provided the would-be purchaser of colonial estates with substantial credit and eased the transfer of West Indian estates.[64] By so doing, it maintained, and even raised, the value of estates, at least in Barbados. Without the guarantee of indemnity, it is unlikely that land values would have risen so dramatically between 1834 and 1839 or that the number of sales would have increased simultaneously.

6

White Women in the Plantation Economy

Throughout the slavery era, white women played a vital role in the economic life of the colonies. As creditors, slave holders, and property owners, they helped to sustain the plantation system, yet their contribution has passed virtually unnoticed. Several factors help to explain this neglect. The tendency to examine the rights of women, especially married women, from the standpoint of common law has obscured their rights under laws of equity, which allowed many married women to retain a "sole and separate estate," which their husbands could not touch. At the same time, the belief that only parents arranged marriage settlements overlooks the part individual women played in designing their own settlements in order to protect their real and personal property. This narrow focus often leads to an overemphasis on such nineteenth-century reforms as the Married Women's Property Acts.[1]

A reassessment of the land and mortgage records places white women in their proper social and economic context and underscores their pivotal role in colonial life. As metropolitan merchants attempted to cut their losses, many women continued to buy or invest in colonial property. Did they lend money only to friends and relations, or were they part of the informal credit that linked British investors to total strangers in the Caribbean? How did they acquire West India property, and to what degree did they control their property and finances?[2]

Although single women and widows enjoyed the same property rights as men, the law restricted those of married women. Common law regarded married couples as one unit, which was represented by the man. It barred married women from mortgaging or selling land or entering into binding contracts. Everything a woman brought to or acquired during marriage automatically became the property of her husband. He could squander her inheritance, sell her lands and slaves, and prevent her from choosing her heirs. If he died in debt, his widow could lose all rights to their personal property, for even if she had no part in amassing the debts, she was held legally responsible.[3]

A wife, nevertheless, did have the right of dower to one-third of the couple's personal property and the life interest on one-third of their real estate. By invoking this right, a woman could prevent her husband from selling or mortgaging any real estate in which her dower was invested. Such property could only be released if she willingly signed away her right, as Eliza Frances Farquharson apparently did when she conveyed the Clifton plantation to her husband, thus enabling him to sell off part of the land.[4]

Despite the severe legal restrictions placed on married women, men did not have complete control of women's property. The laws of equity protected married women to a considerable degree, and the courts of chancery normally upheld their claims against the demands of creditors and male relatives. For women, the most important aspect of equity law related to the safeguarding and disposal of property. Parents, widows, and women marrying for the first time often insisted on liberal marriage contracts. Having complete command of their own "sole and separate estate" during the marriage helped women to guard against unfortunate or dissolute husbands and to guarantee a secure future for themselves and their children. Whenever a separate estate was established, the property was legally conveyed to one or more trustees. The amount of control the trustee exercised varied enormously. In some cases they had total control; in others none at all; and sometimes the trustee and the woman had joint management. For the most part, trusts were intended to protect the property from the husband's creditors.[5]

Property that had been settled on a married woman could not be attached for debt unless it had been included for the express purpose of evading a specific creditor. Men often agreed to generous settlement terms for this very reason. If they tried to safeguard all their property, however, it became extremely difficult to use it as collateral, as Anthony Davis found. In 1836 Davis sold Norfolk, a small Jamaican estate, to his mother-in-law, who bought it on the condition that her daughter Eliza Davis would be the sole owner. Davis had to satisfy his creditors that he had enough other property to cover his debts before they agreed to release Norfolk and allow him to sell it for his wife's "sole and separate estate."[6]

Free women of all classes took an active part in determining the terms of their marriage settlements. This was especially true with regard to wills, and women usually included special clauses in the settlement that allowed them to dispose of their "separate estate" as they saw fit. The specifics of the contracts varied greatly. Some allowed women to change the terms at a later time. In this way a woman could give her husband temporary authority over her property, knowing that she could rescind the arrangement at any time. While some settlements gave women exclusive control over their sole estate, others were more restrictive: settlements that granted a woman the right to bequeath real estate did not necessarily allow her to sell or mortgage the property; those that gave her the rents and profits from a specific property did not usually allow her to spend or invest the principal.[7]

As executrixes and administrators of large plantations women exercised considerable control over colonial real estate. Many men trusted their wives's administrative abilities and expected them to take an active part in managing the family estates. An executor's duties included collecting and paying debts, arranging for the sale of property if necessary, and overseeing the distribution of bequests. When an estate did not sell quickly, the executor was expected to run the property and keep it in good order, maintain the slaves, and hire them out where appropriate.[8]

The Jamaican records identify ninety-eight male estate owners as deceased and provide the names of the executor for thirty-three of them. Seventy-five percent of the time, another man acted as the executor; in the other cases, women acted as the executrix or trustee. Anna Maria Heron, for example, was the sole executrix of the 1,134-acre Wigton coffee estate. James Edgar appointed his wife, Eliza, as one of three trustees for his 1,250-acre Osborne estate, and before she remarried, Sarah Stewart acted as the executrix for the Grange River plantation and two smaller properties. The equivalent records for Barbados identify fifty deceased plantation owners, and in thirty cases the executor was also named. Of the twenty-six male owners, nearly half had appointed an executrix. These women also administered extensive properties, although several were heavily indebted and already in receivership.[9]

In one very unusual case, the Jamaican Court of Chancery appointed a widow, Ann Katherine Storer, as joint receiver of her husband's plantations. The six estates were the center of several lawsuits among members of the Storer family and between the Storers and Armstrong and Bazelgetto, their London consignees. At no other time in the twenty-year period from 1823 to 1843 did the court appoint more than one receiver at a time, and certainly never a woman.[10]

In Barbados only a few women plantation owners appointed an executrix. Most chose men to serve as trustees or executors, but this did not necessarily give the men access to the woman's property. Women appear in the court records as both plaintiffs and defendants in cases dealing with the disposal of property. Where property and inheritances were concerned, they used the court system to prosecute their claims. When Joshua Gitten died in 1819, he left his Bushy Park estate to his wife and named his nephew as executor. In addition, he left legacies to each of his four nieces. When the women had still not received their inheritance eight years later, they filed a complaint against the executor, accusing him of misappropriating their uncle's property and neglecting to pay their legacies. The women pursued the case for another seven years before the court finally decided in their favor. At other times the courts called upon women to account for their actions as administrators. Elizabeth Cadogan appeared in court in 1826 to answer charges that she had failed in her duties as the executrix of her husband's estate. His creditors claimed she had misapplied the rents and proceeds from the Crab Hill plantation instead of paying off his debts and demanded an accounting of her management.[11]

Women owned or controlled approximately 5 percent of the estates for Jamaica, and several ranked among the island's greatest landowners, some with properties in excess of 1,000 acres. The last Jamaican slave register, compiled in 1832, listed at least forty women who owned over 100 slaves each (table 6.1). Lady Cooper, for example, owned the 2,361-acre Duckenfield Hall sugar estate in the Plantain Garden River valley, and in 1832 her Jamaican attorney registered 365 slaves on her behalf. The plantation was held in trust for Lady Cooper who apparently owned the property as part of her "sole and separate estate." Three years later the trustees collected over £6,300 in compensation, although that may have been a mere formality.[12]

The situation of Lady Holland is a little less clear. Lady Holland inherited the 2,252-acre Friendship and Greenwich sugar estates, their satellite Sweet River Pen, and over 350 slaves from her grandfather in 1800. The plantations had originally been separate entities but were operating as a single unit by the time she inherited them. Lady Holland had been married once before and almost certainly had some form of marriage settlement. She may have administered the estates jointly with her husband, for, although she was still living in the late 1840s, her compensation was paid to Lord Holland.[13]

Thousands of British and colonial women received compensation when their slaves were emancipated. Most women owned fewer than 10 slaves, but in Barbados alone their claims accounted for 37 percent of the total claims submitted to the commissioners. In both Jamaica and Barbados, the compensation paid to women who, like Isabella Buckmaster, owned large properties, helped them to reduce their indebtedness or to buy additional land. Buckmaster's 928-acre Windsor Castle plantation produced both coffee and sugar. In 1829 she mortgaged the property to Ambrose Humphrys to secure several legacies. The mortgage remained unpaid until 1832, by which time the accumulated interest had nearly tripled the original debt. In 1839, the commissioners awarded Humphrys approximately £3,300 which, together with the pro-

Table 6.1. *White Women Estate Owners, Jamaica, 1834 (estates over 600 acres)*

Name	Estate	Acres
Lady Cooper	Duckenfield Hall	2,361
Lady Holland	Friendship, Greenwich	2,255
Catherine Wordie	Schwellenberg	2,255
Elizabeth Lydia Reid	Nonpareil, Mount Pleasant	1,749
Elizabeth M. Gayner	Culloden, Friendship Pen	1,724[a]
Frances Dickenson	Barton Estate	1,545
Mary Haughton Reid	Wakefield, Hermitage	1,521
Charlotte A. Quinlan	Wentworth, Charlottenburg	1,419
Elizabeth Burton	Content	1,250[a]
Elizabeth Bullock	Mount Carfax	1,038[a]
Isabella Buckmaster	Windsor Castle	928
Elizabeth Dewar	Richmond Hill	765[a]
Louisa Burke	Newman Hall	703
Sarah G. Bambridge	Lindale	616
Mary Player Smith	Prospect Hill	600
Elizabeth Clarke	Mount Idalia	600
Susannah Hylton	Belvidere	600
Total		21,929

Sources: Slave Registers; Deeds and Conveyances.
[a] Registered between 90 and 100 slaves.

ceeds from the crop, paid off the debt and released the property to Buck-master's heirs.[14]

Other owners met with less success. In order to reduce her debts to Stewart and Westmoreland, Charlotte Ann Quinlan was forced to sell her right to redeem her Wentworth and Charlottenburg plantations. Her creditors collected the compensation for the slaves at Wentworth, but the estates remained the focus of a five-year lawsuit until they were finally sold through the court in 1838. Elizabeth Lydia Reid's 1,749-acre Nonpareil and Mount Pleasant estates remained in receivership throughout the period. So did Susannah Hylton's Belvidere sugar plantation, which until 1830 had made an annual net income of £850.[15]

By 1845, when the Jamaican Assembly reported on the changes that had taken place in sugar and coffee cultivation since 1832, hundreds of owners had abandoned their unprofitable estates. Among the derelict properties were Mary Haughton Reid's Wakefield estate, Mary Player Smith's Prospect Hill sugar plantation, Catherine Wordie's Schwellenberg, and Elizabeth Clarke's Mount Idalia coffee estates. Nevertheless, nearly half of the women who could be classified as large-scale owners of Jamaican slaves claimed their share of the indemnity and among them collected over £56,764.[16]

The extent to which white women engaged in the plantation economy is clearest in Barbados. As creditors and estate owners, women collected 28 percent of the compensation awarded to all women who owned slaves in the colony. Women bought and sold plantations in their own right, controlled others as widows and executrixes, lent money to hard-pressed relatives, and mortgaged their own property. In other cases, they assisted total strangers, and many never set foot in the colonies.[17]

Women provided 13 percent of the 209 private mortgages recorded for Barbados between 1823 and 1843 and over 10 percent of their total value. Although these transactions involved only twenty-four women, their participation far surpassed their small number (table 6.2). Moreover, these women were large-scale creditors, with mortgages averaging £4,535, or 76 percent of the average £6,000 mortgage provided by men.[18] At times mortgages formed an integral part of an estate sale, but at others they were completely separate arrangements. Between 1823 and 1843, women entered into 13 percent of the separate, or simple, mortgage transactions, which ranged in value from a few hundred pounds to over £10,000. At one end of the scale, in Barbados, Margaret Williams White supplied Thorpes estate with a mortgage of £339, while at the other, Margaret Ann Bend supplied Sir Reynold Abel Alleyne with a £12,871 mortgage.[19]

These straightforward mortgages, which totaled slightly over £52,360, involved only fourteen women. In 1824 Elizabeth Bovell accepted a mortgage against the Husbands estate as collateral for a loan of over £6,428. This was not her first financial venture. When the Oxford plantation passed through chancery in 1822, her claim appeared as the second lien against the property. The debt may have been an unpaid legacy, or a mortgage from the registered owners, John and William Bovell.[20]

Few mortgagees, male or female, private or merchant, could expect a rapid repayment of their advances. Most had to wait to collect, or more often accumulate, the interest over the course of many years. Elizabeth Bayne waited nearly fifteen years and undertook a protracted lawsuit in Barbados before collecting on mortgages originally secured against Social Hall in 1816 and 1817.

Table 6.2. *Women Creditors, Barbados, 1823–1843*

Name	Value of Mortgages
Joanna Alleyne[a]	£3,571
Elizabeth Bascom[a]	5,634
Elizabeth Ann Belgrave	8,571
Margaret Ann Bend[a]	22,157
Sarah Bispham	1,143
Elizabeth Bovell	6,429
Ann Boxhill	11,928
Elizabeth Cadogan	1,928
Mary Elizabeth Dalzell[a]	8,571
Elizabeth Gittens[a]	526
Elizabeth Hinds[a]	2,857
Mary Hinds	5,714
Mary Elizabeth Hinds	8,940
Mary Mercy Hinds	10,800
Elizabeth Howell	1,071
Ann Elizabeth Jones	1,071
Ann Isabella Jones	857
Elizabeth Jones	2,857
Priscilla Scantlebury[a]	2,143
Ann Sclater[a]	4,728
Margaret Ann Simpson[a]	4,229
Ann Trotman[a]	11,429
Margaret Williams White[a]	339
Sarah Prescod Williams	6,786
Total	£134,279

Sources: Deeds and Conveyances, RB1/271–306; Minutes of the Court of Chancery, 1829–34, 1835–44; Chancery Sales, 1825–66.
[a]Resident.

In 1835, she entered a counterclaim against the estate's owner, Richard K. Austin. Recognizing that she had received no interest for more than two years, the commissioners ruled in Bayne's favor and awarded her the entire compensation due for Social Hall's 93 slaves.[21] Even so, the award covered only half of her outstanding claim.

In addition to the loans to Social Hall, Elizabeth Bayne also lent money to John Barrow, the owner of the Sunbury, Hampton, and Upton plantations. Three other women held major liens against these estates, which, together with Bayne's, accounted for 6 percent of the total £82,857 secured against the three properties. Only Frances Barrow appears to have been related to the owner, possibly as his widow. If this was indeed the case, the money due to her may have been part of a legacy or marriage settlement. The money owed to Mary Ann Reeves, Elizabeth Senhouse, and Elizabeth Bayne, on the other hand, was clearly specified as mortgages or loans, rather than as marriage settlements, and were secured by court judgments. When the court sold Barrow's heavily encumbered estates in 1832, it paid the four women from the proceeds of the sale of Sunbury, and between them, Barrow, Reeves, Senhouse, and Bayne collected at least 19 percent of the price paid for the estate. The other creditors, mainly merchants, were paid with the money received for Hampton and Upton.[22]

Not all women were so lucky. Some were forced to renew old mortgages in order to protect their original investments. When Ann Boxhill sold the Waterford estate in 1819, she accepted a mortgage for the entire price. Fifteen years later the new owner, James Dottin Maycock, cited the "various causes affecting the price of property and produce in the colonies" as the reason he had paid off less than 9 percent of the debt. Boxhill had little choice but to wait and hope she would eventually be repaid. If she forced the estate into chancery she risked losing everything, especially if other lien holders had stronger claims. This was, in fact, the case when Maycock sold the estate privately in 1835. By then he had mortgaged the estate for a further £6,500, and nearly 85 percent of the price was again secured by mortgages. After the deposit had been used to partially pay other creditors, there was no money left to pay off the Boxhill debt. When the commissioners began their work in 1836, Ann Boxhill's heirs entered a counterclaim against the estate. They hoped to receive at least the indemnity due for the plantation's 112 slaves, but they withdrew the claim when the commissioners awarded the money to a prior lien holder.[23]

Sarah Bispham also disputed an original claim in her unsuccessful attempt to gain the compensation due for the slaves belonging to the Bannatynes estate. She based her counterclaim on an outstanding mortgage originally extended to William Clarke Haynes in 1830, but the commissioners recognized the claim of Robert Reece who had bought the property in 1832. In this particular case, Reece's chancery purchase overrode Bispham's prior mortgage, although no explanation for the decision appears in the records.[24]

Although the surviving records provide the names of all the creditors and give detailed information on indebtedness and the price paid for each property, they rarely disclose any personal relationship between colonial debtors and their mortgagees. In many cases identifiable British merchants were prominent among the creditors. Nevertheless, it is sometimes possible to uncover personal relationships between individuals and to some extent untangle the intricate web of colonial credit.

Although there is no evidence of a personal tie between Elizabeth Bovell and John Poyer Griffith, there was clearly a family relationship between her and the owners of the Oxford estate. The link is documented in an obituary that appeared in *The Barbadian* on 13 August 1834, announcing the death of Elizabeth Bovell, the widow of James Bovell and mother of John and William Bovell, and it is quite possible that the Oxford debt secured a loan from a mother to her two sons.[25]

Other family connections can be traced through the mortgage records. When the court sold Sandy Lane in 1823, Joanna Alleyne and Mrs. G. Alleyne appeared among the list of major creditors. The arrears of Mrs. Alleyne's legacy and the money due to Joanna Alleyne accounted for nearly half of the combined debts. Quite possibly Mrs. G. Alleyne was the mother of John Gay Alleyne and Joanna Alleyne his widow. Shortly before sailing for England in 1819, Alleyne drew up a new will to provide for his wife's security. He gave her an additional settlement of £2,500 and left instructions that after his debts had been paid she should sell Sandy Lane.[26] The new arrangement presumably accounted for at least part of the money owed to Joanna Alleyne.

The two women also appear to have been related to Charles Thomas Alleyne, who administered Sandy Lane as the court-appointed receiver. The probable interrelationship among the three is further supported by a deed of mortgage executed in 1823, which indicates that Charles Thomas Alleyne borrowed over £3,570 from Joanna Alleyne and used the Seniors plantation as collateral. Seniors is one of the very few properties for which a deed of redemption exists. When Alleyne redeemed the mortgage eleven years later, he did not pay interest on the original amount. This unusual arrangement suggests that Joanna and Charles Alleyne were near relatives and that this was a case of a mother providing her son with a substantial interest-free loan.[27]

Women played an equally important role as plantation owners. The triennial slave registers frequently supply alternative information about their own-

Table 6.3. *Widows and Executrixes, Barbados, 1834*

Name	Estate	Number of Slaves	Acres
Ann Trotman	Buckley	231	267
Ann Trotman	Carmichael	178	371
Ann St. John Adams[a]	Adams Castle	216	297
Mary Skeete	Rock Hall	168	60
Mary Skeete	Mangrove	154	572
Margaret Ann Simpson[b]	Hansons	154	274
Margaret Ann Simpson[b]	Haggatts	116	n/d
Catherine Ann Smitten[b]	Mangrove Pond	146	385
Catherine Ann Smitten[b]	Holders	78	203
Rebecca Chessman[b]	Redland	110	151
Mary A. Eversley	Worthing View	94	128
Margaret Foderingham[a]	Ayshford	94	174
Margaret Foderingham[a]	Hopewell	77	140
Frances Als[a]	Shepherd's Cot	78	73
Marie Ann Worrell[b]	Sturges	55	146
Marie Ann Worrell[b]	Neils	n/d	149
Total		1,949	3,390

Source: Barbados Slave Registers, T71/553–64.
Note: No data available for the size of Haggatts estate or the number of slaves at Neils.
[a] Widow and executrix.
[b] Widow.

ership of colonial real estate. The Barbados slave register for 1834 lists twenty-seven women as owners of sugar plantations. Three of these women appear simply as widows (table 6.3). Another nine women were the legal administrators and executrixes of their husbands' estates. Margaret Simpson, for example, controlled Hansons and Haggatts estates as the executrix, and Margaret Fodringham administered the Ayshford and Hopewell plantations in a similar capacity.[28]

The remaining fifteen women appear as plantation owners in their own right (table 6.4). Ten of them lived in the island and represented 5 percent of the 198 known resident proprietors for that year. Among them, these twenty-seven women managed over 6,291 acres and at least 3,870 slaves when the final slave register was compiled. At emancipation they accounted for 11 percent of

Table 6.4. *Women Plantation Owners, Barbados, 1834*

Name	Estate	Number of Slaves	Acres
Mary Lovell,[a] Anne Grassett[a]	Chancery Lane	165	353
Catherine Coulthurst	Bakers	143	301
Mary Salter Dehany	Salters	205	299
Sarah S. Maycock	Mellows	151	248
Sarah and Ann Goodridge[a]	Mt. Brevitor	115	243
Susanna Alsop[a]	Edge Hill	79	238
Mary Jane Callender[a]	Hopefield	154	236
Margaret Ann Bend[a]	Pleasant Hall	136	236
Mary Elizabeth Dalzell[a]	Buttals	176	219
Anna Marie Graham[a]	Bourbon	93	191
Sarah H. Straghan	Mt. All	70	149
Katherine Chase[a]	Stanmore	52	n/d
Fanny P. Howell[a]	Windsor Cot	51	n/d
Mary Licorish[a]	Fords	56	15
Bathseba Lord, deceased[a]	Long Bay	88	n/d
Total		1,734	2,728

Sources: Slave Registers, T71/553–64; Deeds and Conveyances, RB1/271-306.
Note: No data available for the size of Stanmore, Windsor Cot, or Long Bay estates.
[a]Resident.

the 241 persons who owned estates of over 50 acres and supervised the affairs of 11 percent of the total 307 plantations of that size.[29]

These statistics, however, apply only to 1834 and understate the full extent of women's involvement in the management and transfer of real estate. When the full twenty-year span of this study is taken into account, the degree to which a handful of women participated in the plantation economy of Barbados becomes evident. Between 1823 and 1843 forty-five women owned a total of 48 estates. This raises their proportion to 19 percent of the 241 individual owners of properties over 50 acres. Moreover, these forty-five women had access to the labor of 4,484 slaves and effectively controlled more than 9,890 acres of land.[30] Not all of these women kept their estates for the entire period, but their activities in the real estate market are significant, nevertheless.

Throughout the period women participated directly in 10 percent of the 240 sales involving Barbadian plantations. Seven of the transactions took place prior to 1834 and before the British government guaranteed to pay compensation. With only one exception, they concerned the sale rather than the purchase of property.

The major concern of the women who sold estates between 1823 and 1834 was to dispose of economic liabilities in order to protect themselves from their husbands' creditors. Two years after the death of her husband in 1826, Sarah Prescod Williams sold their 327-acre Westmoreland estate for £6,785. Williams took a substantial loss on the transaction, for the 1824 inventory of the property had set a value of £10,633 on the land alone. The price did not cover the mortgage that John Prescod Williams had taken out the previous year, and his widow was also forced to accept a mortgage for the entire amount.[31]

When Elizabeth Jones sold Rowans and Jacob Belgrave's widow, Elizabeth, sold the 218-acre Stirling plantation, the buyers specifically agreed to pay off the outstanding debts against the properties. Neither woman received hard cash, because very few buyers could afford to pay the entire price at the time of a sale. In virtually every case, the buyer paid a deposit and secured the rest of the price with either a mortgage or a court judgment for twice the outstanding sum.[32]

In 1830, shortly after her husband's death, Elizabeth Bascom decided to sell Walkes Spring, an estate that he had bought just four years earlier. The 106-acre plantation had operated with only 35 slaves in the 1820s, and by 1824 it was in receivership. The estate had remained on the market for several months until John Higginson finally bought it at slightly above the appraised value. Higginson had kept the estate only a few months before selling it to John Bascom, who put down nearly 80 percent of the money and immediately mortgaged the estate for the remainder of the price. By the time Elizabeth Bascom sold the property, she was able to make a slight profit. The plantation prospered under the new owner, and over the next eleven years produced an average of 88 metric tons of sugar annually.[33]

Some women did better than others, even when selling heavily indebted plantations, as Susanna Charlotte Duke's sale of Cane Wood estate vividly illustrates. When Duke sold the estate in 1833, John G. Grant paid £5,000 for the property and agreed to pay off all the estate's debts. Duke made a 22 percent profit for the 113-acre plantation, which had been appraised at only £3,887.[34] Was this simple generosity on Grant's part, or did some family relationship exist between the two?

The economic linkage between families in Britain and Barbados often spanned many years. The experience of Mary Lovell and Anne Grassett, the only two women to acquire a plantation between 1823 and 1834, illustrates the point. When Mary Lovell's son-in-law Renn Hamden, and his brother John

Hamden, bought the 350-acre Chancery Lane estate in Christ Church, they had secured the price with a mortgage to the former owner, Lovell and Grassett's brother, William Yard. By the late 1820s the Hamdens found it impossible to continue their mortgage payments and, in 1829, they defaulted on the loan entirely. Normally the property would have reverted back to the previous owner, but Yard had died in the intervening years so the estate passed to Lovell and Grassett, his legal heirs. Although both women lived in Barbados at the time of the transfer, Mary Lovell later moved to England, where she died in 1843. She left all her English and West India property to her son, Philip, and to her daughter, Mary, Renn Hamden's wife, but made no provision at all for her son-in-law. Perhaps she did not trust his ability or financial judgment and saw this as a good way to protect her daughter's future.[35]

The number and value of plantation sales rose substantially in the three years immediately following abolition, and the number of women involved in the transference of Barbadian property rose dramatically. Their participation increased from 9 percent of the 102 sales that took place between 1823 and 1834 to 14 percent of the 138 sales that took place after 1834. The type of their transactions also changed. In the earlier period, women had been predominantly sellers of men's plantations, but after 1834 they began buying estates for themselves.

All but one of the nine women who sold plantations after 1834 were widows disposing of their husbands' property. Only Catherine Anne Smitten had no control over the terms of the sale when her husband's estates passed through the chancery courts in 1836. The other women sold their estates privately at prices ranging from £44 per acre for the 484-acre Lancaster estate, sold in 1840, to £98 per acre for Redland, a 154-acre plantation which was sold in 1838. When Rebecca Cheesman sold Redland, the sole charges against the property were her small annuity and a government mortgage. Cheesman arranged for the buyer, Josiah Heath, to pay off these liabilities and two additional legacies, and divided the remainder of the proceeds between her two daughters.[36]

The purchases that women made after 1834 are of great significance, for they bring to life a previously undocumented sector of the Barbadian plantocracy. The promise of compensation encouraged freer credit, and the subsequent opening up of the land market allowed women to begin buying plantations immediately. Their purchases ranged in size from the 59-acre Mount Harmony estate to the 365-acre Stepney estate in St. George.[37] Their motives for buying land were equally varied. Some apparently wanted to maintain their social position within the planter circle, others to extend their existing landholdings. A few perhaps hoped to join the prestigious plantocracy for the first time.

At least three of the eight women who bought estates after 1834 were already well established through their husbands' ownership of valuable sugar lands. Even after the chancery court sold her husband's three estates, Catherine Anne Smitten retained her position in the landowning elite. In 1836 she bought the 147-acre Maynards plantation although she paid more than the appraised value. Despite the forced sale of her husband's property earlier in the year, Catherine Smitten was able to secure the entire price of Maynard's with a court judgment rather than the more usual mortgage. With Richard Smitten's compensation tied up in lawsuits, his widow clearly could not use the money to buy her new property. Was Catherine Smitten confident of making Maynards a profitable concern? Was she wealthy in her own right, perhaps with other property protected by a marriage settlement or trust? Or was she simply considered an extremely good risk? Whatever the reason, her ownership of Maynards was short-lived. Four years later, the estate was again advertised for sale, but it is impossible to determine how much was paid for the property or if Catherine Smitten made a profit on the sale.[38]

Several women, however, did make profitable sales. When Dr. Samuel Hinds died in 1824 he bequeathed Maynards to his son, Samuel, and Warren's jointly to his five daughters. A conveyance dated 1835 indicates that ownership of Warren's, together with the compensation for its slaves, had been transferred to Mary Mercy Hinds and two of her sisters as tenants-in-common. The three women undertook to repay the estate's debts and provide their other sisters with annuities. Two years later Mary Mercy Hinds sold the property and only her name appears on the conveyance. What had happened to her sisters? Had she bought them out in return for generous annuities? If so, why did she feel that sole ownership of Warren's afforded a better proposition than dividing its liabilities between the five of them? Certainly she made a shrewd decision, for when she sold the estate she made a substantial 29 percent profit.[39]

Among the most economically active women were Sarah Prescod Williams and Elizabeth Bascom. Apart from acting as mortgagees, both women also bought and sold viable sugar plantations. In 1836, ten years after selling Westmoreland, Sarah Prescod Williams bought the 146-acre Warleigh Heights estate and the remaining apprenticeship terms of its thirty-nine laborers. The purchase may indicate her desire to return to the ranks of the landowning elite, although, like Catherine Smitten, she sold her new property before the end of the period.[40]

Elizabeth Bascom, one of the most extensive mortgagees, had made a small profit in 1830 when she sold the Walkes Spring estate. Her financial ventures did not end with the sale of Walkes Spring, for in 1841 she extended a mortgage to John Herbert, the owner of a small property known as The Farm. Bascom may have been related by marriage to the Bascom family of merchants and small landowners. As such she may have held a slightly lower social position than some of the other women, though it is doubtful that she was a great deal poorer.[41]

In the years following abolition, several women bought plantations in order to extend their existing property. In 1838 Ann Pilgrim used a legacy from her husband, John Frere Pilgrim, toward the cost of an estate on the borders of St. John and St. Philip. With the purchase of the 59-acre property known as Mount Harmony, she doubled the size of her landholdings. The original property, known simply as Ann Pilgrim's land, was just under 40 acres, for in the *Barbados Almanack* for 1842 she appears as the owner of a 96-acre estate called Stewart's Hill, the alternative name for the Mount Harmony plantation. At her death, sometime around 1848, she bequeathed the estate to her eight children as tenants-in-common.[42]

The wills that women such as Ann Pilgrim wrote are important social indicators, for they clearly show that women left real as well as personal property. They also illustrate the close interrelationships between the powerful planters of the period. Ann Pilgrim's will is an excellent example of this type of interconnection in Barbados. The names of at least two of her sons and one of her daughters incorporated the names Ellcock, Alleyne, and Forster, all family names of prominent planters or planting attorneys who were among the wealthiest in nineteenth-century Barbados.[43]

The same kind of interrelationship and careful disposal of real estate is evident in the will that Mary Licorish wrote in 1848. In the early 1840s, Mary Licorish expanded her property when she bought the 309-acre Crab Hill plantation in St. Lucy. She already owned the small 15-acre Ford's estate in St. Peter, and her new property, registered to Mary Licorish and Company, made her one of the major female landowners in Barbados.[44]

Mary Licorish may have been a wealthy businesswoman, for in her will she left precise instructions for the disposition of her property. She ordered the sale of both Crab Hill and Ford's and the division of the proceeds among her various grandchildren. Her grandson, Joseph Leacock Licorish, inherited a house and yard in Speightstown, in addition to a share of the money. A granddaughter, Frances Alithea Kellman, inherited another house and unnamed land, also in Speightstown, and several great grandchildren received legacies. Two "late apprentices," Sally and Sally Betsey, received title to their houses and an allotment of land attached to each house. Finally, Mary Licorish stipulated that the £714 owed to her by her son-in-law was to be paid to his wife, rather than become part of the dividable estate.[45] As the use of the names

Kellman, Archer, Stoute, and Redman, for her grandchildren indicates, Mary Licorish's family was well connected in Barbados.

The exact status and family relationships of the three other women who bought estates after 1834 remains unclear, although some relationship may have existed between Mary Catherine Kellman and James Cragg Kellman, the owner of the Prerogative estate in St. George. In 1837, in partnership with William Bynoe, Mary Kellman bought the Seniors estate from Charles Thomas Alleyne. Five years later, when she defaulted on her mortgage payments, Alleyne transferred her debt to John Torrance and James McChlery, partners in Michael Cavan and Company of Bridgetown. Some family connection may also have existed between Rebecca Frances Holligan and James Holligan, who owned the Welches, Coral Hill, Bank Hall, and Mangrove Pond plantations. When she bought the Welches estate in 1843, Rebecca Holligan may have been buying property from her brother or from her husband. If it was the latter, then she almost certainly had a marriage settlement that allowed her to set up her own "sole and separate estate." Finally, Katherine Ann Hinds Cobham appears to have had some connection with the Hinds family. In 1835 Katherine Cobham paid £26,000 for the Stepney estate in St. George. The price included 364 acres of cane and pasture land, the compensation for the 197 ex-slaves, and the remainder of their apprenticeship terms.[46]

This small group of women paid over £78,142 for the 1,286 acres, which they bought between 1834 and 1843. Each paid approximately £60 per acre for an average of 184 acres. This put their purchases squarely between the average of £57 per acre paid by all established proprietors and the average of £64 per acre paid by all those who joined the plantocracy for the first time.

Whereas most of the estates that these women sold were in the fertile parish of St. George, most of the estates they bought were in the more populated parishes of St. Peter and St. Michael. Only Katherine Cobham's Stepney estate, the second largest acquisition, was in St. George. These women must have been aware of the relative fertility of the various parishes, but they preferred to relocate closer to Bridgetown. Why did they sell estates in choice areas? Did they simply want to be closer to the town's amenities, or did some fear social unrest after emancipation and seek the illusory safety of the town?

Regardless of their reasons for relocating, white women in Barbados did more than simply inherit sugar estates and hold on as best they could. Though few in number, they provided 10 percent of all the credit made available to Barbadian planters between 1823 to 1843. While women constituted only 19 percent of all large-scale proprietors, they participated in 10 percent of all plantation sales transacted during the twenty-year period, a figure which was out of all proportion to their small numbers. They demonstrated an active entrepreneurial ability in ridding themselves of indebted estates and at the same time profitting from the changed social and economic circumstances within the colonies. Women played an important role in the complicated world of sugar and slavery—a world made not only more complex but also more precarious by the untidy legal abolition of slavery between 1834 and 1838.

7

Decline and Partition

Although compensation enabled some plantations to survive, it was not an economic panacea. Neither the British government nor the Interest had realistically expect it be. Despite the loud complaints and extended negotiations, both parties knew that the merchants, not the planters, would be the main beneficiaries.

While the majority of the estates in Barbados remained viable entities, plantations in Jamaica rarely enjoyed the same good fortune. By 1834 hundreds of Jamaican estates were already in receivership, and discouraged owners had abandoned hundreds more. People who had expected to live out their lives on the income from West Indian annuities, settlements, and legacies often found themselves embroiled in long and costly court battles with little real hope of success.

Proprietors had always sold land as a means of extending or consolidating their estates, but as the economic decline continued into the nineteenth century many owners began retrenching in earnest. As early as the 1820s, planters began selling off marginal or outlying lands in an attempt to satisfy their creditors. In 1825 the chancery court ordered the sale of 250- and 103-acre sections of the Tremolesworth estate before finally ordering the entire 1,500-acre plantation sold for debt. Yet in spite of the change in ownership, the estate was back in receivership by the late 1830s. Other estates were similarly affected. In 1827 the owners of Cabbage Hall sold off large sections of the 3,290-acre estate and by 1837 had reduced its size by one-fourth. Other properties that could not be sold as complete entities were broken up in the hope of attracting buyers. When Cashew Grove and Southampton Pen were put up for sale in 1833, one-third of the property was offered in three separate lots. When it became clear that even with the addition of the compensation award, the proceeds would not cover the outstanding debts and court costs, the remaining acreage was also split into sections and sold off.[1]

Despite clear evidence of widespread planter indebtedness and the Interest's continual insistence that lack of credit and foreign competition were root causes of the economic decline, planters blamed everyone but themselves. At emancipation they found a new scapegoat, the laborers and their alleged refusal to work. The attitude of Stephen Harmer was typical of the period. Harmer worked as the overseer on the Bull Dead coffee plantation in Manchester. He expressed his opinion of his labor force in a series of letters to friends and family. In early 1840 he wrote, "I regret to say that this once fine country is fast going to destruction through want of continuous labour. One half of the Negroes have scarcely done anything since they were made free and them that do work demand very high wages from 4 to 5 shillings per day and then they will not do even half a day's work for that."[2]

A year later his opinion remained unchanged. The problems confronting the planters of Jamaica were still due to "the natural lazy state of the negroes" and the demands of the British public for cheap sugar which made it "impossible for us here to cultivate Sugar by free labour at so cheap a rate as Foreigners can with slaves." The legislature's efforts to introduce European immigrants as plantation laborers also met with his disapproval. Irish and European immigrants, he informed his friends, were unsuitable for Jamaica. They could not withstand the tropical heat, and the Irish drank themselves to death.[3]

In 1847 the Jamaican House of Assembly met to discuss the condition of the sugar and coffee economy of the island. It found that, just as Harmer had complained, many of the colony's finest plantations had fallen into virtual ruin. Some properties had ceased operations altogether when the laborers had been removed or when the collecting constable had taken off the stock. Others, like Richard Barrett's prized Ramble plantation, had been converted from sugar to livestock pens producing meat for the internal market.[4]

The Assembly reported that over 600 sugar and coffee estates had simply been abandoned since emancipation. While sugar prices remained relatively high, optimistic but inexperienced planters had tried to bring marginal lands into production. Even when faced with declining prices, many continued to hope for an economic revival. When the expected recovery did not occur, they had little choice but to sink more money into worthless land or cut their losses and desert their dreams. Eighty percent of the properties that had been abandoned were over 100 acres in size and the Assembly estimated that at least 344,859 acres no longer had owners interested in maintaining them (table 7.1).[5]

Table 7.1. *Estates Abandoned between 1832 and 1847, Jamaica*

Parish	Sugar	Coffee	Total
Clarendon	17	38	55
Hanover	11	0	11
Manchester	0	109	109
Metcalfe*a*	7	21	28
Portland	12	2	14
Port Royal	1	1	2
Trelawny	8	0	8
Vere	2	0	2
Westmoreland	2	13	15
St. Andrew	10	111	121
St. Ann	8	12	20
St. Catherine	0	14	14
St. David	2	4	6
St. Dorothy	1	7	8
St. Elizabeth	6	14	20
St. George	8	13	21
St. James	18	0	18
St. John	2	21	23
St. Mary	12	6	18
St. Thomas-in-the-East	13	9	22
St. Thomas-in-the-Vale	0	70	70
Total	140	465	605

Source: Votes of the Assembly, app. 57.
*a*The parish of Metcalfe was established in 1841 from parts of St. Mary and St. George.

Coffee plantations were the worst affected and accounted for 77 percent of the abandoned properties. The heaviest concentrations of deserted estates were in the parish of Manchester and the hilly regions of St. Andrew and St. Thomas-in-the-Vale. Coffee production required less capital investment in buildings and machinery and a smaller labor force than sugar. After the initial planting, the coffee bushes needed little more than light maintenance and weeding until they produced their first crop of berries three to four years later. Then, the annual pruning of the bushes, weeding, and the harvesting and dry-

ing of the berries were the only additional requirements. Few coffee plantations relied solely on the British market and few were as heavily involved with
British merchant-creditors as their sugar-producing colleagues.

Nevertheless, after peaking in 1814, coffee production declined even faster
than sugar production—from 15,448 metric tons in 1814, to 4,776 metric tons
in 1835, and 2,307 metric tons in 1845. Over the same period, sugar production
fell from 80,950 metric tons, to 58,380 metric tons, to 37,756 metric tons in
1845—declines of approximately 66 percent and 21 percent respectively. Faced
with a fall off in production, caused partly by soil exhaustion and overextension onto marginal lands, and having fewer liabilities encumbering their properties, coffee growers frequently cut their losses and just abandoned their
estates.[6]

Time after time the chancery court receivers reported on the dilapidated
state of the properties under their control and on the poor condition of the
cottages rented to the laborers. At the Spring sugar estate, the receiver found
only five acres in new cane, another hundred acres in ratoons, and the existing
crop badly affected by a recent drought. At Fellowship Hall conditions were
far worse, and the receiver could not find a single cane on the entire estate.
Most plantation cottages were in a state of general disrepair and generated
little or no revenue. The weekly rent for the fifty cottages at Palmyra was rarely
collected, and even the receiver argued that all sixty cottages at the Spring
estate were in such poor condition that it would have been grossly unfair to
expect the tenants to pay rent.[7]

The breakup or abandonment of many Jamaican estates, the availability of
Crown lands, and laborers' newfound mobility meant that hundreds of laborers could establish themselves as freeholders and become independent of the
plantation economy for the first time. Using money hoarded during slavery
and wages earned during their apprenticeship, thousands of laborers began
buying land. Their purchases ranged from 10 to 50 and occasionally 100 acres,
at prices varying from £2 to £20 per acre. Although in most instances these
low prices indicate that owners were selling off marginal land, this was not
always the case, for whenever possible the laborers wanted developed land
near roads, schools, markets, and churches, rather than isolated acreage.[8]

By 1835 the first group of apprentices had bought themselves out of the
system and founded the free settlement of Sligoville, near Spanish Town. Over
the course of the next six years, at least 3,000 people moved into new villages
in the western sector of the island alone. Others followed their lead, and by
1842 nearly 200 such villages had been established across the island. Laborers
in St. James, St. Mary, and St. Thomas-in-the-East, bought smallholdings and

turned to mixed farming. Others, in Manchester and St. Elizabeth, bought small sections of unwanted coffee estates, sometimes complete with old trees, which they revitalized with drastic pruning. They planted the groves with provision crops for home consumption or sale at the local markets while the trees recovered. Some workers withdrew completely from plantation labor, while others worked on the estates only when it became necessary to supplement their income from the sale of provisions and minor export crops.[9]

Jamaican missionaries, most notably the Baptists, helped the laborers in their quest for land. Many were motivated by a real desire to help, but others were more concerned with holding their congregations together or with making money. In 1838 William Knibb, a leading Baptist minister, began buying land for subdivision and resale to the black population. Two years later, he paid £2,000 for the 1,038-acre Mount Carfax estate, which he renamed Kettering Settlement. He then sold off small sections to various ex-apprentices. Each laborer paid £4 for a lot approximately one-sixth of an acre in size. Knibb had more than the interests of the laborers in mind when he bought the property; he also had a keen appreciation for the kind of profits to be made from their desire for economic independence after the long years of slavery. Land that he had bought for about £1 an acre he now sold for twenty-four times his initial outlay.[10]

Although laborers bought many of the lots at the new settlement, Knibb did not restrict his real estate ventures to the ex-apprentices. In 1840 he bought 58 acres of Content Pen in Trelawny, which he then subdivided as the basis for Hoby's Town. Over the course of the next four years, he sold the house lots to a variety of "gentlemen," including Richard Barrett, for an average of £5 each. His efforts eventually provoked the hostility of the proprietors, who refused to sell to him once they understood his motives, but, undeterred, he continued to buy land through intermediaries.[11]

Overseers and attorneys also took advantage of the laborers' desire for land and at the same time assured themselves of a readily available labor force at crop time. In 1834 William Williams, the overseer at the Fontabelle estate in St. Mary, bought two hundred acres of the plantation's outlying lands. By 1839 he had added another fifty acres of adjoining land and the following year began selling off three- and four-acre lots to ex-apprentices. As late as 1843 William Barron advised the Duke of Buckingham to split up the Hope plantation and sell it to laborers, who were willing to pay as much as £20 an acre. The estate, valued at £10,000, had made an annual loss of almost £2,000 for the previous three years. Nevertheless, Barron believed the duke could get double the value by partitioning the property and selling it off piecemeal.[12]

Despite increasing opposition from many planters, thousands of Jamaican laborers succeeded in becoming freeholders and asserting their independence. Between 1838 and 1845 the number of Jamaican freeholders increased dramatically, from approximately 2,114 freeholders owning 40 acres or less in 1838 to an estimated 19,397 owning less than 10 acres in 1845.[13] Nevertheless, as the situation at the Bamboo estate in Hanover illustrates, selling land to the ex-apprentices was not always a straightforward matter. At times it could be almost as difficult for owners to get rid of unwanted land as it was for laborers to gain access to it.

The Bamboo sugar estate fell into receivership in the 1830s. Throughout the 1830s the 700-acre estate produced an annual average of sixty-six metric tons of sugar, which were consigned to John Graham Clarke of Newcastle-upon-Tyne. The owner of Bamboo, William Carr Walker, also maintained a current account with Clarke for plantation supplies and two mortgages dating from 1815 and 1817. In addition to the mortgages, the plantation expenses for 1834 included rental payments to the Caledonia estate for 80 acres of forest land for use as provision grounds, another 27 acres for cane, and a payment of £18 for one year's use of water from the nearby Friendship Grove plantation. Moreover, despite having 270 slaves of its own, the Bamboo estate paid out £57 for over two years of field labor provided by slaves hired from Frances Walker and Elizabeth Carr Chambers. Faced with this level of expenses, Walker had found it impossible to keep abreast of the mortgage and interest payments, and by 1834 the estate owed Clarke over £19,800.[14] In 1836 William Dyer, the administrator for Clarke's estate, alleged misconduct on the part of the trustee for Bamboo. He accused Richard Chambers, the trustee, of selling the estate goods from his own store at retail prices. At the same time, Dyer claimed that Chambers had bought and resold part of Bamboo's sugar and rum and credited the estate with less than their market value. Moreover, he accused Chambers of selling part of the crop on his own account instead of consigning it to Clarke. Dyer, therefore, petitioned the court to appoint a receiver to control Bamboo affairs until the property could be sold. In its investigations the court found that "[T]he whole estate and premises called Bamboo and the apprentices thereon are not worth and will not realize when sold . . . the debts secured against it."[15]

By 1841 the debts against Bamboo had risen to £42,696, but the court did not put the estate up for sale until two years later. Although several bidders vied for the property, the court deemed the highest offer of £1,000 inadequate and withdrew the premises. When offered again in late 1843, the highest bid was a mere £500, and the court decided that if the entire estate remained unsold twelve months later, it would begin selling off outlying land. In August 1844 the receiver advised the court to sell off 200 acres of back woodlands. The land would sell for £5 to £6 per acre without any difficulty. Many of the nearby laborers planned to build homes on sections they had bought from the adjoining Hopewell estate. The Bamboo lands would make convenient provision grounds, but if the court missed the opportunity, the laborers would look elsewhere for the lands they wanted.[16]

By October the situation had begun to change and the receiver told the court that, "someone has been persuading the people that a good title cannot be given for the land, and it will take some time to disabuse their minds," and he promised to try to reassure them. Later in the year he reported that although the people now wished to rent, he had suggested they wait and buy instead, since the last two crops had been poor and the cost of the land was likely to fall. The problem of the title continued into the next year, when the receiver again reported that although the people were at first eager to buy "some evil-minded person told them the title was bad."[17]

Whoever tried to convince the laborers that they would not receive a good title for Bamboo land appears to have succeeded, for by April 1845 the court would have accepted as little as £3 per acre. If only one sale could be made, the receiver believed, then the rest of the land would sell quickly, but none of the laborers would take the risk. Bamboo remained unsold the following year and by then the majority of the estate's former workers had bought land elsewhere. Those who continued to live in the estate's dilapidated cottages rented land from Cocoon Castle Pen or Maggotty estate. Bamboo itself could no longer continue production. Only ten to twelve acres remained in cane and the last few cattle had already been sold off the year before.[18]

Despite the problems they faced, the number of black freeholders continued to increase until at least the 1880s, when the plantation economy began to recover. As foreign and domestic enterprises consolidated their hold on the most desirable land the title to small plots came increasingly into question. The free villages and settlements had clear titles for their land, but many black freeholders who had bought land independently now found they had never had legal titles or that the same piece of land had been sold to several different people. Nevertheless, by the 1860s the laborers had been able to make enough progress for William Sewell to remark that "the Jamaica laborer of yesterday is a proprietor today. He has bought his acre of land, and is independent."[19] The same certainly could not be said of his Barbadian counterpart.

In Barbados, only two black men, London Bourne and Thomas Ellis, had succeeded in buying land immediately after emancipation, and until 1841 they remained the exception to the general rule. As the two men already knew, buying estates and gaining entrance into the ranks of the white plantocracy were two entirely different matters. The ownership of land did not mean automatic acceptance by the economically and politically dominant elite.

London Bourne, the better known of the two men, had made his mark as a successful Bridgetown merchant. He gained his freedom at the age of twenty-three when his father bought his family out of slavery. When Thome and Kimball met him in 1837, he was reputed to be one of the colony's wealthiest merchants. The Americans reported that Bourne owned three stores in Bridgetown and was worth over 20,000 silver dollars, about £4,350 sterling. His success and business acumen did not, however, guarantee his acceptance into white society, and although he owned the building where the town's merchants held their meetings, as a black man he was barred from membership.[20]

In 1841 Bourne bought Grazette estate in St. Michael. He paid £7,428 for the 169-acre plantation, though it is unclear whether he bought the entire estate or simply a major portion.[21] When the property had been sold in 1834, and again in 1837, it was listed at 188 acres. It is clear, however, that Bourne paid nearly 10 percent more than the previous owner, who had bought the estate only four years earlier. If indeed he purchased a smaller property, he paid £10 per acre more than William Armstrong Griffiths had paid in 1837. The increase may well have reflected the planters' reluctance to sell to nonwhites.

The only other person of color, besides Bourne, to purchase an estate between 1834 and 1841 was Thomas Ellis. In 1837 Ellis bought the 480-acre Clement Castle estate from Hampden Clement for £26,000 and promptly renamed it Ellis Castle. Little is known about Ellis, but it seems probable that, like Bourne, he was a merchant. By 1842 he also owned the 168-acre Cane Field plantation and a smaller 57-acre property called Dalby.[22]

Bourne and Ellis's purchases significantly increased the number of non-whites who owned plantations in Barbados. In 1836 only one other black man in the entire colony owned an estate. Robert Collymore, a civil rights activist in the 1820s, had owned Haggatt Hall in St. Michael. When he died in the early 1830s, the estate passed to his son, Samuel James Collymore, who already owned the Exchange in St. Thomas. The younger Collymore apparently sold both estates sometime after 1836 and before November 1842, when the *Barbados Almanack* listed George Grant as the owner of Haggatt Hall and John William Grogan as the owner of the Exchange.[23]

During the 1820s three men of color, Jacob Belgrave and his sons, had owned sugar plantations but had disposed of them by 1830. The family's original estate had been The Adventure in St. Philip, which Jacob Belgrave had owned in 1803. After his father's death, John Thomas Belgrave had increased the size of the plantation from 98 to 144 acres.[24]

A second son, Jacob Belgrave, Jr., had owned three estates: Graeme Hall in Christ Church and the Sterling and Ruby plantations in St. Philip. In 1823 Belgrave sold the Ruby estate to John Cholmley Roach, who secured the entire price with a mortgage against Ruby and his other estate, Graeme Hall. When Roach defaulted on the mortgage in 1826, Belgrave sued in chancery and bought back Graeme Hall for £14,428.[25]

An inventory of Belgrave's property taken in 1828 valued Graeme Hall at £15,358 and Sterling at £11,833. The 243 acres of Graeme Hall, which together with the mill, utensils, and crop accounted for 57 percent of the total value of the estate, were valued at £36 per acre. A new inventory made three years later when John William Perch owned the property shows that the value of the land had fallen to £29 per acre. The 218 acres of Sterling accounted for 53 percent of the estate's total value and were appraised at £40 per acre. The plantation appears to have retained its value better than Graeme Hall, for Nathaniel Cave paid almost the full inventory value when he bought it from Belgrave's widow in 1829.[26]

With Jacob Belgrave's three estates disposed of by 1828 and John Thomas Belgrave's estate sold by 1826, Samuel James Collymore remained the only plantation owner of color in Barbados until Thomas Ellis and London Bourne bought their estates in the late 1830s and early 1840s. To what extent this was due to the reluctance of other planters to sell to blacks or people of color is difficult to estimate. All of these men were a great deal wealthier than many white proprietors. Although the compensation did not help them financially, it helped them indirectly by easing the transfer of property and providing them with the opportunity to buy land.[27]

The ordinary laborers of Barbados did not have the same success as their counterparts in Jamaica. The changes in land tenure in the smaller island took place within the planter and merchant classes and affected the laborers only in a negative manner. Unlike the landowners of Jamaica, Barbadian proprietors kept their estates intact, and few if any went out of production in the period immediately following emancipation. In Jamaica, at least 231 sugar estates, 243 coffee plantations, and 132 livestock pens valued at £1,743,672 were totally or partially abandoned between 1844 and 1852.[28] Nothing similar occurred in Barbados, where the lack of missionaries willing to act on behalf of the ex-apprentices and the unavailability of Crown or waste land forced the laborers to remain as tenants on the estates and under the close control of their employers.[29]

Laborers in Barbados bought sections of land on only two occasions. In 1841 the workers at Mount Wilton estate in St. Thomas set up Rock Hall, the first free village to be established in the island. Shortly before his death in 1821, the owner of the Mount Wilton estate, Reynold Alleyne Elcock, had left annuities of £5 currency to each of his adult slaves in recognition of their loyalty and good behavior during the insurrection of 1816. Elcock may have mentioned the legacies to his valet, Jeffrey, who was later accused of murdering his thirty-four-year-old master rather than waiting for him to die of natural causes.[30]

The estate's trustees, however, delayed paying the bequest for nearly twenty years. Elcock's heirs later protested that the delay was due solely to the need to pay off the estate's debts. It seems more likely that the trustees simply tried to avoid paying the bequest since, as slaves, the claimants had little legal recourse. Eventually some of the beneficiaries petitioned the governor for help. Others persuaded John Carew, the local police magistrate, to champion their cause. By the time the trustees finally paid the claims in 1840, about thirty of the original 113 slaves had died, but their shares were not divided among the survivors. The remaining 83 claimants each received £85 currency, exactly £5 for each of the seventeen years which had elapsed between Elcock's death and the end of apprenticeship. Nor did the executors feel obliged to pay interest on the awards. The people used the accumulated legacy to purchase land belonging to the Farm and establish the basis of the Rock Hall village.[31]

No other subdivision occurred until 1857, when laborers bought part of the Walkers estate in St. Andrew. The owner, Peter Chapman, divided the estate into one- and two-acre sections and offered them for £70 per acre. Many prospective buyers were unable to pay the full price and eventually lost both their land and their deposits.[32]

The planters' refusal to sell small plots of land to their laborers caused a great deal of private and official comment. In July 1840 Samuel Prescod, the leader of the community of color, wrote to the Colonial Office complaining about the high price of land. He accused whites of deliberately obstructing blacks and people of color in their efforts to become freeholders and thus qualify for the franchise. In reply to a colonial office inquiry into the situation, members of the Council and Assembly admitted that the few hundred proprietors who owned the majority of the land were reluctant to have freeholds cut out of their property. If small parcels of land became available in their neighborhood, the proprietors immediately rented them or bought them outright, often "at some sacrifice," to prevent nonwhites gaining land.[33] Mary Licorish's small bequests to her ex-apprentices were the exception rather than the rule.

Small plots of land were exceptionally expensive, often as much as £200 per acre, and extremely difficult to procure. Although there were over 1,800 landed properties in Barbados only about 1,000 were 10 acres or less. The remainder were properties of between 10 and 900 acres and controlled over 80 percent of the available land. Those who owned the smaller plots were mainly poor whites, free people of color, and free blacks, none of whom had been affected by emancipation.[34]

When questioned in 1842, the special magistrates of Barbados claimed that some people in their particular parishes had bought land but that few had enough to qualify as true freeholders. John Carew of St. Thomas commented on the establishment of the free village at Rock Hall, but the remaining magistrates could only repeat that high prices and the scarcity of small plots of land still continued to prevent most of the laborers from gaining freeholds.[35]

The changes in land tenure in Barbados were neither as radical nor as far-reaching as in Jamaica where the recently emancipated laborers acquired land and the economy gradually moved away from an overwhelming dependency on sugar. By 1855 sugar accounted for only 54 percent of Jamaica's total exports (table 7.2).

Although the opening up of the real estate market enabled a few black or colored merchants to become planters for the first time, the dominate whites successfully excluded the black laborers from the ranks of the landowners. Most of the laborers had little choice but to continue working on the plantations and living in rented cottages in estate villages. Unlike the Baptist and Methodist missionaries who helped the laborers in Jamaica, the Church of England clergy who controlled the spiritual life of Barbados showed no inter-

Table 7.2. *Major Exports from Jamaica, 1830–1860*
(metric tons, with sugar as a percentage of total)

Year	Sugar	Coffee	Rum	Log-wood	Pimento	Ginger	Percentage of Total
1830	70,000	10,000	11,666				76
1835	58,000	4,800	8,893				80
1840	26,270	3,900	4,697				75
1845	37,750	2,300	6,338				81
1850	29,000	1,800	4,069	4,370	1,525	362	70
1855	26,000	2,570	6,377	8,435	3,901	269	54
1860	30,000	1,520	6,189	14,940	3,107	382	53

Source: Derived from Eisner, *Jamaica*, pp. 240–41, table 42.

est in sponsoring the cause of the Barbadian laborers. Indeed, until the final moments of slavery, the church had itself owned sugar plantations in Barbados and received compensation for its slaves. The church viewed its award as "pure gain" but felt it would be "colonial treason" to say so.[36] The absence of vacant land or abandoned estates also served to keep the land-hungry laborers tied to the plantations and the sugar monoculture and to ensure the continued domination of the white landowning elite.

8
International Trade and Finance

The promise of compensation led many people to anticipate a substantial influx of new capital into the British West Indies. Although large-scale proprietors received 57 percent of the money in Jamaica and Barbados, the remaining £3.5 million went to the thousands of small claimants who lived in the islands.[1] Colonial merchants hoped these people would spend their awards locally and expected an imminent, if short-term, economic boom.

In 1833 the British government began systematically collecting reliable annual statistics on social and economic conditions in the West Indies. British officials had previously gathered the relevant information from the journals of the colonial legislatures or from figures submitted to the inspector general's office at the London Customs House.[2] The new measure aimed at providing accurate standardized information on trade, agriculture, education, the judiciary, and other aspects of colonial life.

The new Blue Books of Statistics, which first appeared in 1833, contain only sketchy information on trade and virtually nothing on agriculture. The governors lacked the authority to demand that the appropriate officials make timely returns. In older colonies like Jamaica and Barbados, many of the officials responsible for collecting the data held their offices under patents. Others did not even live in the islands. Instead, they delegated the work to deputies who had little incentive to exert themselves. Consequently, the returns lacked uniformity and most, especially those for Jamaica, were usually incomplete.[3] In Barbados, which had only one major port, cattle imports might be recorded by number or by their value in pounds sterling. Jamaica had several ports of entry, and while Port Antonio reported only the number of cattle imported, Kingston reported both their number and their value.[4]

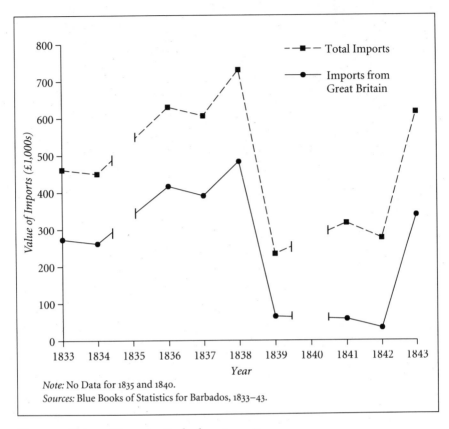

Figure 3. *Value of Imports, Barbados, 1833–1843*

Despite these omissions and discrepancies, the Blue Books contain valuable information concerning important changes in trade patterns and the impact of compensation on the economy of the region. The substantial rise in Barbadian imports coincided precisely with the payment of compensation between 1836 and 1838 (figure 3). Although much of the indemnity went to heavily indebted proprietors and their creditors, the improvement in their credit, together with the money available to smaller owners, resulted in a significant rise in imports during these years. The smaller recipients, who bought their goods from Barbadian merchants, gave a substantial boost to the local economies.

Using the data from the Blue Books, government officials calculated the total value of goods imported into Barbados in 1833 at £461,135. Imports fell the following year, but the economy improved again as soon as the commissioners began paying the compensation claims. The effect of the indemnity became more apparent in 1836, when the value of imports rose 27 percent above the 1833 level. By 1838 the commissioners had paid the majority of the claims, and Barbadian imports rose a further 14 percent, a total increase of 37 percent above the value of imports in 1833.[5]

The higher value of imports represented an important short-term economic change, which was largely attributable to the compensation award. The apprentices received some wages for part of their work after 1834, but this improvement in their purchasing power could not be the sole reason for these particular rises in imports. For the first few years, the apprentices concentrated more on freeing themselves from the system and accumulating money to buy land. Governor Sligo believed that the vast majority of non-praedial apprentices in Jamaica would purchase their release before their terms officially ended.[6] The laborers' wages had a greater impact on imports after apprenticeship finally ended in 1838, as reflected in the second wave of increases which began in 1841. Compensation had been assured since 1833 and local merchants anticipated, and perhaps to some extent created, new demands for imported goods. This would explain the promptness with which imports rose, once the commissioners began paying out the colonial claims.

Between 1833 and 1837 the balance of trade for Barbados changed from a deficit of £73,247 to a credit balance of £291,404 (table 8.1).[7] After 1839, however, the value of imports declined substantially, and the island experienced a 33 percent decrease over a twelve-month period. Within three years the value of imports had fallen a further 13 percent, and by 1838 officials estimated imports at only 60 percent of the value of nine years earlier.[8]

Officials in both Barbados and Britain commented on the decline in imports. In December 1841 local merchants testified before the House of Assembly that the value of their imports had declined since 1838. When William Sharpe, a Barbadian planter, gave evidence before a British select committee the following year, he claimed that imports had been increasing when he left the island but that they had since begun to fall off.[9] His evidence confirmed the claims of the Barbadian merchants and underscored the intense short-lived impact that compensation had on the trade of the island.

The Blue Books also reflect the changing patterns of trade among Barbados, Britain, and the United States after 1840. They identified imports by their country of origin. In 1833 these were divided in the following proportions: 59 percent from Great Britain; 16 percent from British North America (Canada); 15 percent from the United States; 7 percent from the British West Indian colonies; 3 percent from foreign states, and 0.3 percent from other British colonies.[10] The categories remained constant for the ten years between 1833

Table 8.1. *Balance of Trade, Barbados, 1832–1843*

Year	Exports	Imports	Balance of Trade
1832	£408,363	£481,610	− £73,247
1833	553,628	461,135	+92,493
1834	736,006	449,790	+286,216
1835 [a]			
1836	749,193	630,157	+119,036
1837	897,990	606,586	+291,404
1838	960,368	730,763	+229,605
1839	731,262	233,772 [b]	+497,490
1840 [a]			
1841	531,872	317,340 [b]	+214,532
1842	855,712	276,418 [b]	+579,294
1843	668,256	617,131	+51,125

Sources: Blue Books of Statistics for Barbados, 1833–43, CO33/45–54; Levy, *Emancipation*,
   p. 179, app. 2.
[a] No data available.
[b] No data on goods imported from Britain.

and 1843, although their percentage of total imports varied over the period
(table 8.2).

In view of their erratic nature, entries in the Blue Books must be used
with great care; nevertheless, the changes are significant. Throughout the period, imports from the United States and Canada rose substantially, while
those from Britain suffered a corresponding decline. In 1841 the value of
goods imported from the United States was 44 percent above that of 1833, and
their value rose to 58 percent in 1843. Goods from the other British West Indian colonies also increased, with gains of 53 percent and 60 percent in 1841
and 1842.

In the eight years between 1833 and 1840, imports from Great Britain accounted for 59 to 66 percent of the gross value, but in 1841, the balance
changed as the United States challenged British domination of the island's
trade. Imports from the United States tripled in value between 1838 and 1842.
At the same time Canada's percentage of Barbados's imports doubled from
par with the United States in 1838 to 25 percent in 1842. By the time the total
value of Barbadian imports rose again in 1843, Britain had regained its pre-

Table 8.2. *Imports into Barbados, 1833–1843 (percentage by country of origin)*

Year	Great Britain	Foreign	Canada	United States	British West Indies	Other	Total
1833	59	3	16	15	7	0.3	100.3
1834	57	3	13	21	5	0.3	99.3
1835 [a]							
1836	66	4	1 [b]	13	6		90.0
1837	64	5	12	15	3		99.0
1838	66	8	11	11	3	0.2	99.2
1839	27	13	37	4			81.0
1840 [a]							
1841	18	11	23	38	9	0.8	99.8
1842	12	12	25	39	10	1.1	99.1
1843	55	3	9	26	4	0.3	97.3

Source: Blue Books of Statistics for Barbados, 1833–1843, CO33/45–54.
[a] No data recorded.
[b] There seems to be an error in percentage of the imports from Canada.

eminent position but had recovered at the expense of Canada rather than the United States.

Imports from Great Britain were loosely categorized as dry goods, plantation stores, and provisions. These included necessities and luxury items for the white elite and the tiny black middle class; food and clothing for the apprentices; and equipment for plantation boiler houses and mills. Items such as clothes, clocks, furniture, and books would have been subsumed under the general heading of dry goods. These products were available both to whites and to apprentices who were eager to buy a few luxuries after long years of denial.

Imports from "foreign states" included cattle, salt, tobacco, and timber, and these increased in value 76 percent between 1833 and 1838. The value of goods imported from Canada also increased, though somewhat more erratically. In 1833 Canada supplied fish, corn, lumber, shingles, and staves valued at £73,728. The value of these items fell 22 percent the following year but rose again in 1837. By 1838 it had reached 10 percent above the value of goods brought into the island in 1833. Thereafter the level declined slowly until, in 1843, imports from Canada had fallen to 28 percent of the 1833 level.[11]

The most dramatic change occurred in the percentage of goods imported from the United States. In 1833 Barbados had imported £68,208 worth of lumber, flour, horses, shingles, and corn from the United States. By the following year such imports had increased 27 percent. Overall, the United States increased its proportion of Barbadian imports from 15 percent to 21 percent in the course of twelve months. During the next four years, however, the United States lost an advantage that it did not recover until 1841, when its imports amounted to 38 percent of the reported total.

Imports from other British West Indian islands and British possessions, other than Canada, accounted for just over 7 percent of Barbadian imports in 1833. Over the next two years, between 1837 and 1838, their share of the market dropped considerably. Most of these items were provisions, such as corn, rice, cattle, and vegetables, or other British merchandise not described in detail in the Blue Books. When the apprentices were thrown upon their own resources and forced to produce more of their own food after emancipation, their proportion of imported provisions may have gradually decreased. The increase in goods imported from Great Britain, the United States, and Canada, however, compensated for the drop in imports from these areas.

The generalized descriptions of goods imported into Barbados precludes a definitive analysis of their nature or final destination. Unlike the Blue Books for Jamaica, those for Barbados show no importation of machinery, such as plows, engines, or boilers, intended to improve the cultivation and processing of sugar cane. Any machinery brought into the island was probably concealed under the more general heading of "plantation supplies." Even the Jamaican Blue Books limited their entries to the simple description "machinery" without any further details to identify either their nature or the purchaser. In 1834 six pieces of machinery valued at £18 entered the port of Kingston. A year later, in 1835, five pieces worth £91 arrived from Great Britain and the United States.[12] Under the circumstances, it is necessary to rely on individual plantation accounts for information about machinery bought immediately after emancipation. In this way it is sometimes possible to isolate purchases made as a result of improved credit.

The Worthy Park account books record the trustees' annual purchases of plantation equipment between 1835 and 1846. They took control of the heavily indebted estate in 1834 after the death of the owner, Sir Rose Price, and received £4,660 as compensation for the slaves at Worthy Park and Mickelton Pen. They used this money to reduce the debts secured against the properties.[13] The subsequent improvement in their creditworthiness allowed them to buy additional equipment for what had been one of the most productive estates in the entire island.

Despite heavy debts, the administrators continually took advantage of improvements in agricultural technology in an effort to enhance production. The first purchases, made in 1835, consisted of assorted ironmongery, steel hoes, and nails. The following year, Thomas Edbury and Company shipped out a two-horse plow and spares at a cost of £26. In 1837 Davidson, Barkly and Company sent out four more plows and two years later shipped out condensing apparatus, copper tubes, and syphon pipes for use in the plantation's boiler house and distillery. The company sent another plow out in 1840, and the first railway wagons arrived the next year. The most expensive equipment arrived in June 1844, when the trustees bought iron railroad tracks and nearly two tons of guano fertilizer from Thomas Hankey and Company. By October the trustees had added a complete fifteen horsepower horizontal sugar mill to the plantation's equipment.[14]

The plantation accounts that survive for Barbados are less specific about new acquisitions of machinery or fertilizer. Barbadian proprietors did, however, make some efforts to improve their properties after emancipation. The account books and ledgers for the Drax Hall and Newton estates show the overall plantation expenditures for the period, but not the breakdown of expenses. While plantation costs at Drax Hall rose 240 percent between 1833 and 1838 and those at Newton increased 197 percent, this was due more to the need to pay the apprentices' wages than to the cost of additional imports.[15]

Other plantation accounts and sources reveal that a few Barbadian planters bought equipment designed to update their estates. Thomas Yard, for example, spent an average of £343 annually between 1823 and 1834 for the upkeep of the slaves on his Forster Hall, Cottage, and Groves plantations. Although the three estates operated as one unit and the expense accounts were combined between 1825 and 1837, the attorney kept the slave and apprentice expenses separately from those of the general estate. After emancipation the average cost of the apprentices quadrupled, and expenses averaged £1,242 each year between 1835 and 1843.[16] These expenses were kept separately from the plantations' expense account, and it is possible to gain some idea of how Thomas Yard attempted to improve his property and to illustrate how the Blue Books' general import headings hid many important items.

Prior to emancipation, Thomas Yard spent an average of £1,986 annually on repairs, cooperage, and incidental improvements. Some of this went to repairing buildings and equipment damaged in the 1831 hurricane, and three years later, to repairing the slaves' houses. Between 1834 and 1843 plantation expenses almost doubled. The greatest increases came after 1838, when Yard was apparently paying for goods ordered and imported some time earlier. The expenses for 1839 included the purchase of a number of cattle and horses and the cost of improvements to the distilleries at Groves and Cottage and accounted for the increase over previous years.[17] The cattle would have been included in the import figures for foreign states and the horses in with the imports from the United States. The materials for the distilleries almost certainly came from Britain. In order to appear in the expenses accounts for 1839, these items would have entered Barbados in 1838 and fall within the framework of increased imports for that year.

The Blue Books' broad categories may also hide a further item brought into the island for use on the plantations. In his evidence before the select committee of 1842, William Sharpe testified concerning the use of manure, soot, and guano for fertilizing the cane fields. He explained that he had arranged to have 100 pounds of soot and guano sent to one of his own estates.[18] Guano does not appear as a separate item, probably because at that point it was imported in negligible quantities. Until the 1850s, Peru was the major source of guano and transportation costs made it an expensive item. When American and Jamaican diggers began exploiting the guano-rich cays off the coast of Jamaica after 1850, the lower cost made it a better commercial proposition. Even so, during the 1840s enterprising Jamaican merchants had also collected guano, though less intensively. The £50,000 worth of guano imported into Barbados in 1846 could have come from either source, so Sharpe may have bought his supply from Jamaica, rather than from Peru.[19]

These isolated records of items imported for estate improvements do not fully explain the substantial increase in imports between 1836 and 1838. Not all proprietors used their indemnity to pay outstanding debts or to buy land. If Barbadians did not buy luxury items such as wine and glassware or more practical items such as plows and sugarmills, what did they buy?

To some extent the answer lies in an item which appeared in *The Barbadian* in 1842. The newspaper published the report of the finance committee of the House of Assembly on the number of horses and cattle imported since 1833. Concerned about the high death rate among the island's horses, the committee suggested imposing a higher duty in order to raise the quality of imported livestock. In words reminiscent of the abolitionists' comments on slave deaths, the committee claimed that its figures showed a mortality rate of 25 percent and complained that the entire horse population needed renewing every four years.[20]

The committee's figures revealed another startling fact. "the extraordinary and almost incredible number of Horses annually imported into this island." More significantly, the rise in horse imports paralleled the payment of compensation, a fact that did not escape the notice of the committee. The report provided a breakdown of animal imports by type and year.[21] In 1833 Barbados

Table 8.3. *Imports of Horses, Mules, and Oxen, Barbados, 1833–1842*

Year	Horses	Mules	Oxen
1833	294	87	12
1834	557	90	12
1835	986	46	6
1836	1,149	33	0
1837	1,443	37	0
1838	1,172	14	0
1839	810	20	18
1840	728	0	6
1841	850	72	0
1842	326[a]	10[a]	0[a]
Total	8,315	409	54

Source: Report of the Finance Committee of the House of Assembly, app. B, cited in *The Barbadian*, 5 November 1842.
[a] Figures for six months only.

imported 294 horses, 87 mules, and 12 oxen. In the following year, the number of horses imported rose 47 percent while only 3 more mules and 12 oxen arrived in the island. The next year, the number of horses imported increased a further 44 percent and was accompanied by a drop in the number of mules and oxen (table 8.3). The committee pointed out that compensation payments had begun in November 1835 and continued through November 1836, although some Barbadian slave owners had received their awards as late as December 1837.[22]

With the payment of compensation, the number of horses imported into Barbados increased dramatically. In 1836 it reached 1,149 and rose to 1,443 in 1837, increases of 15 and 20 percent respectively. At its height in 1837, the number imported was 80 percent above the number for 1833. Robert Schomburgk, in his *History of Barbados*, commented on this unusually high number and reported the facetious gossip that Barbadians perhaps devoured the horses they bought.[23] These animals must have been purchased from the United States, and the parallel between the two sets of import figures is striking. In 1834 imports from the United States were 27 percent higher than those of 1833 and increased a further 27 percent in 1837, so that at least part of the increase can be attributed to the importation of horses.[24]

The committee also broke down the horse and mule population by parish

Table 8.4. *Horse and Mule Population, Barbados, 1841 (by parish)*

Parish	Horses	Mules	Percentage of Total
St. Michael	810	60	20
St. George	515	38	12
St. John	486	33	12
Christ Church	442	33	11
St. Philip	402	30	10
St. Thomas	393	29	9
St. Joseph	297	22	7
St. Peter	275	20	7
St. Andrew	164	12	4
St. Lucy	161	12	4
St. James	157	12	4
Total	4102	301	100

Source: Report of the Finance Committee of the House of Assembly, app. C, cited in *The Barbadian*, 5 November 1842.

(table 8.4). In 1841, 20 percent of the colony's horses and mules could be found in St. Michael and another 12 percent in St. George and in St. John.[25] The preponderance of horses and mules in St. Michael is not surprising, since it contained Bridgetown, the island's major town and port. The smaller white and colored slave owners who lived and worked in the town may have bought these animals to replace the labor previously supplied by slaves. In other cases, the acquisition of horses may have had a more symbolic meaning. At abolition these small slave owners lost more than their human property, they also lost their most valuable status symbol. Though a white skin remained the primary status symbol, various degrees and classes still existed within the poorer white and colored populations. The ownership of new horses perhaps replaced the ownership of slaves as an easily recognizable symbol of upward mobility in a narrow caste- and class-conscious society, especially among those who were eager to rise literally above their new situation.

Not every slave owner used the indemnity to pay off creditors or to buy horses or land. Metropolitan and colonial financiers viewed anyone who did not simply hoard their money as potential investors. They recognized the need for convenient, and particularly local, institutions in which to invest unused compensation awards. British bankers like the Barclays, Aenaes Barkly, and Sir John Rae Reid and colonial proprietors like George Hewitt and Joseph Connell anticipated the need for banks or similar establishments, through which they could control the investment of the awards, either at the source in Britain or at the destination in the islands.

The flurry of commercial activity following emancipation underscored the need for new ways to initiate and regulate essential credit for the planters. The compensation money "provided huge sums in search of temporary investment outlets or adequate strong boxes and consequently proved to be the motivating stimulus for the establishment of not one, but three banks."[26]

Although no "huge sums" actually found their way into the West Indies, £20 million did become available for investment in one way or another. The mere fact that the money came into circulation was an important psychological factor in stimulating economic expansion within the colonies. Money in circulation meant improved credit, which in turn encouraged trade and investment at virtually all levels of society.

Money repaid to creditors, whether in Great Britain or the West Indies, represented another source of investment. This was particularly true of private creditors who, between 1834 and 1843, provided 87 percent of all mortgages extended to Barbadian proprietors. Unlike the major merchant houses that began withdrawing from the West India trade in the 1830s, these creditors maintained their interest and involvement in the Caribbean economies.[27]

As early as 1824, British merchants had tried to establish some organization capable of handling compensation. Thwarted in its efforts to raise a government loan of £5 million, the Interest had proposed forming a West India Company to advance working capital to planters in exchange for colonial mortgages and consignments of sugar. Although the Interest argued that such a company would stimulate the real estate market and maintain the value of West Indian estates the government refused to lend its official support to the venture.[28]

Initially organized with a capital of £2 million, the company offered 20,000 shares at £100 each to the general public. The company appointed William Manning as its chairman and George Hibbert as deputy chairman. The board of directors included such prominent men as Sir John Rae Reid, Andrew Colville, John Anderdon, Aenaes Barkly, Charles Bosanquet, Samuel Hibbert, Charles Nicholas Palmer, and William Mitchell, all of whom had active connections with the sugar economy either as merchants or bankers.[29]

To counter fears that its activities would divert business from private channels, the company argued that the advantages to the distressed planters outweighed all other considerations. Commenting on the proposed establishment of the West India Company, the *Glasgow Courier* remarked, "If further inducement were wanting it might be addressed to those who advocate the cause of abolition. The insuperable difficulty in the way of this object is the admitted claim for compensation, and the immense sum which would consequently require to be raised in the shape of home taxation."[30]

Though the company intended to make capital available to planters, the *Courier*'s comment implies a more than passing interest in the fate of the indemnity. Presumably the Interest shared this concern and anticipated a new source of investment capital. If it already controlled an established financial organization when emancipation eventually occurred, it could offer a logical place to invest the compensation awarded to British creditors and absentee proprietors.

The West India Company did not survive long, but its foundation underscores the fact that the link between compensation and the establishment of suitable banks was made almost immediately. Buxton and Canning made their parliamentary motions in May 1823 and details of the proposed company appeared in *The Barbadian* less than twelve months later. Yet almost ten years elapsed before the connection was renewed.

Once compensated emancipation became official in 1833, the Interest immediately renewed its efforts to establish a West India bank and between 1836 and 1840 founded four banks in Jamaica and Barbados. With abolition, the demand for specie in small denominations to pay the apprentices' wages and facilitate small-scale trade increased, and the banks represented a response to this new demand. Nevertheless, in the case of at least two of the banks, their sponsors directly cited the expected compensation as a basic reason for their formation.

In 1834 an unsuccessful effort was made to establish a West India Banking Company, designed to operate in the British sugar colonies. As a joint stock company with branches in Liverpool, Glasgow, and Bristol, it expected to replace capital withdrawn from the West Indies and to make advances to planters who could provide suitable collateral. The sponsors claimed their bank would not interfere with the normal relations between planters and merchants. The new organization, they argued, would allow planters to continue production, and at the same time relieve merchants of the need to make immediate cash advances. With a capital of £2.5 million, the bank would extend loans secured against 66 to 75 percent of the value of nonperishable staples shipped to Britain.[31] But West Indian planters already consigned their sugar, rum, and molasses to specific metropolitan merchants. The only remaining nonperishable staples were the coffee, cotton, logwood, rice, arrowroot, and ginger grown in some of the islands, but none of these items were produced on the same scale as sugar. The company's facilities, therefore, would be useful to a very limited number of proprietors.

It was no accident that the four commercial banks designed to handle West India business opened between 1836 and 1839 or that their foundation coincided with the payment of compensation. The sponsors of both the Bank of Jamaica and the Colonial Bank cited compensation as a prime factor in creating the banks. Merchants and bankers closely associated with the Interest were eager to control the investment of the indemnity paid to metropolitan creditors and absentee proprietors or to colonial residents. Banks whose directors lived in England expected to control British investments, while banks with colonial directors expected to regulate investments made in the islands. Such powers would allow the sponsors to tighten their hold on West Indian trade through their various boards of directors.

Among those who proposed the establishment of the Bank of Jamaica in 1836 were Sir John Rae Reid and John Irving of Reid, Irving and Company, Andrew Colville, and the Hibberts. All had been instrumental in founding the short-lived West India Company twelve years earlier. Abolition, they claimed, had brought three great changes in the social and economic life of the island that favored the creation of the bank. First was the widespread purchase of property, presumably facilitated by the indemnity. The second and third changes were more specific: the distribution of new money among the Jamaican proprietary and new methods of cultivation. The sponsors argued that even if British mortgagees and absentees retained nine-tenths of Jamaica's compensation, the remaining £600,000 would find its way to the island and hopefully would eventually be deposited in their bank.[32]

Abolition had also changed the methods of cultivation. The sponsors reasoned that having paid off some of their debts planters would be more willing to dispose of some of their crop locally.[33] Since the bank targeted the resident recipients of compensation, the sponsors clearly hoped that such people would begin to buy their supplies locally and expected that Jamaican merchants would deposit the money with the bank. Moreover, they pointed out, the sale and partition of estates would increase the number of small resident proprietors in Jamaica and simultaneously increase the number of depositors.

In 1836 the Bank of Jamaica set up its headquarters in Kingston. Established as a joint-stock company with limited liability and £500,000 in capital, the bank offered 50,000 shares at £10 each to the general public. Business was scheduled to begin as soon as the sponsors had sold 7,500 shares. The bank particularly encouraged Jamaicans to become shareholders and proposed that, after the disposal of these initial shares, no additional stock should be sold in England for at least one year. Once it had settled the basic details, the bank applied for a royal charter, which would give the bank the respectability and power necessary to attract investors.[34]

Among the original subscribers were Joseph Gordon, the assemblyman for St. Andrew, and John Mais who later served as the president of the bank. Gordon was the attorney for at least fourteen Jamaican properties, including those of Sir Alexander Grant and Lord Seaford. Mais, an attorney, assemblyman, and a receiver for the High Court of Chancery, owned four estates in the island.[35]

At the same time that the Bank of Jamaica was founded, a second bank opened for business. The Colonial Bank was established in London in 1836 and received a royal charter shortly afterwards. Several of its backers, including John Irving, Andrew Colville, John Alexander Hankey, and Samuel Gurney, maintained close ties with the West Indies and also had intimate connections with the Bank of Jamaica.[36] They planned to raise the new bank's capital of £2 million through the sale of 20,000 shares of £100 each. From the outset the bank's shares were in great demand. Several prominent merchants, including William Hibbert, Aenaes Barkly, David Barclay, together with Irving, Colville, Hankey, and Gurney, subscribed a minimum of £2,000 each.[37] Sixty-eight thousand individuals applied for the 17,000 shares available in Britain. Another 5,000 individuals applied for the 3,000 shares reserved for sale in the colonies, an average of 4 applicants per share.

The royal charter allowed the Colonial Bank to operate for a minimum of twenty years, to deal in bullion and bills of exchange, and to lend money, commercial paper or government securities. The bank could also issue and circulate bank notes redeemable in specie on demand. Finally, and most importantly, a limited liability clause protected the shareholders who could be held responsible only for the amount of their original subscriptions. Thus the original shareholders simultaneously protected themselves against possible legal actions and spread the financial risk in the event of bankruptcy. Against this the charter specifically precluded the bank from making loans secured against fixed property, whether in the form of land, houses, shops, or businesses.[38]

In 1837 the bank announced the simultaneous opening of branch offices in Jamaica, Barbados, British Guiana, Trinidad, and St. Thomas. Its proposed to offer short-term cash loans, to facilitate interisland trade, and to improve local transactions by ensuring the prompt payment of bills. Most significantly, the Colonial Bank claimed to offer new evidence of Britain's continued faith in the colonies. The bank's £2 million in capital, its sponsors asserted, was "put out to risk by the British public" and, in conjunction with the £20 million already paid as compensation, provided positive proof of Britain's belief in the future prosperity of the colonies.[39] The directors realized that some of the bank's capital would come from the compensation payments that had already been made and no doubt hoped to pick up additional deposits from the same source.

By 1838 the bank had opened two offices in Barbados: one in Bridgetown managed by Michael McChlery of Cavan and Company and a smaller agency in Speightstown, the second largest town in the island. This smaller office, directed by Robert Challenor of Challenor and Company, simply exchanged the bank's notes for silver and took applications for loans and bills of exchange.[40]

The notes of the neither Bank of Jamaica nor the Colonial Bank were legal tender, but both circulated freely in the island and were generally accepted as a medium of payment. Only the Colonial Bank redeemed its notes in specie. The Bank of Jamaica redeemed its notes in specie or in "island checks" at the discretion of the directors.[41]

The Jamaican legislature had first introduced island checks in 1822, when the supply of specie proved insufficient to meet the normal requirements of the internal trade. The checks were redeemable in specie and were, in essence, non-interest-bearing promissory notes secured against the revenues of the island. Residents could also use the checks when paying public taxes and duties. The legislature had continued to issue checks until, by 1837, approximately £400,000's worth remained in circulation. As long as the government remained solvent, the receiver general could cash the checks if necessary. Unfortunately this was not the normal state of affairs. As the governor, Sir Lionel Smith, informed the Colonial Office in 1839, for years the receiver general had lacked the essential gold or silver to pay off the checks. The government of Jamaica was, in effect, bankrupt.[42]

The council estimated that the Bank of Jamaica had nearly £227,428 in circulation in the form of bank notes redeemable in specie or island checks. The choice of medium was entirely at the discretion of the bank's board of directors. With no specie in the island treasury, the bank was simply replacing one useless form of paper currency with another. A run on the bank would force it to close its doors and lead to a complete financial disaster.[43]

The more circumspect Colonial Bank issued far fewer notes and was better able to survive the financial crises that resulted from the Sugar Duties Acts of 1846 and 1854. The act of 1846 lowered the duties on foreign free-grown sugar entering England and foreshadowed the final equalization of the duties in 1854. The change reduced the duty on sugar, increased competition from foreign producers, and led to a general contraction of trade. Although the Bank of Jamaica survived the panic temporarily, it closed in 1865. The rival Colonial Bank managed to continue operations into the early twentieth century.[44]

Friction and rivalries marred relations between the two banks from the outset. Each hoped to gain deposits from recipients of compensation and in this
respect the Colonial Bank, with its headquarters in England and the prestige
of a royal charter, had a stronger position. In most other respects there was
little to choose between them. Both were limited to short-term advances and
legally prohibited from making large-scale loans secured against plantations.

The Bank of Jamaica blamed its failure to obtain a royal charter on the
opposition of "influential persons in London connected with the Colonial
Bank" who feared competition from local banks. In April 1839 a letter appeared in the *Royal Gazette and Jamaica Times* that reinforced this complaint.
Frederick Verbeke of the British Guiana Bank, accused the Colonial Bank of
manipulating the British government in order to crush local banks, which
had privileges similar to its own.[45] How true these allegations were is difficult
to determine. Nevertheless, some rivalry undoubtedly existed, as can be seen
from the minutes of the Jamaican Legislative Council in 1838.

In late 1838 the Council learned of correspondence between the secretary of
the Colonial Bank and the Colonial Office concerning the affairs of the Bank
of Jamaica. Glenelg asked if the bank's practices contravened the laws of the
island. The secretary replied that although there was no legal infringement,
the Bank of Jamaica might not survive a financial crisis. In such an event
the Colonial Bank would protect itself and refuse to accept its competitor's
notes. This, in turn, would expose the public to considerable risk. In view of
Jamaica's unsettled social conditions, the directors of the Colonial Bank felt it
their duty to bring its rival's overextension to the attention of the imperial
government.[46]

Part of the problem arose from the bank's lack of a charter of incorporation,
which would allow its directors to make bylaws and to sue and be sued. Without the charter, the bank was nothing more than an ordinary commercial
partnership. Its shareholders had no power to demand an inspection of the
books and accounts and had to rely on the president's periodic reports. Five
or six wealthy respected shareholders had originally signed the bank's notes.
When these men sold out around 1839, the bank withdrew the notes and issued new ones bearing only the signatures of the manager and cashier. This
greatly reduced the public's ability to recover its deposits through lawsuits.[47] If
the Colonial Bank did not actively sabotage its competitor, it was not averse
to undermining its credibility.

Two questions arise from the development of West Indian banks. First, why
would the same men originally sponsor both the Bank of Jamaica and the
London-based Colonial Bank? Second, why would the Colonial Bank refuse
to assist, if not actively seek to destroy, its competitor in time of need? The

answer lies with the compensation award, its possibilities as a source of investment, and the speculative opportunities that both banks offered. Sir John Rae Reid, John Irving, Andrew Colville, and their colleagues, who sponsored the two banks, had also been instrumental in founding the West India Company twelve years earlier. Their concern with such ventures sprang from a sense of business, not from any real interest in the immediate needs of West Indian proprietors. To these men, the compensation award represented a potential reservoir of investment to be channeled through colonial and metropolitan financial institutions. As planters repaid their debts to merchants and private creditors, additional funds became available for investment. The new metropolitan bank was designed to serve these investments and to remove most of the risk from the remaining private merchant houses that traded with the West Indies. The Colonial Bank became, in effect, the investment channel for the compensation that remained in the Britain (table 8.5).

When the same financiers also sponsored the Bank of Jamaica, they aimed at serving a similar purpose in the colony. There they could encourage the investment of the compensation money that came into the hands of the resident planters, merchants, and other former slave owners. Whether local owners used their awards to repay colonial merchants, to purchase land, or to buy horses, the sponsors expected the money to pass through their bank. In either case, the sponsors benefited by collecting dividends and directors' fees and through their control of investments.

The opening of branch offices of the Colonial Bank in 1837 ended the useful life of the Bank of Jamaica, as far as Reid, Irving, and Colville were concerned.

Table 8.5. *Debits and Assets of the Colonial Bank (silver dollars)*

Year	Debits	Assets
1837	$2,307,947	$4,204,947
1838	3,990,041	6,452,085
1839[a]		
1840	1,882,921	1,882,921
1841	5,755,706	8,300,610
1842	4,593,068	7,178,517

Sources: The Barbadian, 20 October 1838, 28 August 1839, 3 March 1841, 27 August 1842, 30 September 1843.
[a]No data available.

At that point they may have felt that the Colonial Bank was sufficient to handle the island's financial affairs and saw no further use for their Jamaican enterprise. Financiers like Reid, Colville, and Irving were probably among the shareholders of "known wealth and respectability" who had ended their association with the bank by 1839.[48] Since neither the Bank of Jamaica nor the Colonial Bank could lend money secured against the sugar estates, their use to the colonial proprietors was severely limited. Some institution able to accept land as collateral was sorely needed, and in 1839 the Planters Bank was established to fill the void.

Set up as a joint-stock company with capital of £300,000, the Planters Bank differed from its counterparts in two important respects. It was specifically designed to serve the needs of the proprietors by advancing loans secured against the estates, and its shareholders were subject to unlimited liability. The bank survived for only seven years before sugar prices fell and foreign competition increased after 1846. Alarmed depositors rushed to redeem their bank notes. Unable to meet the sudden demand, the directors applied to the Assembly for assistance. The bank's liabilities amounted to £43,800 in circulating paper and £26,000 in deposits. Its £180,000 in assets were almost entirely in outstanding loans, and only £40,000 of these were secured. The directors petitioned the Assembly for a loan of £40,000 for three years and offered the shareholders' property, valued at £500,000, as collateral. When an Assembly committee investigated the bank's affairs, it found that each loan the directors made had been secured with the signatures of three guarantors. The same signatures had been used so often that they were useless as a guarantee of the bank's ability to pay. The committee rejected the directors' petition and concluded that they had gone "beyond the bounds of strict prudence" in assisting the planters. The Colonial Bank also refused to help its colleague, and when the branch manager at Savanna-la-Mar absconded with part of the deposits, the Planters Bank went into liquidation.[49]

The fourth bank, created shortly after emancipation, was the West India Bank, which was established in 1839 in Barbados. Its board of directors differed radically from those of the Bank of Jamaica and the Colonial Bank. All of its officers, from the chairman to the directors, lived on the island. Joseph Connell, owner of three sugar estates, served as the chairman, and seven other proprietors and three merchants made up the board of directors. The planter contingent included Joseph Heath, owner of Quintynes and Redland estates; George Hewitt, owner of Bloomsbury and Warren's; and Joseph Briggs, the owner of Maynard, Checker Hall, Six Mens, and Hope; together with Charles St. John, Joseph Trotman, Thomas Wilson, and Jonas Wilkinson. Arthur Moore, Samuel Inniss, and Nicholas Walrond represented the local merchant interest.[50] Between them, the directors owned approximately 2,046 acres of plantation land.

In 1839 subscriptions opened to raise the necessary £200,000 capital. The subscribers included Samuel Holder Alleyne; John Bovell, the owner of Oxford and Ports estates; N. W. Carrington, the owner of Content; George Donovan, who owned Chatley Lodge; and William Hinds, the owner of Mount Poyer and The Hope plantations. Though not such extensive landowners as the directors of the bank, these men owned at least 1,190 acres among them. In 1840 the directors began negotiations for a royal charter, but by the late 1840s the bank had followed the Planters Bank into liquidation. Like its Jamaican competitor, it could not survive the economic changes caused by the Sugar Duties Act of 1846.[51]

It is possible that the West India Bank grew out of the West India Banking Company founded in 1834. If so, it differed in that it had its base in Barbados rather than London. Such a connection would mean that the link between compensation and banking survived the change in location as well as a period of seven years. Certainly, the formation of the original West India Banking Company was predicated on the need to provide and employ capital in the colonies. Its backers knew that the greater part of the compensation would eventually return to Britain. The change in location may simply have meant that local sponsors preferred to use the money earlier, in the island, rather than later in Britain.

None of the banks provided any type of service for the laboring population, either during or after apprenticeship. Separate savings banks established for this purpose in 1838 in Kingston, Spanish Town, Manchester, and St. James proved enormously popular. By 1845 the Kingston Savings Bank had 476 depositors and over £6,500 invested in the island Treasury. The bank in St. James fared even better, with 769 depositors and over £9,914 invested.[52]

The indemnity therefore directly influenced the decision to establish at least two colonial banks. Metropolitan and colonial financiers were well aware that recipients who did not hoard or simply fritter their money away would need some avenue for investment. Money repaid to local and metropolitan creditors also became available for investment, and the major British bankers were eager to control these funds both in England and the islands. The banks claimed to assist the hard-pressed sugar planters, but the tension and rivalry that existed between the Colonial Bank and the Bank of Jamaica underscored the financiers' overriding concern for their own control of investments rather than with the economic needs of the islands.

Epilogue

The experience of Jamaica and Barbados underscores the inherent fragility of economies based on credit and protectionism. By the mid-1840s, British merchants and financiers controlled the original indemnity. As many colonists bitterly complained, "very little of the 'monstrous sum' found its way to the West India colonies. It was paid for the most part, to mortgagees, in or about, the small circle of Threadneedle Street."[1] This complaint was what merchants expected and what the government anticipated when it cynically submitted its emancipation plans to the Interest before laying them before Parliament. Any hope that the indemnity would provide the planters with new working capital and ease the transition from slavery to free wage labor was quickly dashed as creditors closed in on their delinquent clients. What merchants could not collect through direct claims, they acquired through counterclaims, lawsuits, and the informal arrangements they forced upon the planters. Nevertheless, some of the money did reach the colonies and affected the local economies in dramatic ways before being reintegrated into the British economy.

The Interest's insistent claims that credit had become virtually unobtainable and that plantations had been "rendered unsaleable" were designed to elicit more favorable compensation terms when emancipation became a reality.[2] Yet in Barbados, at least, the antislavery movement had little impact on the value of plantation land or on the ability of planters to sell or mortgage their estates. While the merchants cut back on their West India trade and sought more lucrative investment opportunities, private individuals continued to provide the planters with essential credit. Many of these private investors were women who played an active part in the transfer of colonial real estate, yet their place in the island economies remains largely unexplored. A better understanding of these shadowy figures would improve our understanding of the diverse roles women played in Caribbean history and expand our knowledge of the intricate workings of colonial society.

The ramifications of compensation stretched far beyond the narrow limits of debt repayment to impinge on other facets of colonial life. In Barbados, where compensation propped up the value of already scarce and valuable land, whites retained control of viable sugar estates and for years avoided selling even small freeholds to their newly emancipated workers. Though some laborers did eventually buy land, the majority lived in rented homes in tenantries close to the estates, providing the planters with a convenient local pool of cheap labor at crop time. Control over land translated into continued control over labor and continued reliance on the sugar monoculture.

In Jamaica, on the other hand, the award could not redress years of debt and mismanagement. As hundreds of planters sold off sections of their estates, or abandoned them entirely, thousands of laborers bought land for the first time. Although most became small farmers or market gardeners producing food for local consumption, others turned to growing crops for export. Within a few years, the increased production of pimento, logwood, ginger, and low grade coffee, all grown or collected by the new workforce, helped to diversify the export economy as sugar and coffee exports continued to decline.

Yet in both cases the local gains were short-lived. The Encumbered Estates Act, adopted in Jamaica in 1864, freed hundreds of plantations from their crippling debts and allowed the courts to sell them with clear title. Though additional land became available to the laborers, British and foreign conglomerates were the major beneficiaries. As resident and absentee capitalists consolidated their landholdings and amalgamated some of the healthier estates, they displaced both the traditional sugar planter and the black freeholder. The trend continued until the end of the century as powerful United States' companies such as Dow Baker and the Boston Fruit Company took advantage of the Aliens Amendment Law of 1871 to expand their Caribbean operations. Much of the engrossed land lay in St. Mary, St. Catherine, Portland, and the reorganized parish of St. Thomas, where bananas had become the principal crop.[3]

Britain's experiment also provided a cautionary model for other slaveholding nations. As France and the Netherlands ended their slave systems they adopted variations of the British theme of compensated emancipation. In 1794, revolutionary France had simply freed all its slaves. Enforcing emancipation in the midst of war and revolution proved impossible. With Napoleon's rise to power, slavery was reinstated in every French colony except Haiti, where, under the leadership of L'Ouverture, Dessalines, and Christophe, the ex-slaves fought a deadly ten-year battle to maintain their freedom. Slavery remained in force in the French colonies until 1848. The following year, the government awarded its slave owners six million francs, far less than the 300 million francs its own commission had originally proposed. The commission suggested that half the indemnity be awarded in money, and the rest as a guaranteed six-year apprenticeship for the ex-slaves. The government refused to consider such a sum and arbitrarily decided on a 6 million franc grant payable in cash within thirty days. But, as with British compensation, most of the award went to pay off the planters' commercial debts.[4]

The Netherlands adopted a more practical system. In 1855, the Dutch government proposed immediate, compensated emancipation. Under its plan, owners of slaves in Surinam would be compensated according to the value of their slaves; those with slaves in Curaçao, Aruba, Bonaire, and the other islands of the Netherlands Antilles, according to the age of their laborers. The ex-slaves would work for their master or another of their choice for one year. Regardless of where they lived, all ex-slaves were expected to repay the State for the expense it incurred in freeing them. The government discussed various other ideas, but did nothing. The Netherlands held comparatively few slaves, about 47,300, and the question of emancipation involved only a very small, tight-knit circle of planters and merchants. Eventually the colonists themselves forced the government to act. Slave owners in Surinam felt particularly vulnerable. If the slaves fled to neighboring British Guiana, where slavery had ended nearly thirty years earlier, or to French Guiana, where it had been abolished fifteen years before, the masters could lose all chance of compensation. Finally, in 1863, the government awarded a flat 300 guilders per slave, about half the market value of the slaves, and ten percent more than British slave owners received.[5]

Every slave-holding nation believed in the right to hold property in people and none seriously considered compensating their slaves. The property argument put forward by vested interests proved too seductive for all but the most radical abolitionists, who lacked the power to implement an alternate plan.

Appendix

Table A.1. *Rate of Compensation, 1834–1837 (by colony)*

Colony	Average Price per Slave, 1822–30	Average Compensation per Slave
Antigua	£32/12/10	£14/12/03
Bahamas	29/18/09	12/14/04
Barbados	47/01/03	20/13/08
Bermuda	27/04/11	12/10/05
British Guiana	114/11/05	51/17/01
Cape Good Hope	73/09/11	34/11/07
Dominica	43/08/07	19/08/09
Grenada	59/06/00	26/01/04
Honduras	120/04/07	53/06/09
Jamaica	44/15/02	19/15/04
Mauritius	69/14/03	31/10/06
Montserrat	36/17/10	16/03/06
Nevis	39/03/11	17/02/07
St. Kitts	36/06/10	16/13/00
St. Lucia	56/18/07	25/03/04
St. Vincent	58/06/08	26/10/07
Tobago	45/12/00	20/03/07
Trinidad	105/04/05	50/01/01
Virgin Islands	31/16/01	14/02/10

Source: PP, 1837–38 (64).

Table A.2. *Compensation to Private Individuals, Barbados*

Name	Number of Slaves	Compensation
Haynes Family	1,609	£35,191
Best Family	1,181	25,952
Alleyne Family	1,137	24,815
William Hinds	894	18,757
Joseph W. Jordan	710	14,761
William T. Sharpe	722	14,608
Samuel Hall Lord	625	13,763
Total	6,878	£147,847

Source: PP, 1837–38 (215).

Table A.3. *Compensation to Private Individuals, Jamaica*

Name	Number of Slaves	Compensation
Neill Malcolm	2,091	£38,719
Abraham Hodgson	1,408	27,421
John Morant	1,016	20,957
Sir Edward Hyde East	1,156	20,495
William Rae	957	18,003
William Beckford	917	17,889
Lord Seaford	947	17,762
Benjamin Scott Moncrieffe	683	17,428
William Parke	1,095	15,881
Sir Henry Fitzherbert	847	14,752
William Dehaney	918	14,188
William Jackson	705	13,969
Isaac Higgins	707	13,442
Bishop of Exeter	665	12,728
Total	14,112	£263,634

Source: PP, 1837–38 (215).

Table A.4. *Estates in Receivership, Jamaica, 1823–1843 (by parish)*

Parish	Number of Estates	Percentage of Total
Clarendon	12	6.0
Hanover	12	6.5
Manchester	13	6.5
Portland	7	3.5
Port Royal	3	2.0
Trelawny	23	12.0
Vere	4	2.0
Westmoreland	17	8.5
St. Andrew	10	5.0
St. Ann	11	6.0
St. Catherine	1	0.5
St. David	4	2.0
St. Dorothy	1	0.5
St. Elizabeth	13	6.0
St. George	11	5.5
St. James	11	5.5
St. John	4	2.0
St. Mary	17	9.0
St. Thomas-in-the-East	14	7.5
St. Thomas-in-the-Vale	6	3.5
Total	194	100.00

Source: Deeds and Conveyances, Jamaica; Chancery Court Records, High Court of Chancery, Master's Reports.

Table A.5. *Distribution of Estates with over 100 Slaves, Jamaica, 1834 (by product)*

Parish	Product					Total
	Sugar	Coffee	Livestock	Mixed	Unassigned	
Clarendon	19	9	5	1	25	59
Hanover	44		7		25	76
Manchester		60		2		62
Portland	13	1		1	9	24
Port Royal	1	4			17	22
Trelawny	23		3	5	52	83
Vere	3	1	2		23	29
Westmoreland	7		10		45	62
St. Andrew	9	18	3		9	39
St. Ann	11	9	12	6	28	66
St. Catherine	3	3	9		6	21
St. David	9	8	1	1	6	25
St. Dorothy	11	1	2		1	15
St. Elizabeth	9	10	14	3	19	55
St. George	10	3	2		16	31
St. James	34		3	1	29	67
St. John	5	3	1		6	15
St. Mary	38	6	7	1	30	82
St. Thomas-in-the-East	23	6	4		44	77
St. Thomas-in-the-Vale	2	14	1		21	38
Totals	274	156	86	21	411	948

Source: Deeds and Conveyances; Chancery Court Records; Accounts Current; Accounts Produce; Slave Registers.

Table A.6. *Distribution of Estates with over 50 Slaves, Barbados, 1834 (by parish)*

Parish	Total
Christ Church	45
St. Andrew	22
St. George	35
St. James	19
St. John	25
St. Joseph	18
St. Lucy	20
St. Michael	24
St. Peter	26
St. Philip	42
St. Thomas	31
Total	307

Sources: Deeds and Conveyances, RB1/271–306; Chancery Court Records; Slave Registers, T71/553–64.

Table A.7. *Number of Estate Sales, Barbados, 1823–1843*

Year	Private	Chancery	Total
1823	3	2	5
1824	2	2	4
1825	8	5	13
1826	5	5	10
1827	7	1	8
1828	12	6	18
1829	5	1	6
1830	12	4	16
1831	3	0	3
1832	4	8	12
1833	2	5	7
1834	2	1	3
1835	10	5	15
1836	15	5	20
1837	29	1	30
1838	25	1	26
1839	10	0	10
1840	7	0	7
1841	6	1	7
1842	11	4	15
1843	5	0	5
Total	183	57	240
Percent	76.25	23.75	100

Sources: Deeds and Conveyances, RB1/271–306; Chancery Sales, 1825–64; Minutes of the Court of Chancery, 1829–34, 1835–44.

Table A.8. *White Women Slave Owners (of over 100 slaves), Jamaica, 1834*

Name	Estate	Product	Number of Slaves
Susannah Gordon	Home Castle, Cromwell		689
Jemima C. Munro	Tulloch		382
Lady Cooper	Duckenfield Hall	sugar	365
Mary Chandler, deceased	Seven Plantation		337
Sarah Grey	Friendship	sugar	302
Lady Holland	Friendship, Greenwich	sugar	273
Frances Jennings	Coley		248
Mary Haughton Reid	Hermitage, Wakefield	sugar	241
Elizabeth Marhshall	Mount Moses	coffee	238
Susannah Hylton	Belvidere	sugar	237
Charlotte Ann Quinlan	Wentworth, Charlottenburg		223
Ann Hill	Hermitage	coffee	209
Judith Gatteres, deceased	Palm		200
Mary Ann Turner	Dumbarton	sugar	196
Isabella Brickmaster	Windsor Castle	coffee/ sugar	189
Ann Sill	Providence		184
Mary Forster	Richmond Hill	coffee	184
Espine Batty	Lambkin Hill		183
Elizabeth Osborne	Mount Pelier		168
Mary McKenzie	Harmony Hill		165
Mary S. Morris	Kensington	sugar	149
Eliza Parker	Chudleigh	coffee	142
Mary Gilpin	Cascade		140
Louisa Burke	Newman Hall	sugar	134
Frances Lee	Wheelerfield	sugar	132
Mary Smith	Prospect Hill	coffee	131
Sarah G. Bambridge	Lindale		129
Rose Milles	Georgia		125
Elizabeth Simpson	Bounty Hall		125
Elizabeth L. Reid	Nonpareil	sugar	122
Catherine Wordie	Schwellenberg	coffee	115
Ann McLean	McLean's Mocha	coffee	114
Frances Cox	Carlton Pen	livestock	108
Ann Shickle	Shickle's Pen	livestock	107

(Continued)

Table A.8. (*Continued*)

Name	Estate	Product	Number of Slaves
Mary Walker	Success	sugar/ livestock	106
Mary Adams	Lemon Ridge, Friendship		105
Catherine Davies	New Battle	coffee	103
Magdalen McLeod	Keynsham	coffee	103
Elizabeth Clarke	Mount Idalia	coffee	102
Lydia Baker	Bardowie	coffee	100
Total			7,605

Sources: Deeds and Conveyances; Slave Registers.

Notes

ABBREVIATIONS

CO	Colonial Office
DM	Deposited Manuscript
PP	Parliamentary Papers
RB1/271–306	Deeds and Conveyances, Barbados
T71	Treasury Papers relative to slave registration and compensation.
1B/11	Slave Registers for Jamaica (National Archives of Jamaica)

Chapter 1

1. Great Britain, *Parliamentary Debates*, Commons, 2d ser., 9 (1823): 274–75, 282–86 (hereafter *Debates*, Commons). Emphasis added. For general background on British abolition see Burn, *Emancipation*; Ragatz, *The Fall of the Planter Class*; Temperley, *British Anti-Slavery*; Anstey, *The Atlantic Slave Trade*; Davis, *The Problem of Slavery in the Age of Revolution*; Green, *British Slave Emancipation*; and Walvin, ed., *Slavery and British Society*.

2. The planters, merchants, and their parliamentary lobbyists were known colloquially as the "Interest."

3. Judd, *Members*, pp. 67–68. Ragatz, *The Fall of the Planter Class*, pp. 51–53. The term "monoculture" is used for convenience, for although sugar dominated, the colonies also exported coffee, and some logwood, ginger, cotton, and pimento. Murray, *The West Indies*, p. 91. Higman, "The West India 'Interest,'" p. 2. Penson, "The London West India Interest," pp. 379–90. The two Societies remained separate until 1843, when they merged to form the West India Company.

4. Pares, *A West India Fortune*, pp. 186–88. Bills of exchange were payable at thirty, sixty, or ninety days after receipt and carried an interest rate of about 20 percent. Original Correspondence: General, West Indies, CO318/117. Checkland, "Finance for the West Indies," p. 461. Karch, "The Transformation," p. 88. Pares, *Merchants and Planters*, p. 46.

5. Buxton, ed., *Memoirs*, p. 243. Higman, "The West India 'Interest,'" p. 3, table 1. Murray, *The West Indies*, p. 197. Judd, *Members*, pp. 205, 271, 317.

6. Knaplund, *James Stephen*, p. 97. Checkland, "John Gladstone," pp. 222–23. Higman, "The West India 'Interest,'" p. 11, n. 61. T71/41–42, 56, 150, 176–77; 1B/11/7, no. 124; T71/329–31, Slave Register for Grenada; T71/1300, Adjudication List: St. Lucia, Contested Claims. PP, 1837–38 (215): 1–79, 94–101, 285–308, 312–13.

7. PP, 1837–38 (215): 1–79, 94–101. T71/222–23. Higman, "The West India 'Interest,'" p. 8.

8. T71/553–64, Slave Registers for Barbados, 1834. T71/32, 18. Judd, *Members*, pp. 250–51.

9. Penson, *The Colonial Agents*, pp. 228–29.

10. See Higman's article, "The West India 'Interest,'" for an analysis of the composition and conflicts of the Interest.

11. *Debates*, Commons, 2d ser., 9 (1823): 311, 342. *Debates*, Commons, 2d ser., 14 (1826): 994. William Smith belonged to a group of evangelical philanthropists known as the Clapham Sect. See Higman, "The West India 'Interest,'" p. 10.

12. Stephen, *Anti-Slavery Recollections*, p. 63; Murray, *The West Indies*, pp. 128–29. Ragatz, *The Fall of the Planter Class*, pp. 411–14.

13. *The Barbadian*, 23 March 1824.

14. *Quarterly Review*, October 1825, April 1831. Mayers to the Committee of Correspondence, 1 March 1833, Agent's Letterbook.

15. *St. Jago de la Vega Gazette*, 30 March–6 April 1833. The Jamaican and Barbadian newspapers frequently quoted the *Glasgow Courier*. Davis, *The Problem of Slavery in the Age of Revolution*, pp. 366–67.

16. Beaumont, *Compensation to Slave Owners*, pp. 5–6. Ragatz, *The Fall of the Planter Class*, p. 441.

17. *Royal Gazette and Jamaica Times*, 9–16 July 1831.

18. PP, 1831–32 (381). Sheridan, "The West India Sugar Crisis," p. 540.

19. RB1/271–306.

20. PP, 1831–32 (381): 115, 1216, 1570, 1573 (evidence of Joseph Marryat and Alexander Macdonnell). *Report of the Select Committee on the State of the West India Colonies* (1832) (hereafter *Report*): 7–8, 103. Eisner, *Jamaica*, p. 190. Williams, *Capitalism*, pp. 112, 116, 121. Sheridan, "The West India Sugar Crisis," p. 539.

21. PP, 1831–32 (381): 87, 91 (evidence of Alexander Macdonnell). For Louisiana see Deerr, *The History of Sugar* 1:250, and Sitterson, *Sugar Country*. For Cuba see Moreno Fraginals, *El Ingenio*, 3:67–69, cuadro 6. For Puerto Rico see Scarano, *Sugar and Slavery*, p. 13, table 1.4.

22. Hall, *Five of the Leewards*, pp. 119, n. 53. Pares, *A West India Fortune*, p. 192. Williams, *Capitalism*, pp. 79–80.

23. PP, 1831–32 (381): 35 (evidence of Alexander Macdonnell). *Report*, pp. 6–9. Pares, *A West India Fortune*, p. 192. The Interest had suggested this earlier. See Minutes of General Meeting of West India Planters and Merchants, 12 May 1829, and the *Quarterly Review* 45 (April 1831): 238.

24. PP, 1831–32 (381): 30 (evidence of Alexander Macdonnell). These prices include the duty.

25. For a "pessimistic" view of the standard-of-living debate of the early nineteenth-

century see Hobsbawm, "The Standard of Living." Hartwell presents a more optimistic view in "The Rising Standard of Living." See also Mintz, *Sweetness and Power*, pp. 165–67, 175.

26. PP, 1831–32 (381): 1421 (evidence of Alexander Macdonnell). Green, *British Slave Emancipation*, p. 40. Deerr, *The History of Sugar*, 2:430, 531.

27. PP, 1831–32 (381): 989, 1413–15 (evidence of James Colqhoun and Alexander Macdonnell).

28. PP, 1831–32 (381): 1409–21 (evidence of Alexander Macdonnell). Green, "The Planter Class," p. 453.

29. PP, 1831–32 (381): 1433 (evidence of John Pollard Mayers).

30. PP, 1831–32 (381): 502, 1433–34 (evidence of Thomas Phillpotts and John Pollard Mayers). Madden, *A Twelve Month's Residence*, 2:230. Although it was illegal to charge compound interest on West Indian mortgages, merchants often did so by requiring the planter to re-fund the entire debt, including the interest, at frequent intervals, see Pares, *Merchants and Planters*, p. 44.

31. PP, 1831–32 (381): 6–12, 298 (evidence of Alexander Macdonnell and Andrew Colville). Sheridan, "The West India Sugar Crisis," p. 540. *Report*, pp. 4, 15.

32. PP, 1831–32 (381): 850 (evidence of James McQueen). Mayers to Committee, 3 March 1831, Agent's Letterbook. Schomburgk, *The History of Barbados*, p. 288.

33. Memorial to Parliament, 23 February 1832. Minutes of the West India Merchants, 1828–43, *Report*, pp. 15–16, 44.

34. These figures do not take account of the higher death rate among a resident slave population exposed to a continual influx of new Africans. CO318/117. The Colonial Office pointed out that in 1830 the Interest had put the cost of rearing slaves at £135. For discussions of the slave population of Cuba, see Knight, *Slave Society in Cuba*; Kiple, *Blacks in Colonial Cuba*. For Brazil, see Karasch, *Slave Life in Rio*, and Stein, *Vassouras*.

35. Curtin, "The British Sugar Duties," p. 159. Appendix to the *Report*.

36. *Report*, pp. 18, 21, 46, 89 (evidence of Simon Taylor and Andrew Colville).

37. *The Barbadian*, 28 June 1823.

38. Brathwaite, *The Development of Creole Society*, pp. 111–12. Pares, *Merchants and Planters*, p. 47. PP, 1831–32 (381): 259, 1081 (evidence of Andrew Colville).

39. RB1/302, fol. 352.

40. T71/157, High Court of Chancery, Master's Report (June 1837), no. 139, fol. 1, Wright v. Venables.

41. PP, 1831–32 (381): 1076–77, 1081–88 (evidence of Andrew Colville). See for example John Brewer, "Commercialization and Politics," *The Birth of a Consumer Society*, ed. McKendrick, et al.

42. Pinney Papers, 1740–1848, p. 415. Georgia Estate Letterbooks and Accounts, vols. 1, 2. 23 February 1832, Minutes of the West India Merchants, 1828–43. PP, 1831–32 (381): 688, 694–96 (evidence of Simon Taylor).

43. Hurwitz, *Politics*, pp. 57, 67–68, 84. Read, *Press and People*, pp. 39–41.

44. Thompson, *The Making of the English Working Class*, pp. 807–27. Harrison, *Poor Men's Guardians*, p. 58. CO318/117, Position of Government and Two Alternative Plans of Proceeding Considered, 1833.

45. Murray, *The West Indies*, p. 198. Address to Earl Grey, 1 February 1833, Minutes of the West India Merchants, 1828–43.

46. Goderich to West India Body, 4 February 1833, CO318/116. Murray, *The West Indies*, pp. 200–201.

47. Minutes of Standing Committee (Special), 10–11 May 1833, West India Committee 1829–34.

48. *The Times*, 11 May 1833. *Debates*, Commons, 3d ser., 17 (1833): 1194, 1230.

49. *Debates*, Commons, 3d ser., 17 (1833): 1222–31, 1234–37. Murray, *The West Indies*, p. 201. Temperley, *British Anti-Slavery*, p. 17.

50. Taylor, "Our Man," p. 68.

51. CO318/117, 13 March 1833. Committee of Correspondence, Out-Letter Book of the Agent in England: William Burge, 1832–34, 5 March 1833.

52. *Annual Register*, 30 May 1833. Petition to the House of Commons from the West India Planters and Merchants, 18 May 1833. Minutes of the Society of West India Planters and Merchants, 1829–34. *St. Jago de la Vega Gazette*, 6–13 July 1833.

53. CO318/117, 13 March 1833.

54. 29 May, 3 June 1833, Minutes of the Acting Committee, 1829–33; 29 May, Minutes of the Standing Committee (Special), 1833. *Annual Register*, 30 May 1833. The request for the additional £10 million was raised on two later occasions.

55. *Annual Register*, 30 May 1833.

56. *Debates*, Commons, 3d ser., 19 (1833): 1063. 7 June 1833, Minutes of the Acting Committee (1829–33). *Liberal*, 18 April 1838. Murray, *The West Indies*, pp. 202–3.

57. *Debates*, Commons, 3d ser., 20 (1833): 201.

58. Stephen, *Anti-Slavery Recollections*, pp. 127–32. Temperley, *British Anti-Slavery*, pp. 12–13.

59. Stephen, *Anti-Slavery Recollections*, p. 161. Davis, *The Problem of Slavery in the Age of Revolution*, pp. 366–67. Temperley, *British Anti-Slavery*, p. 17.

60. The letters were written by Richard Oastler, the factory reformer: see Read, *Press and People*, p. 30.

61. Hollis, *The Pauper Press*, p. 278. Harrison, *Poor Men's Guardians*, p. 94. Betty Fladeland, "Our Cause Being One and the Same: Abolitionists and Chartism," pp. 77–78, in *Slavery and British Society*, ed. Walvin. *The Poor Man's Guardian* claimed a readership of over 16,000.

62. Buxton, *Memoirs*, p. 282. Stephen, *Anti-Slavery Recollections*, p. 206.

63. *Barbados Globe and Colonial Advocate*, 20 November 1834. *St. Jago de la Vega Gazette*, 9–16 November 1833, no. 46.

64. Hendy to Stanley, 15 July 1833, CO28/112.

65. *St. Jago de la Vega Gazette*, 26 October–2 November 1833.

66. Vidal to Mitchell and Company, 8 July 1833, Agent's Letterbook. Smith to Stanley, 13 July 1833, 29 July 1833, CO28/111.

67. Buxton, ed., *Memoirs*, p. 134. *Quarterly Review* (1823): 484. *Debates*, Commons, 2d ser., 9 (1823): 351–52.

68. *St. Jago de la Vega Gazette*, 13–20 July 1833.

Chapter 2

1. PP, 1833 (492): 5, 41, 47.

2. PP, 1833 (492): 29, 33, 34. Three commissioners, Henry Frederick Stephenson, Hastings Elwin, and James Lewis received £3,000 each over the three-year term. Wastell, "The History of Slave Compensation," pp. 35–38.

3. Murray, *The West Indies*, pp. 120–22, 147, 228.

4. Wastell, "The History of Slave Compensation," pp. 138–40. Murray, *The West Indies*, pp. 121–22. Stephen's wife, Jane Venn, and his father also belonged to the Sect. See David Spring, "The Clapham Sect."

5. PP, 1833 (492): 33.

6. T71/553–564, Slave Registers for Barbados, 1834. Smith to Stanley, 21 December 1833, CO28/111.

7. T71/1596, Commissioners of Compensation: Colonial Office Correspondence, 5 May 1834. Samuel Murphy, James Bernard, and George Atkinson completed the board.

8. Sligo to Glenelg, 11 March 1836, no. 377. Votes of the House of Assembly, message from the governor, 17 November 1836, no. 3.

9. PP, 1833 (492): 19. Fogel and Engerman, "Philanthropy," pp. 395, n. 22. Wastell, "The History of Slave Compensation," pp. 56–58, 64–65.

10. Wastell, "The History of Slave Compensation," pp. 70–71. PP, 1833 (492): 19. Burn, *Emancipation*, p. 116, n. 5.

11. T71/1499, Commissioners of Compensation, Minute Book, 7 July 1835. Engerman, "Economic Change," p. 142, table 2.

12. Minutes of the General Meeting of the West India Planters and Merchants Committee, 19 July 1833. Sligo to Stanley, 22 June 1834, no. 7, (Confidential), Private Letterbook of Lord Sligo. Smith to Stanley, 1 August 1833, CO28/111.

13. Mayers to Goderich, 9 July 1833, CO28/112. Taylor, "Our Man," pp. 65, 72–77.

14. Mayers to Committee of Correspondence, 11 February 1833, Agent's Letterbook. Taylor "Our Man," p. 74.

15. Mayers to Goderich, 2 March 1833, Agent's Letterbook.

16. PP, 1837–38 (215): 189, 190, 195–98, 202, 327. Owners of over fifty slaves submitted 368 claims.

17. Ibid., 189–201. Barbados Almanack, 1842.

18. Mayers to Goderich, 2 March 1833, Agent's Letterbook. Smith to Stanley, 28 September 1833, Confidential, CO28/111.

19. T71/1499, Commissioners of Compensation, Minute Book, 9 March 1835. Charles M. Willick, the secretary of the University Life Assurance Office, did the calculations independently of the commission. Wastell, "The History of Slave Compensation," p. 32.

20. PP, 1833 (492): 5, 42. Gisela Eisner estimated that in 1830–31 merchants employed about 3,200 slaves on dock work. See Eisner, *Jamaica*, p. 37.

21. W. K. Marshall, ed., *The Colthurst Journal*, p. 69. Wastell, "The History of Slave Compensation," p. 77. Pitcairn and Amos to Mayhew, 11 May 1835, Chiswick Plantation Papers, vol. 2 (1832–35). MS WIs s17–19. The valuers' returns also contain details of the number of slaves, their places of residence, and their value.

22. T71/500; T71/553–64. Although the evaluators were expected to donate their services

they were in fact paid on a per capita basis for the slaves they valued. See Wastell, "The History of Slave Compensation," pp. 74–6.

23. Committee of Correspondence Out-Letter-Book of William Burge, 21 September 1833. As half-pay army officers inured to strict discipline, the stipendiary magistrates were not expected to be "soft" on the ex-slaves. Since they depended on the whites for company and social comfort, they risked ostracism if perceived as favoring the apprentices. Some openly sided with the whites and received testimonials when their terms expired. Others tried to be fair, and the whites despised them for their efforts. Thirty-one officers went to Jamaica and received £300 per year, in addition to their half pay from the army. The smaller colonies got fewer magistrates. Excellent accounts of the apprenticeship appear in Burn, *Emancipation*, and Green, *British Slave Emancipation*.

24. W. K. Marshall, ed., *The Colthurst Journal*, p. 111 (emphasis in the original).

25. T71/500, Slave Register for St. Vincent, 1834. W. K. Marshall, ed., *The Colthurst Journal*, pp. 68–69, 94–95, 147.

26. Knapland, *James Stephen*, p. 101, n. 13. Green, *British Slave Emancipation*, p. 133, n. 12.

27. PP, 1837–38 (215). See W. K. Marshall, ed., *The Colthurst Journal*, p. 238 for the returns from St. Vincent. Sligo to Glenelg, 11 April 1836, no. 414. Duncan Hamilton made the allegation.

28. T71/1622, General Rules of the Commissioners of Compensation. T71/1596, Commissioners of Compensation: Colonial Office Correspondence, 18 September 1834. T71/790–803, Valuers' Returns for Barbados. Wastell, "The History of Slave Compensation," pp. 112–13.

29. T71/1622. Wastell, "The History of Slave Compensation," pp. 45–46, 69, 120.

30. T71/1622. PP, 1833 (492): 42. T71/1596, 8 September 1834. Wastell, "The History of Slave Compensation," pp. 115, 258.

31. T71/1596, 28 January 1834, 20 January 1835. PP, 1833 (492): 47.

32. PP, 1833 (492): 4. T71/1622. The certificates carried an interest rate of 2 percent for the first year and 3 percent for each consecutive year until the claim was settled. Wastell, "The History of Slave Compensation," p. 116.

33. Report of meeting with West India Committee, 23 April 1833, CO318/116. Wastell, "The History of Slave Compensation," p. 106.

34. Stephen, *Anti-Slavery Recollections*, p. 190. *Annual Register*, 30 May 1833, p. 199. Murray, *The West Indies*, p. 201.

35. Mitchell and Deane, *Abstract*, no. 17, pp. 392–93.

36. Report of meeting held 29 July 1835, PP, 1835 (463). *Debates*, Commons, 3d. ser., 20 (1833): 198–200.

37. Report of meeting held on 29 July 1835, PP, 1835 (463).

38. Wastell, "The History of Slave Compensation," p. 104.

39. Report of John Finlaison, Actuary of the National Debt and Government Calculator, PP, 1836 (597), 5. Wastell, "The History of Slave Compensation," pp. 120–22.

40. Wastell, "The History of Slave Compensation," pp. 138–40.

41. Pares, *A West India Fortune*, p. 186. Wastell, "The History of Slave Compensation," p. 227.

42. T71/1607, In-Letters, Jamaica, Original Correspondence, 10 April 1837, letter from R. Tippler.

43. T71/1596, 15 August 1834, letter from [John] Lefevre.

44. PP, 1837–38 (215).

45. *The Barbadian*, 9 March 1836. The costs were about 3.8 percent. W. K. Marshall, ed., *The Colthurst Journal*, p. 213. Wastell, "The History of Slave Compensation," pp. 209–11.

46. Sligo to Stanley, 5 June 1834, Private Letterbook of Lord Sligo, MS 281.

47. *Royal Gazette and Jamaica Times*, 21–28 November 1836, and 28 November–5 December 1835. *The Barbadian*, 1835–36.

48. *Barbados Globe & Colonial Advocate*, 29 October 1835, CO33/4.

49. Circular Despatches, 12 October 1835, CO854/1. Votes of the House of Assembly, p. 120, message from the Governor, 26 November 1835. "A Proprietor" to Glenelg, 9 March 1836, CO318/125.

50. Votes of the House of Assembly, letter from Glenelg, 12 October 1835. Glenelg was Colonial Secretary from April 1835 to February 1839.

51. W. K. Marshall, ed., *The Colthurst Journal*, pp. 211–14 (emphasis in the original).

52. Votes of the House of Assembly, letter from Glenelg, 12 October 1835.

53. *Royal Gazette and Jamaica Times*, 28 November–5 December 1835; See also *Royal Gazette and Jamaica Times*, 5 September 1835–12 September 1835; *The Times*, 7 September, 2 October 1835, and Pitcairn and Amos to Mayhew, 6 October 1834, Chiswick Plantation Papers, MSS WIs s17–19, vol. 2, for comments on the delays.

54. Deeds and Conveyances, Jamaica, vol. 795, fols. 160–62, fols. 173–75. Burge to Stanley, 30 January 1834, CO137/195. *Royal Gazette and Jamaica Times*, 26 May 1838. Minutes of the Society of West India Planters and Merchants, Standing Committee (Special), 26 March 1838. W. K. Marshall, ed., *The Colthurst Journal*, pp. 94–95.

55. Sligo to Stanley, 5 June 1834, Private Letterbook of Lord Sligo, MS 281. Votes of the House of Assembly, message from the governor, 19 November 1835.

56. Smith to Glenelg, no. 14, 1836, CO28/117.

57. T71/1596, Lefevre to the Colonial Office, 15 August 1834. T71/1611, In-Letters: Barbados, Chalmers and Guthrie to the Commissioners of Compensation, 18 December 1838.

58. Blue Books of Statistics for Barbados, CO33/45–54. Blue Books of Statistics for Jamaica, CO142/51, 52.

59. Blue Books of Statistics for Jamaica, CO142/51, 52; Eisner, *Jamaica*, p. 237.

60. George Smith, receiver general, to the Island Secretary, 27 January 1835, CO142/47.

61. Mayers to Committee, 18 May 1831, Agent's Letterbook.

Chapter 3

1. Sligo to Glenelg, 10 February 1836, no. 316. Pares, *A West India Fortune*, p. 330 Eisner, *Jamaica*, p. 196.

2. High Court of Chancery, Master's Report, (6 April–3 July 1841), vol. 529 fols. 305–7, Payne v. Palmer. PP, 1837–38 (215): 293.

3. T71/555; T71/557. Mortgage of Fairey Valley to Thomas and John Daniel, 24 May 1838; DM 89/2/9–10. RB1/281, fol. 97. PP, 1837–38 (215): 189, 194.

4. PP, 1842 (479): 5892 (evidence of Hinton Spalding).

5. Pares, *A West India Fortune*, pp. 243–50. See also Ragatz, *The Fall of the Planter Class*, pp. 340–41.

6. Beachey, *The British West Indies*, pp. 10−11.

7. 1B/11/5/27, fols. 206−10 (1827), Accounts Current. Mortgagees-in-possession could not "clog" the mortgage by undertaking repairs in excess of the value of the debt. Beachey, *The British West Indies*, pp. 9−12. Pares, *A West India Fortune*, p. 272.

8. 1B/11/5/27, fols. 206−10, Accounts Current for Hope plantation (1827).

9. Beachey, *The British West Indies*, p. 9.

10. T71/553−564. High Court of Chancery, Masters' Reports (1832−41). Chancery Sales. Minutes of the Court of Chancery (1829−34, 1835−44).

11. See the first report of the Dwarris Commission, which inquired into the civil and criminal justice system in the West Indies in the 1820s, PP, 1827 (559): 19−30, 64−69. Beachey, *The British West Indies*, p. 14.

12. Chancery Sales, Bovell v. Rollock. RB1/290 fol. 172.

13. Chancery Sales. PP, 1831−32 (381): 1138 (evidence of Andrew Colville). *The Barbadian*, 28 June 1823.

14. See for example the sales of Pickerings, Chancery Sales, 1835, Wilson v. Hall; and Ayshford, Minutes of the Court of Chancery, 1836, Hardy v. Fotheringham.

15. Chancery Sales. RB1/274, fol. 392; RB1/275, fol. 154; RB1/290, fol. 187.

16. High Court of Chancery, Master's Report, no. 142 (17 March−19 July 1838). Master's Report, no. 150 (6 April−3 July 1841).

17. Mayers to Goderich, 2 March 1833, CO28/112. Roughley, *The Jamaica Planter's Guide*, pp. 3−10. Beachey, *The British West Indies*, p. 14.

18. Pares, *A West India Fortune*, pp. 271−72.

19. RB1/286, fol. 71; RB1/301, fol. 58. RB1/271-306. Prior Park was in St. James.

20. Beachey, *The British West Indies*, p. 13; Pares, *A West India Fortune*, pp. 266−69.

21. Deeds and Conveyances, Jamaica, vol. 802, fol. 1.

22. RB1/271-306. Chancery Sales; Minutes of the Court of Chancery. The figure does not include mortgages from the imperial government to cover damage from the 1831 hurricane. Twenty-five of the 120 estates carried more than one mortgage, although this seems very conservative and 50 percent seems more realistic. I am grateful to Ronald Hughes for bringing a further twenty-six eighteenth-century mortgages to my attention. If these were still unpaid in 1834, the percentage of mortgaged estates could rise to 45.

23. T71/1174−18, app. to counterclaim no. 128, Newry estate. Charles Rose Ellis became Lord Seaford in 1826.

24. T71/1174−18, app. to counterclaim no. 134, Nutfield estate. Mortgage of Nutfield and Newry estates, Ellis Papers, DM 54/4/45. Statement for the Advice of Mr. Burge, DM 54/4/21. The £9,000 was part of a marriage settlement dating from 1785. See also Mortgage of Nutfield, Newry and Greencastle to Timperon and Dobinson, DM 54/4/16. The mortgage also included Tulloch Castle.

25. Ellis Papers, DM 54/4/45; DM 54/4/21.

26. Ellis Papers, DM 54/4/45; DM 54/4/21.

27. T71/1174−1218, appendix to counterclaim no. 128, Newry estate.

28. PP, 1837−38 (215): 285, 287−88, 301.

29. Deeds and Conveyances, Jamaica, vol. 730 fol. 104, James v. Allen; vol. 808 fol. 141. 1B/11/7-130.

30. Claims for Compensation Filed with the Commissioners for Jamaica, 0.3268. Deeds

and Conveyances, Jamaica, vol. 808 fol. 141; vol. 817 fol. 43. Hawthorn and Shedden to William Lake, 1836, MS at U.W.I., Mona. PP, 1837–38 (215): 69, 290, 305. The Colliston claim was for £2,004.

31. CO318/117. RB1/297, fol. 160. *The Barbadian*, 26 January 1827.

32. RB1/300, fol. 288. PP, 1837–38 (215): 326.

33. Minutes of the Court of Chancery (1829–34), Alleyne v. Corbin. *The Barbadian*, 12 September 1832, RB1/284, fol. 123; RB1/290, fol. 89.

34. PP, 1837–38 (215).

35. Estimates range from 527 to 646 estates devoted to sugar in the 1830s. See Hall, *Free Jamaica*, p. 82, and Higman, *Slave Population and Economy*, pp. 11–14, table 1.

36. Based on the 1832 slave registers and chancery court records and limited to estates with over 100 slaves. A few were assigned according to the dominant crop in their region.

37. PP, 1837–38 (215). T71/1499, Commissioners of Compensation Minute Book, 7 July 1835. In some cases, two conflicting claims were entered for the same property, so that the number of claims for more than 100 slaves is actually closer to 953.

38. Phillips "The Changing Role," p. 45. Sheridan, "The West India Sugar Crisis," pp. 548–49. Pares, *A West India Fortune*, p. 317.

39. Peter Marshall, *Bristol*, appendix, p. ii. PP, 1837–38 (215): 1–79, 285–308.

40. PP, 1837–38 (215): 1–79, 285–308.

41. T71/150; T71/242; 1B/11/7/130. PP, 1837–38 (215): 50, 66–69, 307. Williams put Miles's indemnity at £17,850 for his plantations in Jamaica and Trinidad. See Williams, *Capitalism*, pp. 74–75. Peter Marshall put the figure at £36,000.

42. Checkland calculated Gladstone's total awards at £93,526; see Checkland, *The Gladstones*, pp. 320–21. Williams put the figure at £85,600; see Williams, *Capitalism*, p. 90. Gladstone actually received at least £110,332 and perhaps as much as £114,677.

43. Deeds and Conveyances, Jamaica, vol. 795, fol. 65. T71/176–77; T71/150. Claims for Compensation, 0.326.8. Checkland, *The Gladstones*, pp. 41–42, 196–97.

44. John Dawkins to John Randall, 7 August 1836; John Randall to Henry Dawkins, 12 August 1836; miscellaneous documents dated 1812 and 5 September 1817, Dawkins Family Papers, MSS D. D. Dawkins, C47. PP, 1837–38 (215): 1, 4, 19–21.

45. Paisley and Windsor Lodge Accounts, MS 32. PP, 1837–38 (215): 71. PP, 1831–32 (561): 40. The government loan was secured against the estates and slaves. Individuals could request sums equal to the value of the property destroyed and had six to ten years to repay their loans at 4 percent interest. Althorp to the Committee, 17 April 1832, Minutes of the Society of West India Merchants, 1828–43.

46. Edwards, *The History Civil*, p. 221. At the height of Puerto Rico's sugar production in 1845, the average estate in Ponce province was 273 acres with 49 slaves and produced an average of 85 metric tons. When Cuba was in full production in 1860, the average estate was 1,486 acres and produced 157 metric tons. The average for Louisiana in 1820 was 117 metric tons on 1,365 acres with 70 slaves. See Scarano, *Sugar and Slavery*, pp. 63–68.

47. T71/557. Drax Hall Ledger, 1825–41, fols. 30, 35, 82, 106, Z9/2/6.

48. T71/564, Abstract of Barbados Slave Register, 1834. This estimate is based on 396 estates with 50 or more slaves. Higman put the figure at 77.5 percent for 1830. See Higman, *Slave Populations of the British Caribbean*, p. 70, table 3.8.

49. T71/564, Abstract of the Barbados Slave Register, 1834. These crops were cultivated

by poor whites and slaves in the Scotland district of the northeast coast and in St. Philip and St. Lucy. See Handler, *The Unappropriated People*, pp. 99–100, and "The History of Arrowroot," pp. 70–81. Karch, "The Transformation," p. 70. Higman, *Slave Populations of the British Caribbean*, pp. 52, 70. See also Levy, *Emancipation*, for the continued reliance on sugar after 1845.

50. I was able to match 307 of the 326 large claims with their appropriate estates; only these are included here.

51. Eisner, *Jamaica*, p. 197.

52. Mayers to Goderich, 2 March 1833, CO28/112. According to Mayers, only 25 percent of owners were absentee. My estimate for 1834 is based on 241 owners.

53. Checkland, *The Gladstones*, p. 264. Richard Barrett to the Duke of Buckingham, 18 March 1832, 22 Aug. 1835, Stowe Collection. Accounts Current, fols. 206–10, 1827. 1B/11/5/27.

54. Roughley, *The Jamaica Planter's Guide*, pp. 3–10. Curtin, *Two Jamaicas*, p. 16.

55. T71/553–64.

56. John Gale Vidal to Rowland Mitchell, 5 August 1833, Attorney's Letterbook, 1B/5/83.

57. Vidal to Mitchell and Company, 22 June 1833, ibid.; Vidal to Roland Mitchell, 5 August 1833, ibid. T71/32; T71/687.

58. Vidal to Mitchell and Company, 26 October 1835, 22 January 1836, 14 February 1836, 24 June 1836, Attorney's Letterbook, 1B/5/83.

59. Vidal to Mitchell and Company, 12 February 1836, ibid.

60. Vidal to Mitchell and Company, 24 June 1836, ibid. High Court of Chancery, Master's Report (July–December 1838), no. 143, fol. 189, Mitchell v. Stoney. Master's Report of Sale, 8 August 1839, fol. 262. The Mitchells received £4,415 for the Grange River slaves. The court then sold the estate to James Allwood for £2,500.

61. *St. Jago de la Vega Gazette*, 7–14 May 1836, T71/150. John Gale Vidal to Mitchell and Company, 27 June 1836, 18 July 1837, Attorney's Letterbook, 1B/5/83.

62. Brathwaite, *The Development of Creole Society*, p. 41. PP, 1837–38 (215): 48.

63. When Grossett arrived in Jamaica in 1834, his slaves had been working for wages, but he ended the practice because he felt it was a bad habit. Later he complained that his apprentices would not work for wages. Private Letterbook of Lord Sligo, 1835–36, MS 281.

64. T71/895–900, claim no. 488, Register of Claims, Barbados. RB1/290, fol. 254.

65. RB1/262, fols. 307, 309; RB1/282, fols. 211, 218; RB1/292, fols. 3, 27. Apes Hill was valued at £29,642 in 1831. Inventory of Apes Hill, the estate of John William Perch, 1831.

66. Richard Barrett to Ambrose Humphrys, 24 December 1834, 5 November 1835, Stowe Collection. Conveyances and Mortgages for Richmond, Hope, Middleton, and Constant Spring, 11 September 1844, BRA 1272 file 7/14, no. 16. PP, 1837–38 (215): 297.

67. Minutes of the Court of Chancery, 1829–34, Gibbes v. Storey; Chancery Sales, 1825–64. *The Barbadian*, 5 December 1832.

68. RB1/295, fol. 7.

Chapter 4

1. Pares, *A West India Fortune*, p. 261.

2. Mortgages that the British government extended to cover damage to Barbadian plan-

tations during the slave rebellion or the hurricane of 1831 are not included since they fall into the class of emergency relief funds and do not reflect true commercial credit. The hurricane affected St. Lucia, St. Vincent, and Barbados and caused an estimated £2 million in damage. Levy, *Emancipation*, p. 26. Ragatz, *The Fall of the Planter Class*, p. 375, n. 9.

3. RB1/271-306.

4. RB1/285, fol. 320; RB1/292, fol. 191; RB1/297, fol. 188, 261; RB1/298, fol. 181; RB1/300, fol. 174. When the marriage settlement fell due in 1830, the money was not available, and the estate became the subject of a complex chancery suit (Mapp v. Ellcock), which was still not settled in 1838. In 1840, in addition to all these liabilities, Prettyjohn encumbered the estate even further, with a £300 annuity for his wife. RB1/298, fol. 226.

5. Sheridan, "The West India Sugar Crisis," pp. 542–43. Murray, *The West Indies*, p. 191.

6. Mayers to Committee, 3 August 1831, Agent's Letterbook, 6 September 1829–6 June 1833.

7. Digest of the United Society for the Propagation of the Gospel (hereafter SPG) Records, 1701–1892, Papers of SPG. *Annual Report*, 1837, p. 82. *Debates*, Commons, 3d ser., 17 (1833): 1209–11. *Report*, p. 21. See also Sheridan, "The West India Sugar Crisis," p. 540. James Stephen, 27 February 1833, CO318/116.

8. Karch, "The Transformation," p. 38. The Daniels may have been established even earlier. They traded with the Colbeck estate in Jamaica and properties in Tobago, Antigua, Nevis, Monserrat, and British Guiana. The compensation for Colbeck's 237 slaves became the subject of a lawsuit, Faulkner v. Daniel. Accounts Current, Colbeck Estate with Thomas Daniel, no. 27, fol. 164; no. 34, fol. 157, 1B/11/5.

9. In 1702 Christopher Codrington bequeathed the Codrington and Consett plantations to the SPG. By 1712 the two estates were being operated as one unit known as the Society estate; Bennett Collection, West India Papers, Codrington Estate Papers, C-MSS, box 1, folder 16; boxes 4, 6. Codrington Estate, C-WI, box 6, folder 25; C/COD/129, Accounts with Thomas Daniel, 1794–1838. See also Butler, "Mortality," pp. 49–50, and Bennett, *Bondsmen and Bishops*, pp. 1–2.

10. Emphasis added. Digest of SPG Records. Bennett Collection, West India Papers, Codrington Estate Papers, C-MSS, box 6, folder 25. Correspondence of Thomas Daniel and Company with Rev. Anthony Hamilton, 26 May 1830, 29 Sept. 1831, C/COD/128. Thomas Daniel with Major Moody, 26 February 1830, C/COD/71.

11. PP, 1837–38 (215). Thomas Daniel and Company, Liquidation Papers, 1895.

12. RB1/271-306. Minutes of the Court of Chancery, 1829–34, 1835–44. Chancery Sales, 1825–64. The parent company originally consisted of Sir William Barton, George Barton Irlam, and John Higginson and operated simultaneously with the colonial subsidiary, at least after 1816.

13. Forster Hall, Cottage, and Groves Estate Accounts, 1817–55. RB1/271-306. Minutes of the Court of Chancery, 1829–34, 1835–44. Chancery Sales, 1825–64. T71/557, Slave Register for Barbados. Yard also assigned sugar to Ranken and Wilson of Glasgow, Thomas Lee and Company of Liverpool, and the Daniels in London and Bristol.

14. John Brewer, "Commercialization and Politics," in *The Birth of a Comsummer Society*, ed. McKendrick et al., pp. 203–4. Pares, *Merchants and Planters*, p. 47.

15. RB1/271-306.

16. Private Letterbook of Lord Sligo, 1835–36, MS 281.

17. T71/41, T71/49. PP, 1837–38 (215): 12, 289.

18. Private Letterbook of Lord Sligo, 1835–36, MS 281. PP, 1837–38 (215). Henry Cox owned Industry, Spring Garden, Epping Plantation, and Tower Hill. T71/41. Hodgson received £16,400 for Cox's slaves.

19. PP, 1837–38 (215). Hodgson received £7,581 for his own slaves. Hamilton Brown also owned Minard Pen, Antrim estate, and Colliston plantation.

20. Peter Marshall, *Bristol*, p. 27. Philips, "The Changing Role," p. 69. Pares, *A West India Fortune*, p. 184.

21. Checkland, "John Gladstone," pp. 216–29. Williams, *Capitalism*, pp. 123–24.

22. Checkland, *The Gladstones*, pp. 59, 120–26, 179, 195, 273. Checkland, "John Gladstone," p. 216. Gladstone also owned the Waller's Delight and Covenden estates.

23. Checkland, *The Gladstones*, pp. 327; pp. 414–15. Checkland, "John Gladstone," pp. 216–29. Gladstone bought shares in the London to Brighton railroad.

24. Pares, *A West India Fortune*, p. 331. Charles's brother, John Frederick Pinney, preferred to hold on to his West India assets.

25. Hobsbawm, *The Age of Revolution*, p. 65. Ragatz, *The Fall of the Planter Class*, p. 3.

26. Checkland, *The Gladstones*, p. 179.

27. Brewer, "Commercialization and Politics," in *The Birth of a Consumer Society*, ed. McKendrick et al., pp. 204–5.

28. RB1/271-306. These mortgages totaled £1,490,000.

29. Beachey, *The British West Indies*, pp. 24–25.

Chapter 5

1. Mr. Milles to Francis Graham, 20 June 1806, Georgia Estate Letterbooks and Accounts, vol. 1, Mst 132. Mackenzie to Alston, 23 January 1825, 10 July 1825, Georgia Estate Letterbooks and Accounts, vol. 3, Mst 132. Pitcairn and Amos to Mayhew, 8 June 1831, Chiswick Plantation Papers, vol. 1, MSS WIs s17–19.

2. *St. Jago de la Vega Gazette*, 2 February 1833. Vidal to Mitchell, 6 June 1833, Attorney's Letterbook, 1B/5/83.

3. Sligo to Glenelg, 3 March 1836, Despatches, no. 359, 1B/5/18-11. Sligo to Seaford, 10 March 1836, Private Letterbook of Lord Sligo, MS 281. Sligo to Glenelg, 17 April 1836, Despatches, no. 422, 1B/5/18-11. Oldham's purchases included Caen Wood, a 1,072-acre estate in St. George. Deeds and Conveyances, Jamaica, vol. 797, fol. 107.

4. Sligo to Glenelg, 21 March 1836; Private Letterbook of Lord Sligo, MS 281. Sligo to Glenelg, 18 October 1835, ibid.

5. Vidal to Mitchell and Company, 6 June 1833, Attorney's Letterbook, 1B/5/83.

6. Sligo to Glenelg, 3 March 1836, Despatches, no. 359, 1B/5/18-11.

7. Deeds and Conveyances, Jamaica, vol. 804, fol. 165. T71/222. CO142/51, Blue Book of Statistics for Jamaica, 1837. The Blue Books show that Barrett received ten land grants of between 100 and 500 acres in Middlesex county, giving him at least 2,915 more acres in addition to the 7,736 acres he bought.

8. The purchase of New York Pen also included another 520 acres bordering his new property. In 1838 Barrett also bought the 652-acre Union Pen in St. Catherine. Deeds and

Conveyances, Jamaica, vol. 822, fol. 147; vol. 819, fol. 7; vol. 821, fol. 61; vol. 812, fols. 119, f195. PP, 1837–38 (215): 74, 306.

9. Sligo to Seaford, October 1835, 10 March 1836, Private Letterbook of Lord Sligo, MS 281. Sligo to Glenelg, June 1836, Despatches February–August 1836, no. 511, 1B/5/18/11. PP, 1837–38 (215): 5, 19, 21, 27, 35. Bravo was also the Custos, or chief magistrate, of Clarendon.

10. Deeds and Conveyances, Jamaica, vol. 806, fols. 229, 230; vol. 824, fol. 61. No Barbadian estates were sold for such a low price per acre.

11. Sligo Estate Papers, MS 275d, 6 September 1844; Alexander Bravo to William Ramsay, 5 July 1845; Thomas Land to Sligo, 18 August 1846. Bravo purchased the estates through Vidal, Allwood, and Vidal. Green, *British Slave Emancipation*, p. 209.

12. Sligo thought Brown "good-hearted but violent and inconsiderate," October 1835, Private Letterbook of Lord Sligo, MS 281. Bridges, a virulent opponent of emancipation and the Baptists, wanted to expel all missionaries and advocated armed resistance to the abolition effort. Benjamin Scott Moncrieffe, was also a member. See Turner, *Slaves and Missionaries*, pp. 166–68, 180–81 and Heuman, *Between Black and White*, p. 77.

13. Brown's creditors, who included Hawthorne and Shedden, collected over £9,440. PP, 1837–38 (215): 13, 16, 17, 290, 291. Deeds and Conveyances, Jamaica, vol. 824, fol. 128. He may also have owned Farm Pen in St. Ann.

14. T71/553–64, Slave Register for Barbados, 1834. John Davy claimed that 508 estates operated in Barbados in 1840 but he included all estates between 10 and 879 acres. See Davy, *The West Indies*, p. 109.

15. RB1/271-306. Chancery Sales, 1825–64; Minutes of the Court of Chancery, 1829–34, 1835–44.

16. RB1/271-306; Chancery Sales, 1825–64; Minutes of the Court of Chancery, 1829–34, 1835–44. Karch, "The Transformation," p. 144. Karch estimates that 450 estates still operated at this point.

17. Thome and Kimball, *Emancipation in the West Indies*, pp. 59–68.

18. The other estates were Egerton; Locust Hall, and Rowans in St. George and Endeavour and Cane Garden in St. Thomas. RB1/229, fol. 16; RB1/294, fol. 320; RB1/295, fols. 281, 340; RB1/296, fols. 170, 110; RB1/297, fol. 94; RB1/299, fol. 324; RB1/302, fol. 333.

19. RB1/271-306; Chancery Sales, 1825–64; Minutes of the Court of Chancery, 1829–34, 1835–44. Schomburgk, *The History of Barbados*, pp. 217–51.

20. RB1/274, fol. 312; RB1/275, fol. 154; RB1/290, fol. 187. Beachey, *The British West Indies*, especially chap. 1.

21. Harrow, 392 acres, and Four Square, 287 acres, both in St. Philip, were appraised at £25,837 and £12,752 respectively. When Joseph Connell bought Harrow and Nathaniel Kirton bought Four Square, both paid the appraised value. RB1/286, fol. 251; RB1/287, fol. 110.

22. RB1/275, fol. 118; RB1/278, fol. 11. The Gibbes and Bright mortgage secured £2,621. Lee and Garner's mortgage for £3,383 covered the debts to Charles Thomas Alleyne and the earlier mortgage to Gibbes and Bright. Mangrove Pond was 385 acres; the Farm, 150 acres, and Black Rock, 206 acres. RB1/293, fol. 310; RB1/301, fol. 104; RB1/298, fol. 8.

23. Chancery Court Case Papers, Daniel v. Barrow (1832). Minutes of the Court of Chancery, 1829–34; Master's Report, 31 December 1834. RB1/299, fols. 326, 333, 321. Sunbury and Hampton were in St. Philip.

24. BT31/14843/23260, Board of Trade papers pertaining to Thomas Daniel and Co. When the company ceased operations in 1894, it still had interests in Brewsters, Four Square, Kent, Ruby, Joe's River, Mellows, and Balls estates in Barbados and the Felicite Cocoa estate in Trinidad. Liquidation Papers, 1894, Thomas Daniel and Company.

25. Thomas and John Daniel were major creditors for Scantlebury, Pilgrim, Kirton's, Jackmans, The Pine, Bagatelle, Social Hall, Morgan Lewis, and Prior Park. Barton, Irlam, and Higginson were the major creditors for Sandy Lane, Joe's River, Black Rock, Walkes, Foul Bay (or Grettons), Palmers, Pilgrim Place, Mount Harmony, and Mount Clapham. See RB1/271-306. Minutes of the Court of Chancery, 1835-44. T71/1306, Adjudications of Contested Claims, Barbados.

26. Gibbes and Bright were major creditors of Rices and Richmond Hill, and Lee and Garner had an interest in Contented Retreat. See RB1/271-306. Minutes of the Court of Chancery, 1829-34; Chancery Sales, 1825-64.

27. The total debts against Bagatelle were £8,317. RB1/298, fol. 255.

28. Bezsin King Reece held a lien for £5,449 against the Pine in St. Michael. RB1/294, fol. 323.

29. When Sandy Lane was appraised at £14,084 in 1820, the total debts against the estate were £19,663. By 1829 the debts had increased to £23,560. RB1/281, fol. 237; RB1/276, fol. 26.

30. Two estates in St. Philip were known as Foul Bay. This one was also called as Grettons; the other, Rices. Minutes of the Court of Chancery, 1829-34, 1835-44, Irlam v. Brathwaite. RB1/295 f12.

31. Inventory of Estate of John Higginson, 1832. Department of Archives, Barbados. T71/ 559. Higginson paid £28,796 for Joe's River in 1826 and £16,860 for Foul Bay. Chancery Sales, 1825-64, Barton v. Asheham. John Spooner and Hall, McGarrell and Company, both of London, each held liens against Foul Bay. RB1/295, fol. 12; RB1/288, fol. 37; RB1/283, fol. 12.

32. See for example the arguments in *The Barbadian*, 28 June 1823, and evidence given before the 1832 select committee.

33. *The Barbadian*, 4 February 1837, Minutes of the Court of Chancery, 1835-44, Higginson v. Louis. RB1/295, fol. 23. The company bought Mount Clapham for £16,882 and sold it for £19,857.

34. RB1/303, fol. 84.

35. Karch, "The Transformation," p. 97. Handler, *The Unappropriated People*, p. 40.

36. Karch, "The Transformation," p. 96. T71/558. The Barbados Almanack, 1842. James Holder Alleyne entered an unsuccessful counterclaim for Holder's slaves. See T71/1505, Assistant Commissioners' Proceedings, Barbados and Trinidad, List of Counter-Claims.

37. RB1/274, fol. 312; RB1/275, fol. 108; RB1/288, fol. 37. Chancery Sales, 1825-64. The family may have owned Black Rock, an estate in St. Michael, which was also known as Holders. Ronald Hughes, conversations with author.

38. Ronald Hughes, conversations with author. RB1/272, fol. 140.

39. Henry Alleyne may have been an uncle. The debts totaled £29,428. RB1/271, fol. 353; RB1/275, fols. 76, 154; RB1/278, fol. 58; RB1/290, fols. 135, 142, 149, 162.

40. PP, 1837-38 (215): 182, 196, 197. RB1/301, fol. 260; RB1/292, fols. 241, 199; RB1/294, fol. 42.

41. Most of the Alleyne's property was in St. James and St. Thomas. Minutes of the Court

of Chancery, 1829–34. RB1/275, fol. 154. James Holder Alleyne bought Swans out of chancery in 1833 for £8,034. Alleyne paid £21,500 for Lancaster. RB1/298, fol. 121.

42. Prescod owned Dayrells and Searles in Christ Church; Rock Dundo, Small Hope, Carlton and Sion Hall in St. James; and Kendall and Barrys in St. John. He received £2,694 compensation for the slaves at Barrys, but another £23,016 (for 1,101 slaves valued at £60,365) went directly to William Hinds and John Gay Golding. T71/555; T71/558; T71/562. Prescod to commissioners, 18 December 1835, CO28/116. T71/800–801, Valuers' Returns for Barbados. PP, 1837–38 (215): 184, 196, 202.

43. Mount Harmony, in St. John, cost Robert Haynes £5,035. RB1/274, fol. 296. The Haynes family owned Newcastle, Clifton Hall, Bath, Guinea, and Clifden in St. John and Friziers and Bissex Hall in St. Joseph. Their smaller properties were the Retreat (23 acres), Forster Lodge (14 acres), and Passage (acreage unknown). T71/554–59.

44. PP, 1837–38 (215): 173, 189, 193–96. Clifton Hall was valued at £35,714 in 1835. Cracknell, ed., *The Barbadian Diary*. The Haynes held liens worth £2,874 against Mount Poyer in 1824, and £4,788 against Bannatynes in 1832. RB1/290, fol. 178; RB1/281, fol. 17.

45. T71/555–62. DM 89/2/9–10, Deed of Charge and Direction against Fairey Valley and Moonshine Hall.

46. RB1/300, fol. 54; RB1/229, fol. 197; RB1/284, fols. 152, 157. PP, 1837–38 (215): 189, 190, 195, 198. T71/797, Valuers' Returns for Barbados. The government mortgage was for £8,575.

47. T71/561, 564. Minutes of the Court of Chancery, 1829–34, Gibson v. Thornhill. Briggs, the sole bidder, paid £10,000 for the estate.

48. RB1/296, fol. 111; RB1/297, fol. 94; RB1/302, fol. 403. The Barbados Almanack, 1842. T71/560–63.

49. Reece paid £20,000 for Yorkshire and sold it in 1842 for £24,464. RB1/284, fols. 152, 157. RB1/301, fol. 154. PP, 1837–38 (215): 182, 199, 201.

50. Minutes of the Court of Chancery, 1829–34, 1835–44. Chancery Sales, 1825–64. RB1/294, fol. 330; RB1/294, fol. 323. Thomas and John Daniel received the compensation for the slaves at The Pine. PP, 1837–38 (215): 325.

51. RB1/271-306. Minutes of the Court of Chancery, 1829–34, 1835–44. Chancery Sales, 1825–64.

52. T71/562. RB1/294, fol. 223; PP, 1837–38 (215): 197.

53. RB1/292, fol. 346. CO318/117.

54. RB1/292, fol. 350; RB1/298, fol. 24; RB1/301, fol. 131.

55. RB1/300, fols. 166, 83.

56. RB1/295, fols. 249, 281; RB1/296, fol. 37. Nathaniel Forte also owned Bennetts, a 289-acre estate in St. Thomas, and Warleigh Heights, 146 acres, in St. Peter. He sold the latter for £6,428 in 1836 and received £4,615 compensation for 215 slaves. PP, 1837–38 (215): 193, 198. T71/561, 563.

57. RB1/292, fols. 132, 136; RB1/295, fol. 219; RB1/296, fol. 111. Briggs paid £30,000 for the two properties. Warren paid Edmund Knight £19,285 for Cane Garden in St. Thomas, RB1/295, fol. 340.

58. RB1/271-306. Chancery Sales, 1825–64. Minutes of the Court of Chancery, 1829–34, 1835–44. The remaining 16 percent of the sales were allocated to an "unknown" category.

59. RB1/292, fol. 248; RB1/294, fol. 225; RB1/295, fol. 281. Rogers also owned Parks in St. Joseph.

60. T71/553. PP, 1837–38 (215): 173. RB1/289, fol. 271; RB1/293, fol. 292; RB1/295, fol. 197. John Colthurst complimented Holligan on his use of a horse plow when he visited Bank Hall in 1837 and commented that he had never seen a "more prominent crop." See W. K. Marshall, ed., *The Colthurst Journal*, pp. 141–42.

61. RB1/295, fol. 143; RB1/296, fol. 106. In 1843 Holligan bought Welches, a 71 acre estate in St. Michael, from Ann Sclater, RB1/302, fol. 487.

62. RB1/295, fol. 23.

63. RB1/293, fols. 310, 292; RB1/289, fol. 345. RB1/292, fol. 355. Nathaniel Cave collected the compensation for the slaves at Sterling, an estate which may also have been called Moncrieffe. PP, 1837–38 (215): 188.

64. Pares, *A West India Fortune*, p. 317. Davy, *The West Indies*, pp. 16–17. Eisner, *Jamaica*, p. 196.

Chapter 6

1. Erickson, "Common Law," pp. 23–24. Salmon, *Women and the Law*, p. 81.

2. See Butler, "Slave Compensation and Property." On the intricacies of metropolitan and colonial credit see John Brewer's excellent article "Commercialization and Politics."

3. A married woman could not write a will without her husband's permission. As a "feme covert" her property was vested in him and she had no legal property to bequeath. Lebsock, *The Free Women*, p. 23. Salmon, "Women and Property," pp. 655–56.

4. Erickson, "Common Law," p. 24. Salmon, "Women and Property," pp. 655–56. Lebsock, *The Free Women*, p. 24. Deeds and Conveyances, Jamaica, vol. 847, fols. 74, 77.

5. Lebsock, *The Free Women*, p. 60. Salmon, *Women and the Law*, pp. 80–89. Salmon, "Women and Property," p. 656.

6. Lebsock, *The Free Women*, p. 55. Salmon, "Women and Property," pp. 656, 662. Deeds and Conveyances, Jamaica, vol. 862, fol. 11. Real property could not be legally transferred without at least a nominal payment, usually 10 shillings.

7. Berg, "Women's Property," pp. 233–35. Salmon, *Women and the Law*, pp. 86–87. Salmon, "Women and Property," pp. 668–69, 674, 677.

8. Berg, "Women's Property," pp. 237–39. Lebsock, *The Free Women*, p. 37.

9. Master's Report (July–December) 1838, no. 143. 1B/11/7-127, Slave Register for Clarendon, 1B/11/7, Slave Register for St. George. The executrixes included Mehitabelle Ann Simmons for Harrow and Four Square and Catherine Ann Smitten for Mangrove Pond, Black Rock, and the Farm. RB1/287, fol. 110; RB1/286, fol. 251; RB1/274, fol. 312; RB1/293, fol. 310. Two of the four women appointed executors, and the other two appointed women.

10. Ann Katherine Storer administered the 1,423-acre Fontabelle estate, the 2,157-acre Haddo Pen, the 643-acre Ormiston plantation, Bellcastle, the Farm, and Long Wharf. Master's Reports (December–April), vol. 526, fol. 61, Armstrong v. Storer; Chancery Quarterly Returns (1847), vol. 707, fols. 15, 16. Chancery Court Records (1824–27), vol. 388, fol. 129, Storer v. Storer.

11. RB1/305, fol. 422; RB1/298, fol. 154; RB1/293, fol. 12. Bushy Park was valued at nearly £15,000. Elizabeth Cadogan held a mortgage for £1,928 against Buttals, RB1/302, fol. 251. Erickson, "Common Law," p. 28.

12. PP, 1837–38 (215): 114.

13. PP, 1837–38 (215): 27, 30, 31. Higman, *Jamaica Surveyed*, pp. 105–11. Lord Holland received £2,211, and James Leman and Robert Curry collected another £5,000.

14. PP, 1837–38 (215). Deeds and Conveyances, Jamaica, vol. 831, fol. 29.

15. PP, 1837–38 (215): 20, 263. Deeds and Conveyances, Jamaica, vol. 792, fol. 118; vol. 747, fol. 8. 1B/11/7-136; T71/727; CO318/17.

16. Court of Chancery Minutes, Votes of the House of Assembly, Jamaica Legislature, 1661–1866, 1847–48, appendix 57, J281438.

17. PP, 1837–38 (215). Brewer, "Commercialization and Politics."

18. RB1/271-306. Minutes of the Court of Chancery, 1829–34, 1835–44. Chancery Sales, 1825–64.

19. RB1/299, fol. 39; RB1/272, fol. 17.

20. RB1/289, fol. 13; RB1/273, fol. 51.

21. T71.1306, Adjudication of Contested Claims, Barbados. Minutes of the Court of Chancery, 1829–34, Bayne v. Young.

22. Minutes of the Court of Chancery, (31 December 1834), Daniel v. Barrow. RB1/299, fol. 321. PP, 1837–38 (215): 264. The estate was sold for £24,179.

23. RB1/289, fols. 76, 165; RB1/287, fol. 279. T71.1306. PP, 1837–38 (215): 264. The estate owed Barton, Irlam, and Higginson £4,000 from 1821, so the compensation went to Higginson's estate.

24. RB1/285, fol. 54; RB1/290, fol. 178, King v. Haynes. PP, 1837–38 (215): 3285.

25. *Journal of the Barbados Museum and Historical Society* 3, no. 4 (1936): 65.

26. *Journal of the Barbados Museum and Historical Society* 4, no. 4 (1937): 190–92.

27. RB1/275, fol. 76; RB1/276, fol. 26; RB1/292, fol. 241.

28. T71/564; T71/557; T71/561, Slave Registers for Barbados.

29. T71/553-64. Minutes of the Court of Chancery, 1829–34, 1835–44. Chancery Sales, 1825–64.

30. RB1/271-306. Minutes of the Court of Chancery, 1829–34, 1835–44. Chancery Sales, 1825–64.

31. RB1/274, fols. 341, 346.

32. RB1/296, fol. 53; RB1/283, fols. 12, 53. Elizabeth Ann Belgrave was the widow of Jacob Belgrave, a politically active freedman during the 1820s. She may have been the only woman of color to buy or sell a sugar estate during the entire period. See Handler, *The Unappropriated People*, p. 121.

33. RB1/279, fol. 69; RB1/286, fol. 237. Walkes Spring Ledger, 1832–76, sugar production, 1832–48, fol. 47. The plantation was in Christ Church.

34. RB1/286, fol. 365.

35. RB1/284, fol. 300. Wills: Mary Lovell, 1851, Department of Archives, Barbados.

36. RB1/298, fols. 245, 121; RB1/293, fol. 310; RB1/296, fol. 5.

37. RB1/294, fol. 207; RB1/289, fol. 258.

38. RB1/291, fol. 140.

39. RB4/63/72, Wills: Samuel Hinds, Sr., 1824, Department of Archives, Barbados. RB1/294, fol. 80.

40. RB1/291, fol. 183.

41. RB1/298, fol. 245. Ronald Hughes, conversations with author.

42. RB1/294, fol. 207.

43. Wills: Ann Pilgrim, 1848, Department of Archives, Barbados. Berg, "Women's Property," p. 245.

44. Barbados Almanack, 1842. In 1828 Crab Hill had carried debts of over £21,000, nearly 85 percent due to Mary Cadogan and Elizabeth Christina Miller. RB1/293, fol. 12.

45. Wills: Mary Licorish, 1848, Department of Archives, Barbados.

46. RB1/301, fol. 26; RB1/299, fol. 145; RB1/302, fol. 477; RB1/289, fol. 258.

Chapter 7

1. Deeds and Conveyances, Jamaica, vol. 740, fol. 191. Master's Report (September–February), 1837–38, no. 141, Thompson v. Higson. Deeds and Conveyances, Jamaica, vol. 747, fol. 183; vol. 806, fol. 229. Master's Report (June 1837), no. 139, Wright v. Wright.

2. Stephen Harmer to Henry, 11 February 1840, Letters of Stephen Harmer, MS 765.

3. Stephen Harmer to Saul, 4 December 1841, 21 June 1842, ibid., MS 765.

4. See for example the Peru estate in Trelawny. 1A/3, Chancery Quarterly Returns, 1846–47, vol. 707, fol. 295. Deeds and Conveyances, Jamaica, vol. 707, fol. 119, Vidal v. Barrett; vol. 839, fol. 72. Barrett Hall was also in receivership, see 1A/3, vol. 707, fol. 111.

5. Votes of the House of Assembly, app. 57, 1847–48.

6. Eisner, *Jamaica*, p. 240, table 42. Holt, *The Problem of Freedom*, p. 122. Higman, *Slave Population and Economy*, pp. 21–23. Hall, *Free Jamaica*, pp. 184–85.

7. 1A/3, Chancery Quarterly Returns, 1846–47, vol. 707, fols. 79, 111. Davis v. Barrett; fol. 179, Palmer v. Montague; fol. 375, Neate v. Pink.

8. W. K. Marshall, "Notes on Peasant Development," p. 255. Hall, *Free Jamaica*, pp. 18, 20–21. Holt, *The Problem of Freedom*, p. 160. In several colonies the state, and by extension the British Crown, owned unassigned land that was usually unsuitable for sugar and from which they collected no rents or revenues. At emancipation, laborers sometimes moved onto these lands as squatters, although, as Hall and Holt point out, most preferred more developed areas close to markets and churches.

9. Eisner, *Jamaica*, pp. 210–11. Curtin, *Two Jamaicas*, p. 115. Hall, *Free Jamaica*, pp. 24, 182, 187–88. Holt, *The Problem of Freedom*, p. 156.

10. Deeds and Conveyances, Jamaica, vol. 833, fol. 225; vol. 862, fol. 199; vol. 855, fols. 48–55.

11. Knibb also bought Weston Favel Pen in 1844. Deeds and Conveyances, Jamaica, vol. 831, fol. 127; vol. 862, fol. 193. Governor Sligo once described him as "Mr. Knibb, the notorious," who drove a two-horse phaeton and appeared to live above his means; see Sligo to Stanley, 5 April 1834, no. 2 (Private), Private Letterbook of Lord Sligo, MS 281. Eisner, *Jamaica*, p. 211.

12. Deeds and Conveyances, Jamaica, vol. 825, fol. 81; vol. 831, fols. 21, 162. William Barron to the Duke of Buckingham, 1843, Stowe Collection, microfilm no. 510.

13. Eisner, *Jamaica*, pp. 210–11. Hall, *Free Jamaica*, p. 163. Green, *British Slave Emancipation*, pp. 170–71.

14. Bamboo paid for 774 days of field labor by hired slaves. Master's Report (3 December–10 May) 1841–43, vol. 530, no. 3. Master's Report (1844–46), vol. 533, no. 263.

15. Master's Records (1835–36), vol. 761, fol. 188, Dyer v. Chambers.

16. Henry Edward Walcott to W. W. Ramsey, Master-in-Chancery, 19 August 1844, Mas-

ter's Reports (1844–46), vol. 533, fol. 263. Master's Reports (1844–46), vol. 533, fol. 263, Dyer v. Chambers.

17. Letters dated 28th October 1844; 25th November 1844; 2 March 1845, Master's Reports (1844–46), vol. 533, fol. 263.

18. Master's Reports (1844–46), vol. 533, fol. 263. 1A/3, Chancery Quarterly Returns (1846–47), vol. 707, fol. 286, Dyer v. Chambers.

19. Satchell, *From Plots to Plantations*, pp. 79, 115. Hall, *Free Jamaica*, p. 163, n. 6. Veront Satchell has recently shown that foreign enterprises such as the Boston Fruit Company and the West Indies Improvement Company, both U.S.-based, were among the major beneficiaries of the economic recovery and of Jamaican legislation dealing with the property rights of married women and aliens. Sewell, *The Ordeal of Free Labor*, p. 279.

20. Thome and Kimball, *Emancipation in the West Indies*, p. 75. Handler, *The Unappropriated People*, pp. 132–33. The silver dollar was the basis of Jamaica's currency and was worth 4s.4d. sterling, or 6s.8d. currency. So Bourne's $20,000 would have translated into over £4,348 sterling. See Green, *British Slave Emancipation*, p. 181, n. 60 and Hall, *Free Jamaica*, pp. 224–26 for rates of exchange.

21. RB1/313, fol. 669. Bourne paid £714 more than the previous owner and renamed the estate Industry Hall. By 1860 he also owned the 164-acre Friendship estate in St. Michael. Barbados Almanack, 1860.

22. RB1/293, fol. 59. Barbados Almanack, 1842. Both estates were in St. Thomas.

23. Handler, *The Unappropriated People*, p. 121. Barbados Almanack, 1842. Collymore collected £1,879, but the compensation for Haggatt Hall went to Thomas and John Daniel. PP, 1837–38 (215): 325.

24. Handler, *The Unappropriated People*, p. 121.

25. RB1/273, fol. 16; RB1/284, fol. 6; RB1/283, fol. 53. Condition of Sale (Chancery), 1825–64. The estates were advertised on 18 April and sold on 4 May 1826. Samuel Hall Lord bought the Ruby.

26. Inventory of Estate of Jacob Belgrave (1828), Inventory of Estate of John William Perch (1831), Department of Archives, Barbados. RB1/283, fol. 53. Sterling was advertised on 30 September 1828 and sold in 1829. *The Barbadian*, 30 September 1828.

27. London Bourne received £127, and Thomas Ellis received nothing. PP, 1837–38 (215): 175.

28. Memorial to Sir John Packington, Secretary of State for the Colonies, from St. George's Jamaica, 1852. Original Correspondence, Barbados, Report of Joint Committee of Honorable Board of the Council and General Assembly on a Despatch from Lord John Russell dated 5 August 1840, CO28/140. PP, 1842 (479): 1686–89, 1691–1700 (evidence of William Sharpe).

29. W. K. Marshall, "The Establishment," p. 87.

30. W. K. Marshall, "Rock Hall," pp. 10–13. Mount Wilton's debts totaled £92,000. Elcock also owned Dayrells estate but lived at Mount Wilton. His estranged wife, Mary Mercy, lived at Dayrells. See the *Journal of the Barbados Museum and Historical Society* 8, no. 4 (August 1941): 166–71.

31. MacGregor to Russell, 3 July 1840, CO28/134, no. 59. W. K. Marshall, "Rock Hall," pp. 23–28. By the time the Mount Wilton people bought their land, the Farm had passed into the hands of Joseph Bayley.

32. W. K. Marshall, "Rock Hall," p. 3.

33. Samuel Prescod to Lord John Russell, 13 July 1840, Minutes of the House of Assembly, Barbados, 1838–1842. Original Correspondence, Barbados, Report of Joint Committee on a Despatch from Lord John Russell, 1841, CO28/140.

34. Report of the Joint Committee, CO28/140. W. K. Marshall, "The Establishment," pp. 85–88. Davy, *The West Indies*, p. 108.

35. Despatch from Grey to Stanley, 19 April 1842, enclosure 1; Report of Stipendiary Magistrates, Barbados, app. 6 to Report from the Select Committee on the West India Colonies (no. 479), 1842, 13.

36. 28 September 1833, Bishop Coleridge Correspondence, United Society for the Propagation of the Gospel Archives. West Indian Papers.

Chapter 8

1. Lobdell, "Patterns of Investment," p. 36. Hall, *Free Jamaica*, pp. 87–88. Eisner, *Jamaica*, p. 196.

2. The move coincided with the establishment of the Statistical Office of the Board of Trade and the formation of statistical societies in Manchester and London. Perkin, *The Origin*, p. 326.

3. Report from the Select Committee on the Accounts of the Colonial Receipt and Expenditure, PP, 1837 (516): 884 (evidence of G. R. Porter).

4. See CO33/45–54, Blue Books of Statistics for Barbados, 1833–43; CO142/47–52, Blue Books of Statistics for Jamaica, 1834–35, 1838–39.

5. CO33/45–54.

6. Sligo to Glenelg, 13 January 1836, no. 270, Despatches, vol. 3, MS 228.

7. Schomburgk, *The History of Barbados*, pp. 154–55. Levy, *Emancipation*, p. 179, app. 2.

8. CO33/45–54.

9. 7 December 1841, Minutes of the House of Assembly, 1838–42. Minutes of Evidence before Select Committee on the West Indies, PP, 1842 (479): 1561 (evidence of William Sharpe).

10. CO33/45–54.

11. Ibid.

12. CO142/47–48.

13. PP, 1837–38 (215): 6, 286, 287. The award for the slaves at Spring Garden went to Sir Rose Price's estate. Worthy Park was the first estate sold under the Encumbered Estates Act of Jamaica in 1863. By then its debts totaled £68,000. Beachey, *The British West Indies*, p. 7.

14. Worthy Park Plantation Books, 1836–46, 4/23, no. 7. Between October 1835 and September 1846, the estate spent over £4,900 on plantation equipment.

15. Drax Hall Plantation Ledger, 1825–41, Z9/2/6. Newton Papers, 1706–1890, MS 523.

16. Forster Hall, Cottage, and Groves Estate Accounts, Slave and Estate Expenses, 1823–43.

17. Ibid., Estate Expenses, 1839.

18. PP, 1842 (479): 1629–30 (evidence of William Sharpe). Sharpe owned the Claybury, Maxwell, and Brewster estates.

19. Davy, *The West Indies*, pp. 115–16. Green, *British Slave Emancipation*, p. 56. Hall, *Free Jamaica*, pp. 64, 114. Beachey, *The British West Indies*, p. 88.

20. *The Barbadian*, 5 November 1842, Report of the Finance Committee of the House of Assembly.

21. Ibid., app. B.

22. PP, 1838–39 (215): 171–327. Nearly all the late awards were litigated claims and 47 percent of them were paid in 1837.

23. Schomburgk, *The History of Barbados*, p. 168.

24. CO33/45–54.

25. *The Barbadian*, 5 November 1842, Report of the Finance Committee of the House of Assembly, app. C.

26. Callender, *The Development of the Capital Market*, p. 7. See also *A Banking Centenary*, p. 26.

27. Phillips, "The Changing Role," p. 69. Phillips also includes the Barclays, Bourkes, Briscoes, Campbells, Chambers, Dawkinses, Grays, Jacksons, and Pennants.

28. *The Barbadian*, 11 June 1824. Ragatz, *The Fall of the Planter Class*, pp. 354, 381.

29. *The Barbadian*, 11 June 1824. Ragatz, *The Fall of the Planter Class*, p. 381.

30. Reprinted in *The Barbadian*, 11 June 1824.

31. *The Barbadian*, 8 November 1834. Ragatz, *The Fall of the Planter Class*, p. 381.

32. *The St. Jago de la Vega Gazette*, 13–20 February 1836.

33. Ibid.

34. Ibid. Laws of Jamaica, 1830–37, 1B/11.

35. *St. Jago de la Vega Gazette*, 13–20 February 1836. Callender, *The Development of the Capital Market*, p. 8. Sligo once described Gordon as a man of "liberal principles and little moral courage." Private Letterbook of Lord Sligo, October 1835, MS 281.

36. Jamaica Almanack, 1839. *A Banking Centenary*, pp. 24–31. *St. Jago de la Vega Gazette*, 13–20 February 1836. Laws of Jamaica, 1830–37, 1B/11.

37. *The Barbadian*, 11 January 1837. Callender, *The Development of the Capital Market*, p. 7.

38. Laws of Jamaica, 1830–37, 1B/11. *A Banking Centenary*, p. 29. Callender, *The Development of the Capital Market*, p. 7.

39. *Royal Gazette and Jamaica Times*, 6 May 1837, Laws of Jamaica, 1830–37, 1B/11. *The Barbadian*, 3 June 1837. Lobdell, "Patterns of Investment," p. 37.

40. *The Barbadian*, 21 April 1838.

41. Callender, *The Development of the Capital Market*, pp. 8–9, 161.

42. Smith to Glenelg, 15 February 1839, no. 43, Despatches, no. 13, Jamaica to England, 1838–41. 1B/5/18. Armstrong, "Island 'Checks,'" pp. 2–3. Callender, *The Development of the Capital Market*, pp. 2–3.

43. Callender, *The Development of the Capital Market*, p. 3.

44. Minutes of the Council, Jamaica, 3 May 1839. Curtin, "The British Sugar Duties," p. 159. Lobdell, "Patterns of Investment," pp. 38–39. *A Banking Centenary*, pp. 24–31.

45. *Royal Gazette and Jamaica Times*, 29 April 1839. Committee of the Privy Council on the State of Banking in Jamaica, 3 May 1839. Callender, *The Development of the Capital Market*, pp. 8, 162.

46. Glenelg to Smith, 13 July 1838, no. 384, Minutes of the Council, Jamaica. 1/B/5/3/24. Letter from the director of the Colonial Bank dated 29 November 1838, Minutes of the Council, Jamaica.

47. Committee of the Privy Council Report on the State of Banking in Jamaica, 3 May 1839. Minutes of the Council, Jamaica. Callender, *The Development of the Capital Market*, p. 9.

48. Report of the Privy Council on the State of Banking in Jamaica, 3 May 1839.

49. Callender, *The Development of the Capital Market*, pp. 9, 19. Armstrong, "Island 'Checks,'" p. 38. Hall, *Free Jamaica*, pp. 112–13.

50. *The Barbadian*, 29 April 1840. Levy, *Emancipation*, p. 95. RB1/298, fol. 208. Callender, *The Development of the Capital Market*, pp. 19, 162.

51. *The Barbadian*, 4 December 1839. Hall, *Free Jamaica*, p. 91.

52. Jamaica Almanack, 1839, 1846. *Royal Gazette and Jamaica Times*, 26 May 1838.

Epilogue

1. *The Barbadian*, 14 April 1841.

2. *The Barbadian*, 23 August 1834.

3. Satchell, *From Plots to Plantations*, pp. 133, 148. Karch, "The Transformation," p. 143. The Encumbered Estates Act went into force in most West Indian colonies in 1854. Barbados refused to pass the law, claiming that its chancery system was sufficiently efficient.

4. Cochin, *L'Abolition de l'Esclavage*, pp. 148–51. Priestley, *France Overseas*, p. 68. Venezuela, Cuba, and Brazil all bound their ex-slaves for varying terms when they finally abolished slavery in 1854, 1886, and 1888 respectively. Although the planters in each country demanded compensation, none was awarded. See for example John V. Lombardi's work on Venezuela, Franklin W. Knight and Rebecca Scott on Cuba, and Robert Conrad on Brazil.

5. Emmer, "Between Slavery and Freedom," pp. 87–89. See also Cochin, *L'Abolition de l'Esclavage*, pp. 148–51, 274–78; Hiss, *Netherlands America*, p. 107.

Bibliography

Manuscripts and Official Documents

Barbados

Barbados Museum and Historical Society, St. Ann's Garrison
  Barbados Almanack: 1832, 1838
  Colleton Plantation Ledger, 1818–57 and Journal, 1818–44
  Forster Hall, Cottage, and Groves Estate Accounts, 1817–55
  Newcastle and Bissex Hall Ledger, 1816–38
  Shilstone, E. M. *Plantation Records*, 1796–1849, 1851–88
  Thomas Daniel and Company, Liquidation Papers, 1895
  Walkes Spring, Over Hill, and Ashton Hall Accounts, 1832–76
Barbados Public Library, Bridgetown
  The Barbardian, 1822–1861 (microfilm)
  Correspondence of Special Magistrates, 1836–39 (microfilm)
  Mount Gay Plantation Journal, 1809–36 (microfilm)
Department of Archives, Black Rock
  Agent's Letterbook: John Pollard Mayers, 1829–33
  Barbados Almanack: 1842, 1860, 1870
  Blue Books of Statistics for Barbados, 1833–43
  Chancery Court Papers
    Minutes of the Court of Chancery, 1829–34, 1835–44
    Chancery Court Case Papers
    Chancery Sales, 1825–64
  Deeds and Conveyances, RB1/271-306
  Diary of General Robert Haynes, 1787–1836
  Drax Hall Plantation Records, Ledgers and Accounts, 1825–1854
  Hopewell Papers, Ledger, 1860–62
  Inventories

Journal of the Barbados Museum and Historical Society
Minutes of Barbados Mutual Life Assurance Society, 1840–47
Minutes of the House of Assembly, 1836–42
Power of Attorney Index
Wills RB4: Susan Alsop, 1839; Elizabeth Bayne, 1851; Margaret Ann Bend, 1841; Mary
    Katherine Chase, 1844; Renn Hamden, 1838; Mary Elizabeth Hinds, 1842; Samuel
    Hinds, Sr., 1824; Mary Licorish, 1848; Mary Lovell, 1851; Ann Pilgrim, 1848; Bezsin
    King Reece, 1833
University of the West Indies, Cave Hill
  West India Collection
    Original Correspondence, Barbados, 1833–40, CO28 (microfilm)
    Barbados Slave Registers, T71/553–64 (microfilm)
    Messrs. Robert Challenor and Company, Speightstown, Ledgers 1830–60, 5 vols.
    Newton Papers, 1706–1890, MS 523 (microfilm)
    Substance of the Debate in the House of Commons, 1823

Jamaica
Island Record Office, Spanish Town
  Counterclaims filed before Commission of Compensation against Baxter's Estate, Bar-
      bados, 1834
  Deeds and Conveyances, Jamaica, vols. 722–830
  Wills
National Archives of Jamaica, Spanish Town
  Accounts Current, 1832–37, 1841–42
  Accounts Produce, 1838–39
  Attorney's Letterbook: John Gale Vidal, 1831–38
  Blue Books of Statistics for Jamaica, 1834–40, CO33/45-54
  Chancery Court Records, 1A/3
    Chancery Court Accounts, 1836–43
    Chancery Court Minutes
    Chancery Index, 1837–82
    Chancery Quarterly Returns, 1846–47
    High Court of Chancery Reports
    Masters' Reports and Records
  Conveyances and Mortgages for Richmond, Hope, Middleton, Constant Spring, BRA
      1272 file 7/4, no. 16
  Despatches: Sligo to Glenelg, 1835–36, 1B/5/10-11
  House of Assembly, Committee of Correspondence Out-Letter Book, 1794–1833
  Inventories: Estates of John Tharp and Walter Minto
  Journal of Benjamin Scott Moncrieffe, 1828–40
  Laws of Jamaica, 1830–37
  Letterbook of Daniel Levy, merchant, 1836–50
  Minutes of the Council, 1832–39
  Minutes of the House of Assembly, 1795–1846

Titles of Lands, 1833–41
Out-Letter Book of William Burge, 1832–34
Private Letterbook of Lord Sligo, 1835–36, MS 287
Slave Registers, 1832
Votes of the House of Assembly, 1832–34, 1836–37
Wills: Robert Hibbert, 1835; Benjamin Scott Moncrieffe, 1849; John Gale Vidal, 1851
Worthy Park Plantation Books, 1836–46
National Library of Jamaica, Kingston
    Almanack: 1820, 1822, 1824–26, 1830–33, 1835–41, 1845
    Barbados Almanack: 1830, 1832, 1833, 1835, 1836, 1837
    Claims for Compensation Filed with the Commissioners for Jamaica
    Dawkins Papers, 1749–1812
    Despatches: Sligo to Glenelg, 1–26, MS 275c
    Estate maps and surveyors platts
    Georgia Estate Letterbooks and Accounts, 1805–35, 3 vols.
    Hope Estate Letterbook, 1770s
    Inventory, Irwin Estate, 1820–27
    Jamaica Manuscript, circa 1848
    Letters of Stephen Harmer, 1830–42, MS 765
    Old Montpelier Estate, Account Book, 1828
    Paisley and Windsor Lodge, Accounts Books, 1827–37, 2 vols. MS 32.
    Private Letterbook of Lord Sligo, 1834, MS 281
    Slave lists, Ellis's Caymanas and Crawle Pen, 1834
    Sligo Estate Papers, 1788–1845, 1844–47
    Springfield and Grimmett Estates, letter, 1838
Registrar of Titles, Kingston
    Mortgages on Chiswick Estate, Jamaica, 1924–77
    Records of Titles, vols. 153–69
University of the West Indies, Mona
    West India Collection
        Counterclaims against Baxter's estate, Barbados
        Letter from Hawthorn and Shedden to William Lake re: Haughton Hall, Burnt
            Ground, and Colliston estates, 1836
        Returns of slaves on various estates in Barbados, 1834
        Review of the Report of a Select Committee on the State of the West India Colonies,
            1832
        Stowe Collection, correspondence relative to Hope and Middleton estates (microfilm)

Trinidad
University of the West Indies, St. Augustine
    West India Collection
        Minutes of the Society of West India Planters and Merchants (General), 1822–29,
            1829–34, 1834–50
        Minutes of the Standing Committee (Special), 1833

Minutes of the Acting Committee, 1829–33, 1833–43
Minutes of Special Subcommittee, 1828–30
West India Documents Submitted to the Board of Trade, 1830
Minutes of the Society of West India Merchants, 1804–27, 1828–43
Slavery Tracts and Pamphlets, West India Committee Collection

Great Britain
Bristol University, Bristol
  Deeds of lease, release, and mortgage on Lears estate (1809); Swans plantation, 1830; Fairey Valley, Moonshine Hall, and Newcastle estates (Barbados), 1838, 1839; Arcadia plantation and Cedar Grove Pen (Jamaica)
  Ellis Family Papers, 1815–71
  Pinney Papers (Pares's transcripts), 1813–14
  Valuation of slaves on Albany estate, 1814
British Library, London
  Holland House Papers, 1677–1845
  House of Lords Journal, 1833–37, 1846
  Keene Papers, Lowther's Plantation, Barbados, 1756, 1825–35
  Peel Papers, 1841
  Rose Papers
  Windham Papers, 1829, 1833
Fulham Palace, London
  Papers of the United Society for the Propogation of the Gospel
Guildhall Library, London
  Boddington Family Papers, 1640–1843
  Deeds and mortgages for Fairey Valley, Moonshine Hall, Newcastle, Lears, Swans, and Friendship with Thomas and John Daniel
  Ellis Papers, 1823–36
London University: Goldsmiths Library, London
  West India Pamphlets
Oxford University: Rhodes House and Bodleian Libraries, Oxford
  Barham Family Papers, 1825–30.
  Chiswick Plantation Papers, 1815–46, 3 vols.
  Dawkins Family Papers, 1666–1839, 1814–65
  Pinney Papers (Pares's transcripts), 1740–1848
  Young Papers, 1768–1835
Public Record Office, London
  Audit Office Papers, Slave Compensation Commission, 1835–46
  BT31 14843/23260, Incorporation papers of Thomas Daniel and Sons, 1886
  Colonial Office Papers
    CO28: Original Correspondence, Barbados, 1835–39.
    CO137: Original Correspondence, Jamaica, 1833–38.
    CO318: Original Correspondence, West Indies, General, 1833, 1836–37, 1840
    CO441: Encumbered Estates Commission, Worthy Park Papers
    CO854: Circular Despatches, Colonies, General, 1808–38

Digest of Records of the United Society for the Propagation of the Gospel, 1701–1892

Great Britain, *Parliamentary Debates*, Commons, 1823–43.

———, *Parliamentary Debates*, House of Lords, 1833.

———, House of Commons, Parliamentary Papers

    1825, XV (517), "First Report of the Commissioner of Inquiry into the Administration of the Civil and Criminal Justice in the West Indies."

    1831–32, XX (381), "Minutes of Evidence taken before the Select Committee on the State of the West India Colonies."

    1831–32, XX (721), "Minutes of Evidence taken before the Select Committee on the Extinction of Slavery Throughout the British Dominions."

    1831–32, XX (721), "Report from the Select Committee on the Extinction of Slavery Throughout The British Dominions."

    1831–32, XLVII (561), "Jamaica: Slave Insurrection; Copy of Report of a Committee of the House of Assembly of Jamaica."

    1833, IV (492), Slavery Abolition Act 1833.

    1835, LI (463), "Slavery Abolition Act: Copy of Contract for Loan of 15,000,000l."

    1835, LI (591), "Apprenticed Negroes: Copies of Instructions given relative to Compensation claimed for Negroes who have not been registered as Slaves."

    1836, XLIX (597) "Accounts and Papers: Returns relating to West India Compensation."

    1837, VII (516), "Report from the Select Committee on the Accounts of Colonial Receipt and Expenditure with Minutes of Evidence."

    1837–38, XLVIII (64), "An Account of the Average Sales in the Colonies Affected by the Slavery Abolition Act."

    1837–38, XLVIII (215), "Slavery Abolition Act: An Account of all Sums of Money awarded by the Commissioners of Slavery Compensation."

    1842, XIII (479) "Report from the Select Committee on the West India Colonies."

House of Commons Journal, 1836–37

House of Lords Journal, 1833–36, 1846.

National Debt Office Records, West India Slave Compensation, 1835–42

Treasury Papers, T71, relative to Slave Registers and Compensation and Valuers' Returns

United States

Johns Hopkins University, Milton S. Eisenhower Library, Baltimore

    Newton Papers, Barbados (microfilm)

    Slavery Tracts and Pamphlets from the West India Committee Collection (microfilm)

University of Texas, Nettie Lee Benson Library, Austin

    Bennett Collection: United Society for the Propogation of the Gospel: Codrington Estate Records (microfilm)

Newspapers and Periodicals

Annual Register (London), 1832–35

The Barbadian, 1823–43

Barbados Globe and Colonial Advocate, 1834, 1839

Edinburgh Review, 1833, 1838
Liberal (Bridgetown), 1837–40
Manchester Guardian, 1833
Mirror (London), 1834, 1840
Morning Chronicle (London), 1836
Quarterly Review (London), 1825–33
Royal Gazette and Jamaica Times, 1830–32, 1834–36
St. Jago de la Vega Gazette (Jamaica), 1833–35
The Times (London), 1833–38
Watchman and Jamaica Free Press, 1836
Westminster Review, 1834–35

Contemporary Books and Pamphlets

"A Reply to Mr. Jeremie's Pamphlet by an Inhabitant of St. Lucia." London: Effingham Wilson, 1832.

Beaumont, Augustus Hardin. *Compensation to Slave Owners Fairly Considered*, 4th ed. London: Effingham Wilson, 1826.

Bosanquet, Charles. "A Letter to W. Manning Esq. MP on the Causes and the rapid and progressive depreciation of West India property." 2d. ed. McDowal, 1807.

Buxton, Charles, ed. *Memoirs of Sir Thomas Fowell Buxton, Bart*. Philadelphia: Henry Longstreth, 1849.

Cracknell, Everil M. W., ed. *The Barbadian Diary of General Robert Haynes, 1787–1836*. Medstead: The Azania Press, 1934.

Cropper, James. "The Interests of the Country and the Prosperity of the West India Planters mutually secured by the immediate Abolition of Slavery: Being a Review of the Report of the Select Committee of the House of Commons on the State of the West India Colonies." 2d ed. London: J. and A. Arch, 1833.

———. *A Vindication of a Loan of £15,000,000 to the West India Planters*. London: J. and A. Arch, 1833.

Davy, John. *The West Indies Before and Since Slave Emancipation*. 1854; reprint, London: Frank Cass & Co., 1971.

Dickson, William. *Letters on Slavery*. 1789; reprint, Westport, Conn.: Negro Universities Press, 1970.

Edwards, Bryan. *The History Civil and Commercial of the British Colonies in the West Indies*. London, 1798.

An Ex-Member of the Jamaican Assembly. "Twenty Millions Thrown Away and Slavery Perpetuates." Reprinted from the *Radical*. London: G. Morgan, n.d.

Horton, Rt. Hon. R. Wilmot. "First Letter to the Freeholders of the County of York: Being an Enquiry into the Claims of the West Indians for Equitable Compensation." London: Edmund Lloyd, 1830.

Ligon, Richard. *A True and Exact History of the Island of Barbadoes*. 1657; reprint, London: Frank Cass & Co., 1976.

Madden, R. R. *A Twelve Month's Residence in the West Indies During the Transition from Slavery to Apprenticeship*. 2 vols. Philadelphia: Carey, Lea & Blanchard, 1835; reprint, Westport, Conn.: Negro Universities Press, 1970.

Nugent, Maria. *Lady Nugent's Journal of her Residence in Jamaica from 1801 to 1805*. 4th rev. ed. by Philip Wright. Kingston: Institute of Jamaica, 1966.

Phillippo, James M. *Jamaica: Its Past and Present State*. London: J. Snow, 1843; reprint, Westport, Conn.: Negro Universities Press, 1970.

Roughley, Thomas. *The Jamaica Planter's Guide*. London: Longman, Hurst, Rees, Orme & Brown, 1823.

Schomburgk, Robert A. *The History of Barbados*. 1848; reprint, London: Frank Cass & Co., 1971.

Sewell, William G. *The Ordeal of Free Labor in the British West Indies*. London: Sampson, Low, Son & Co., 1862; reprint, London: Frank Cass & Co., 1968.

Stephen, Sir George. *Anti-Slavery Recollections in a Series of Letters to Mrs. Beecher Stowe*. London: Thomas Hatchard, 1854; reprint, London: Frank Cass & Co., 1971.

Sturge, Edmund. *West India Compensation to the Owners of Slaves: Its History and Results*. Gloucester: John Bellows, 1893.

Thome, J. A., and J. H. Kimball. *Emancipation in the West Indies: A Six Month's Tour of Antigua, Barbadoes, and Jamaica in the Year 1837*. New York: American Anti-Slavery Society, 1838; reprint, New York: Arno Press, 1969.

Bibliographies

Handler, Jerome S. *A Guide to Source Materials for the Study of Barbados History, 1627–1834*. Carbondale: Southern Illinois University Press, 1971.

Ingram, K. E. *Manuscripts Relating to Commonwealth Caribbean Countries in United States and Caribbean Repositories*. Barbados: Caribbean University Press, 1975.

———. *Sources of Jamaican History*. 2 vols. London: Inter Documentation Company (U.K.), 1976.

Marshall, Trevor, comp. *A Bibliography of the Commonwealth Caribbean Peasantry, 1834–1974*. Cave Hill, Barbados: I.S.E.R., 1975.

Marshall, W. K. "A Review of Historical Writing on the Commonwealth Caribbean Since Circa 1940." *Social and Economic Studies* 24 (1975).

Ragatz, L. J. *A Guide for the Study of British Caribbean History, 1763–1834, Including the Abolition and Emancipation Movements*. Washington, D.C.: U.S. Government Printing Office, 1932.

Walne, Peter. ed. *A Guide to Manuscript Sources for the History of Latin America and the Caribbean in the British Isles*. Oxford: Oxford University Press, 1973.

Secondary Sources

Adamson, A. H. *Sugar without Slaves: The Political Economy of British Guiana, 1838–1904*. New Haven: Yale University Press, 1972.

Albert, Bill, and Adrian Graves. *Crisis and Change in the International Sugar Economy, 1860–1914*. Edinburgh and Norwich: ISC Press, 1984.

Anstey, Roger. *The Atlantic Slave Trade and British Abolition, 1760–1810*. London: Macmillan Press, 1975.

Armstrong, Eric. "Island 'Checks' and the Advent of Commercial Banks in Jamaica, 1819–1888." Seminar Paper no. 8, Department of History, University West Indies, Barbados, 1981–82.

Aron, Harold G. *The Gist of Real Property Law*. New York: Writers Publishing Co., 1916.

Asiegbu, Johnson U. J. *Slavery and the Politics of Liberation*. New York: Africana Publishing, 1969.

Bagehot, Walter. *Lombard Street*. London: Smith, Elder & Co., 1915; reprint, Arno Press, 1979.

A Banking Centenary: Barclays Bank (Dominion, Colonial and Overseas) 1836–1936. Great Britain: Mayflower Press, William Breadon & Son, 1938.

Bartlett, C. J. "A New Balance of Power: The Nineteenth Century." *Chapters in Caribbean History*, vol. 2. London: Ginn & Co., Caribbean University Press, 1971.

Beachey, R. W. *The British West Indies Sugar Industry in the Late Nineteenth. Century*. Oxford: Basil Blackwell, 1957.

Bennett, J. Harry. *Bondsmen and Bishops: Slavery and Apprenticeship on the Codrington Plantations of Barbados, 1710–1838*. Berkeley: University of California Press, 1958.

Berg, Maxine. "Women's Property and the Industrial Revolution." *Journal of Interdisciplinary History* 24, no. 2 (1993): 232–50.

Bolt, Christine, and Seymour Drescher, eds. *Anti-Slavery, Religion and Reform: Essays in Memory of Roger Anstey*. Kent, England: William Dawson and Sons, 1980.

Brathwaite, Edward. *The Development of Creole Society in Jamaica, 1770–1820*. Oxford: Clarendon Press, 1971.

Buffon, Alain. *Monnaie et Crédit en Économie Coloniale: Contribution à l'Histoire Économique de la Guadeloupe, 1635–1919*. Basse-Terre: Société d'Histoire de la Guadeloupe, 1979.

Burn, W. L. *Emancipation and Apprenticeship in the British West Indies*. London: Jonathan Cape, 1937; reprint, New York: Johnson Reprint, 1970.

Butler, Kathleen Mary. "Slave Compensation and Property, Jamaica and Barbados, 1823–1843." Ph.D. diss., Johns Hopkins University, 1986.

Butler, Mary. "A Fair and Equitable Consideration: The Distribution of Slave Compensation in Jamaica and Barbados." *Journal of Caribbean History* 22, nos. 1–2 (1988): 138–52.

———. "Mortality and Labour on the Codrington Estates, Barbados." *Journal of Caribbean History* 19, no. 1 (1984): 48–67.

Callender, Charles V. *The Development of the Capital Market Institutions of Jamaica*. Supplement to *Social and Economic Studies* 14, no. 3. I.S.E.R.; University West Indies, Mona, 1965.

Campbell, M. C. *The Dynamics of Change in a Slave Society: A Socio-Political History of the Free Coloreds in Jamaica, 1800–1865*. Madison, Wis.: Fairleigh Dickinson University Press, 1976.

Checkland, S. G. "Finance for the West Indies, 1780–1815." *Economic History Review* 10 (1957–58): 461–69.

———. *The Gladstones: A Family Biography, 1784–1851*. Cambridge: Cambridge University Press, 1971.

———. "John Gladstone as Trader and Planter." *Economic History Review* 7 (1954–55): 216–29.

Cochin, Augustin. *L'Abolition de L'Esclavage*. 2 vols. Paris: Guillaumin, 1861.

Cohen, D., and J. Greene, eds. *Neither Slave Nor Free: The Freedmen of African Descent in the Slave Societies of the New World*. Baltimore: Johns Hopkins University Press, 1972.

Conrad, Robert. *The Destruction of Brazilian Slavery, 1850–1888*. Berkeley: University of California Press, 1972.

Corwin, A. *Spain and the Abolition of Slavery in Cuba, 1878–1886*. Austin: Institute of Latin American Studies, University of Texas Press, 1967.

Coupland, Reginald. *The British Anti-Slavery Movement*. London: T. Butterworth, 1933.

Craton, Michael, and James Walvin. *A Jamaican Plantation: The History of Worthy Park, 1670–1970*. New York: W. H. Allen, 1970.

Craton, Michael, James Walvin, and David Wright. *Slavery, Abolition and Emancipation*. New York: Longman, 1976.

Craton, Michael. "Hobbesian or Panglossian? The Two Extremes of Slave Conditions in the British Caribbean, 1783–1834." *William and Mary Quarterly* 35 (April 1978): 325–56.

———. "Jamaican Slave Mortality: Fresh Light from Worthy Park, Longville and the Tharp Estates." *Journal of Caribbean History* 3 (November 1971): 1–27.

———. *Searching for the Invisible Man: Slaves and Plantation Life in Jamaica*. Cambridge, Mass.: Harvard University Press, 1978.

———. *Sinews of Empire: A Short History of British Slavery*. London: Temple Smith, 1974.

Curtin, Philip D. "The British Sugar Duties and West Indian Prosperity." *Journal of Economic History* 14 (1954): 157–64.

———. *Two Jamaicas: The Role of Ideas in a Tropical Colony, 1830–1865*. Cambridge, Mass.: Harvard University Press, 1955; reprint, New York: Atheneum, 1975.

Davis, David Brion. *The Problem of Slavery in the Age of Revolution, 1770–1823*. Ithaca: Cornell University Press, 1975.

———. *The Problem of Slavery in Western Culture*. Ithaca: Cornell University Press, 1966; Cornell Paperbacks, 1969.

Debien, G. *Les Esclaves aux Antilles Francaises (XVIIe–XVIIIe Siècles)*. Basse-Terre: Société d'Histoire de la Guadeloupe, 1974.

Deerr, Noel. *The History of Sugar*. 2 vols. London: Chapman & Hall, 1950.

Drescher, Seymour. *Econocide: British Slavery in the Era of Abolition*. Pittsburgh: University of Pittsburgh Press, 1977.

Dunn, Richard S. "The Barbados Census of 1680: Profile of the Richest Colony in English America." *William and Mary Quarterly* 26 (October 1969): 2–30.

———. *Sugar and Slaves: The Rise of the English West Indies, 1624–1713*. New York: W. W. Norton & Co., 1973.

———. "A Tale of Two Plantations: Slave Life at Mesopotamia in Jamaica and Mount Airy in Virginia, 1799–1828." *William and Mary Quarterly* 34 (January 1977): 32–65.

Eisner, Gisela. *Jamaica, 1830–1930: A Study in Economic Growth*. Manchester: Manchester University Press, 1961; reprint, Westport, Conn.: Greenwood Press, 1974.

Eltis, David. "Dr. Stephen Lushington and the Campaign to Abolish Slavery in the British Empire." *Journal of Caribbean History* 1 (1970): 41–56.

———. "The Traffic in Slaves between the British West Indian Colonies, 1807–1833." *Economic History Review* 25 (1972): 55–64.

Emmer, Pieter. "Between Slavery and Freedom: The Period of Apprenticeship in Suriname (Dutch Guiana), 1863–1873." *Slavery and Abolition* 14:1 (1993): 87–105.

Engerman, Stanley L. "Economic Change and Contract Labor in the British Caribbean: The End of Slavery and the Adjustment to Emancipation." *Explorations in Economic History* 21, no. 2 (April 1984): 133–50.

———. "Some Considerations Relating to Property Rights in Man." *Journal of Economic History* 33 (1973): 43–65.

———. "Some Economic and Demographic Comparisons of Slavery in the United States and the British West Indies." *Economic History Review* 29 (1976): 258–75.

Engerman, Stanley L., and Eugene D. Genovese, eds. *Race and Slavery in the Western Hemisphere: Quantitative Studies*. Princeton: Princeton University Press, 1975.

Erickson, Amy Louise. "Common Law versus Common Practice: The Use of Marriage Settlements in Early Modern England." *Economic History Review*, 2d ser., 43, no. 1 (1990): 21–39.

Fogel, Robert. W., and Stanley L. Engerman. "Philanthropy at Bargain Prices: Notes on the Economics of Gradual Emancipation." *Journal of Legal Studies* 3 (1974): 377–401.

Goldin, C. D. "Economics of Emancipation." *Journal of Economic History* 33 (1973): 66–85.

Goveia, Elsa V. *Slave Society on the British Leeward Islands*. New Haven: Yale University Press, 1965.

———. *A Study of the Historiography of the British West Indies to the End of the Nineteenth Century*. Mexico City: Instituto PanAmericano de Geographia e Historia, 1956.

———. "The West Indian Slave Laws of the Eighteenth Century." *Chapters in Caribbean History*, vol. 2. London: Ginn & Co., Caribbean University Press, 1971.

Green, W. A. "The Apprenticeship in British Guiana, 1834–1838." *Caribbean Studies* 9 (1969–70): 44–66.

———. *British Slave Emancipation: The Sugar Colonies and the Great Experiment, 1830–1865*. Oxford: Clarendon Press, 1976.

———. "Caribbean Historiography, 1600–1900: The Recent Tide." *Journal of Interdisciplinary History* 7, no. 3 (1977): 509–30.

———. "James Stephen and British West India Policy, 1834–1847." *Caribbean Studies* 13–14 (1974): 33–56.

———. "The Planter Class and British West Indian Sugar Production, before and after Emancipation." *Economic History Review* 26 (1973): 448–63.

Gross, Izhak. "Parliament and the Abolition of Negro Apprenticeship, 1835–1838." *English Historical Review* (July 1981): 560–76.

Halévy, Elie. *The Liberal Awakening, 1815–1830*. Trans. E. T. Watkin. London: Ernest Benn, 1961.

———. *The Triumph of Reform, 1830–1841*. Trans. E. T. Watkin. London: Ernest Benn, 1927.

Hall, Douglas. "Absentee-Proprietorship in the British West Indies to about 1850." *Jamaican Historical Review* 4 (1964): 15–35.

———. "The Apprenticeship Period in Jamaica, 1834–1838." *Caribbean Quarterly* 3 (1953–54): 142–66.

———. *A Brief History of the West India Committee*. Barbados: Caribbean University Press, 1971.

———. *Five of the Leewards, 1834–1870*. 1971; reprint, London: Ginn & Co., Caribbean University Press, 1981.

———. "The Flight from the Estates Reconsidered, 1838–42." *Journal of Caribbean History* 10–11 (1978): 7–24.

———. *Free Jamaica, 1838–1865: An Economic History*. New Haven: Yale University Press, 1959.

———. "Slaves and Slavery in the British West Indies." *Social and Economic Studies* 4, no. 11 (1962): 305–18.

Hall, Gwendolyn Midlo. *Social Control in Slave Plantation Societies*. Johns Hopkins University Studies in Historical & Political Science, 39th ser. Baltimore: Johns Hopkins University Press, 1971.

Handler, Jerome S. "The History of Arrowroot and the Origin of Peasantries in the British West Indies." *Journal of Caribbean History* 2 (1971): 46–93.

———. *The Unappropriated People: Freedmen in the Slave Society of Barbados*. Baltimore: Johns Hopkins University Press, 1974.

Harrison, Stanley. *Poor Men's Guardians: A Record of the Struggles for a Democratic Newspaper Press, 1763–1973*. London: Lawrence & Wishart, 1974.

Hartwell, R. M. "The Rising Standard of Living in England, 1800–1850." *Economic History Review* 12–13 (April 1961): 397–416.

Heuman, Gad J. *Between Black and White: Race, Politics and the Free Coloreds in Jamaica, 1772–1865*. Westport, Conn.: Greenwood Press, 1981.

Higman, Barry W. *Jamaica Surveyed: Plantation Maps and Plans of the Eighteenth and Nineteenth Centuries*. Kingston, Jamaica: Institute of Jamaica Publications, 1988.

———. *Slave Population and Economy in Jamaica, 1807–1834*. New York: Cambridge University Press, 1976.

———. *Slave Populations of the British Caribbean, 1807–1834*. Baltimore: Johns Hopkins University Press, 1984.

———. "The West India 'Interest' in Parliament, 1807–1833." *Historical Studies* 13, no. 49 (October 1967): 1–19.

———, ed. *Trade, Government and Society in Caribbean History, 1700–1920: Essays Presented to Douglas Hall*. Kingston: Heinemann Educational Books (Caribbean), 1983.

Hiss, Philip Hanson. *Netherlands America: The Dutch Territories in the West*. London: Duell, Sloan and Pearce, 1943.

Hobsbawm, E. J. *The Age of Revolution, 1789–1848*. New York: Mentor Books, 1962.

———. "The Standard of Living During the Industrial Revolution: A Discussion." *Economic History Review* 16 (1963): 119–34.

Hobsbawm, E. J., and G. Rude. *Captain Swing*. London: Lawrence & Wishart, 1969.

Hobhouse, Stephen. *Joseph Sturge: His Life and Works*. London: J. M. Dent & Sons, 1919.

Hollis, Patricia. *The Pauper Press: A Study in Working-Class Radicalism of the 1830s*. Oxford: Oxford University Press, 1970.

Holt, Thomas C. *The Problem of Freedom: Race, Labor, and Politics in Jamaica and Britain, 1832–1938*. Baltimore: Johns Hopkins University Press, 1992.

Hurwitz, Edith. *Politics and the Public Conscience: Slave Emancipation and the Abolitionist Movement in Britain*. London: George Allen & Unwin, 1973.

Judd, G. P. *Members of Parliament, 1734–1832*. New Haven: Yale University Press, 1955.

Karasch, Mary C. *Slave Life in Rio de Janeiro, 1808–1850*. New Jersey: Princeton University Press, 1987.

Karch, Cecilia Ann. "The Transformation and Consolidation of the Corporate Plantation Economy in Barbados, 1860–1977." Ph.D. diss., Rutgers University, 1979.

Kiple, Kenneth F. *Blacks in Colonial Cuba, 1774–1899*. Gainesville: University Presses of Florida, 1976.

Knaplund, Paul. *James Stephen and the British Colonial System, 1813–1847*. Madison: University of Wisconsin Press, 1953.

Knight, Franklin W. *Slave Society in Cuba during the Nineteenth Century*. Madison: University of Wisconsin Press, 1970.

Klingberg, Frank J. *The Anti-Slavery Movement in England: A Study in English Humanitarianism*. New Haven: Yale University Press, 1926; reprint, Hamden, Conn.: Archon Books, 1968.

Lebsock, Suzanne. *The Free Women of Petersburg: Status and Culture in a Southern Town, 1784–1860*. New York: W. W. Norton & Co., 1984.

Levy, Claude. "Barbados: The Years of Slavery, 1823–1833." *Journal of Negro History* 44 (1959): 308–45.

———. *Emancipation, Sugar, and Federalism: Barbados and the West Indies, 1833–1876*. Gainesville: University Presses of Florida, 1980.

———. "Slavery and the Emancipation Movement in Barbados, 1650–1833." *Journal of Negro History* 55, no. 1 (January 1970): 1–14.

Lobdell, Richard A. "Patterns of Investment and Sources of Credit in the British West India Sugar Industry, 1838–97." *Journal of Caribbean History* 4 (1972–73): 31–53.

Lombardi, John V. *The Decline and Abolition of Negro Slavery in Venezuela*. Westport, Conn.: Greenwood Publishing, 1971.

McKendrick, Neil, John Plumer, and J. H. Plumb, eds. *The Birth of a Consumer Society: The Commercialization of Eighteenth Century England*. Bloomington: Indiana University Press, 1982.

McPherson, J. M. "Was West Indian Emancipation a Success?" *Caribbean Studies* 4 (1964): 28–34.

Marshall, Peter. *Bristol and the Abolition of Slavery: The Politics of Emancipation*. Bristol: Bristol Branch of the Historical Association, 1975.

Marshall, W. K. "The Establishment of a Peasantry in Barbados, 1840–1920." In *Social Groups and Institutions in the History of the Caribbean*, ed. T. Mathews. Mayaguez, P.R.: Association of Caribbean Historians, 1975.

———. "Notes on Peasant Development in the West Indies Since 1838." *Social and Economic Studies* 17 (1968): 252–61.

———. "Rock Hall, St. Thomas: The Search for the First Free Village in Barbados." Paper presented at the Ninth Annual Conference of Caribbean Historians, Barbados, July 1977.

———. "The Termination of the Apprenticeship in Barbados and the Windward Islands: An Essay in Colonial Administration and Politics." *Journal of Caribbean History* 2–3 (1971): 1–45.

———, ed. *The Colthurst Journal*. New York: KTO Press, 1977.

Mathieson, W. L. *British Slave Emancipation, 1823–1849.* Longmans, Green & Co., 1932; reprint, New York: Octagon Books, 1967.

Mintz, Sidney. *Sweetness and Power: The Place of Sugar in Modern History.* New York: Viking Penguin, 1985.

Mitchell, B. R., and Phyllis Deane. *Abstract of British Historical Statistics,* no. 17. Cambridge: Cambridge University Press, 1971.

Moreno Fraginals, Manuel. *El Ingenio: Complejo Económico Social Cubano del Azúcar.* Havana: Editorial de Ciencias Sociales, 1978.

Moreno Fraginals, Manuel, Frank Moya Pons, and Stanley L. Engerman, eds. *Between Slavery and Free Labor.* Johns Hopkins University Studies in Atlantic History and Culture. Baltimore: Johns Hopkins University Press, 1985.

Murray, D. J. *The West Indies and the Development of Colonial Government, 1801–1834.* Oxford: Clarendon Press, 1965.

Osborne, George E. *Handbook on the Law of Mortgages.* St. Paul, Minn.: West Publishing Co., 1970.

Pares, Richard. *Merchants and Planters.* Economic History Review Supplements no. 4. Cambridge: Cambridge University Press, Economic History Society, 1970.

———. *A West India Fortune.* London: Longmans, Green & Co., 1950; reprint, Hamden, Conn.: Archon Books, 1968.

Penson, Lillian M. *The Colonial Agents of the British West Indies: A Study in Colonial Administration, Mainly in the Eighteenth Century.* 1924; reprint, London: Frank Cass & Co., 1971.

———. "The London West India Interest in the Eighteenth Century." *English Historical Review* 36 (1921): 372–92.

Perkin, Harold. *The Origin of Modern English Society, 1780–1880.* London: Routledge & Kegan Paul, 1969.

Phillips, Glen O. "The Changing Role of the Merchant Class in the British West Indies, 1834–1867." Ph.D. diss., Howard University, 1976.

Pitman, F. W. "Slavery on the British West India Plantations in the Eighteenth Century." *Journal of Negro History* 11 (1926): 584–668.

Prestley, Herman Ingram. *France Overseas: A Study in Modern Imperialism.* London: D. Appleton-Century Co., 1938.

Ragatz, L. J. *The Fall of the Planter Class in the British Caribbean, 1763–1833: A Study in Social and Economic History.* New York: Century Co., 1928; reprint, New York: Octagon Books, 1963.

Read, Donald. *Press and People, 1790–1850: Opinion in Three English Cities.* London: Edward Arnold (Pub.), 1961.

Reckord, Mary. "The Colonial Office and the Abolition of Slavery." *Historical Journal* 14 (1971): 723–34.

Reid, Molly A. "The Growth of a Twentieth Century Fiction: The Foreclosure Suit in Barbados." *Social and Economic Studies* 22, no. 3 (1973): 358–83.

Rice, C. Duncan. "Humanity Sold for Sugar! The British Response to Free Trade in Slave-Grown Sugar." *Historical Journal* 13 (1970): 402–18.

Riviere, W. Emmanuel. "Labour Shortage in the British West Indies after Emancipation." *Journal of Caribbean History* 4 (1972): 1–30.

Salmon, Marylynn. "Women and Property in South Carolina: The Evidence from Marriage Settlements, 1730 to 1830." *William and Mary Quarterly*, 3d ser., 39, no. 4 (1982): 655–85.

———. *Women and the Law of Property in Early America*. Chapel Hill: University of North Carolina Press, 1986.

Satchell, Veront M. *From Plots to Plantations: Land Transactions in Jamaica, 1866–1900*. Mona, Jamaica: I.S.E.R., University West Indies, 1990.

Scarano, Francisco A. *Sugar and Slavery in Puerto Rico: The Plantation Economy of Ponce, 1800–1850*. Madison: University of Wisconsin Press, 1984.

Schnakenbourg, Christian. *Histoire de l'Industrie Sucrière en Guadeloupe aux XIXe et XXe Siècles, tome 1: La crise du système esclavagiste (1835–1847)*. Paris: Éditions L'Harmattan, 1980.

Shepherd, Verene A. "The Effects of the Abolition of Slavery on Jamaican Livestock Farms (Pens), 1834–1845." *Slavery and Abolition* 10, no. 2 (1989): 187–211.

Sheridan, Richard B. "The Crisis of Slave Subsistence in the British West Indies During and After the American Revolution." *William and Mary Quarterly* 33 (October 1976): 615–41.

———. *The Development of the Plantations to 1750: An Era of West Indian Prosperity, 1750–1775*. Barbados: Caribbean University Press, 1970.

———. *Sugar and Slavery: An Economic History of the British West Indies, 1623–1775*. Baltimore: Johns Hopkins University Press, 1974.

———. "'Sweet Malefactor': The Social Costs of Slavery and Sugar in Jamaica and Cuba, 1807–54." *Economic History Review* 29 (1976): 236–59.

———. "The West India Sugar Crisis and British Slave Emancipation, 1830–1833." *Journal of Economic History* 21 (1961): 539–51.

Sires, Ronald V. "Negro Labor in Jamaica in the Years Following Emancipation." *Journal of Negro History* 25 (1940): 484–97.

Sitterson, J. Carlyle. *Sugar Country: The Cane Sugar Industry in the South, 1753–1950*. Lexington: University of Kentucky Press, 1953.

Spring, D. "The Clapham Sect: Some Social and Political Aspects." *Victorian Studies* (1961): 35–48.

Stein, Stanley. *Vassouras: A Brazilian Coffee County, 1850–1890*. New York: Atheneum, 1976.

Taylor, Bruce M. "Emancipation in Barbados, 1830–1850." Ph.D. diss., Fordham University, 1975.

———. "Our Man in London: John Pollard Mayers, Agent for Barbados, and the British Abolition Act, 1832–1834." *Caribbean Studies* 16 (October 1976–January 1977): 60–84.

Temperley, Howard. *British Anti-Slavery, 1833–1870*. London: Longman, 1972.

———. "Capitalism, Slavery and Ideology." *Past and Present* 75 (1977): 94–118.

Thomas, R. P. "The Sugar Colonies of the Old Empire: Profit or Loss for Great Britain?" *Economic History Review* 21 (1968): 30–45.

Thompson, E. P. *The Making of the English Working Class*. New York: Random House, 1963; reprint, New York: Vintage Books, 1966.

Turner, Mary. *Slaves and Missionaries: The Disintegration of Jamaican Slave Society, 1787–1834*. Chicago: University of Illinois Press, 1982.

Walsh, William F. *A Treatise on Mortgages*. Chicago: Callaghan & Co., 1934.

Walvin, James, ed. *Slavery and British Society, 1776–1846*. Baton Rouge: Louisiana State University Press, 1982.

Ward, J. R. *British West Indian Slavery, 1750–1834: The Process of Amelioration*. Oxford: Clarendon Press, 1988.

———. "The Profitability of Sugar Planting in the British West Indies, 1650–1834." *Economic History Review*, ser. 2, 31 (May 1978): 197–213.

Wastell, R. E. P. "The History of Slave Compensation, 1833–1845." Master's thesis, London University, 1932.

Williams, Eric. *Capitalism and Slavery*. Chapel Hill: University of North Carolina Press, 1944; reprint, New York: Capricorn Books, 1966.

———. *From Columbus to Castro: The History of the Caribbean 1492–1969*. New York: Harper & Row, 1970.

———. *The Negro in the Caribbean*. Westport, Conn.: Negro Universities Press, 1942.

Index